"The use of the notion of negativity in psychoanalysis is double-edged: while it definitely remains the philosophical concept which provides the key to what Freud called death-drive, it simultaneously opens up the path to the philosophical colonization of psychoanalysis – psychoanalytic theory is de facto reduced to another version of 'philosophy of negativity' with no links to clinical experience. Here the volume edited by Murphy and Rousselle sets the record straight: it articulates negativity as a concept immanent to psychoanalytic experience and practice, as well as in our social reality. For this reason alone, it deserves to be read by thousands!"

– **Slavoj Žižek**, *Professor,*
European Graduate School; International Director,
Birkbeck Institute for the Humanities, Birkbeck College,
University of London; senior researcher, Institute of Sociology,
University of Ljubljana, Slovenia

Negativity in Psychoanalysis

Negativity in Psychoanalysis examines the role of negativity in psychoanalytic theory and its application in clinical settings.

While theories around negativity and death drive have become routinized within philosophical interpretations of Freudian and Lacanian psychoanalysis, they often mask an inherent positivity. This volume assembles highly esteemed psychoanalytic theorists and clinicians for an in-depth discussion on the topic. It features comprehensive introductions to Freudian and Lacanian perspectives, alongside contemporary clinical and cultural issues. The book also investigates how psychoanalytic negativity influences and is influenced by social, theological, and philosophical dialogues.

This work will prove invaluable for practicing psychoanalysts and those in training, while also appealing to academics and scholars in critical and cultural theory, continental and post-continental philosophy, and sociology, especially those whose research intersects clinical and theoretical traditions.

Duane Rousselle, PhD, is a Canadian sociological theorist and practicing Lacanian psychoanalyst. He is a visiting associate professor of sociology at the University Colleges of Dublin and Cork.

Mark Gerard Murphy is an editor for the political journal and blog *Taiwan Insight* and a lecturer at St. Mary's University, Scotland, Gillis Centre, where he convenes courses on ethics, philosophy, and mystical theology and spirituality. His research interests include the relationship between psychoanalysis and mystical theology. He has published in the *Journal for Cultural and Religious Theory* and the *European Journal of Psychoanalysis*.

Negativity in Psychoanalysis

Theory and Clinic

Edited by Duane Rousselle &
Mark Gerard Murphy

Routledge
Taylor & Francis Group
LONDON AND NEW YORK

Designed cover image: Getty | Ihor Tsyvinskyi

First published 2024
by Routledge
4 Park Square, Milton Park, Abingdon, Oxon OX14 4RN

and by Routledge
605 Third Avenue, New York, NY 10158

Routledge is an imprint of the Taylor & Francis Group, an informa business

British Library Cataloguing-in-Publication Data
A catalogue record for this book is available from the British
Library

ISBN: 9781032452104 (hbk)
ISBN: 9781032452098 (pbk)
ISBN: 9781003375920 (ebk)

DOI: 10.4324/9781003375920

Typeset in Times New Roman
by Apex CoVantage, LLC

Contents

Editor Biographies   *ix*
List of Contributors   *x*
Acknowledgements   *xiii*
Introduction   *xiv*
DUANE ROUSSELLE

SECTION 1
Foundations   1

1 Who Is Transferring What to Whom? Resistance to Lacan   3
ELLIE RAGLAND

2 On Sigmund Freud's "Negation"   61
SERGIO BENVENUTO

SECTION 2
Drive and Desire   89

3 Turning Opportunities into Crises: The Lacanian Antidote to
Toxic Positivity   91
COLIN WRIGHT

4 The Ethics of the Death Drive   98
TODD MCGOWAN

5 Humility and Humiliation of the Drive: Comedy and Tragedy
in Philosophy and Psychoanalysis   111
SIMONE A. MEDINA POLO

6 Apophatic Psychoanalysis: The Plenitude of the Negative   118
MARK GERARD MURPHY

SECTION 3
Clinical Implications   135

7   Negation beyond Neurosis   137
LEON S. BRENNER

8   Spiraling   147
CYRUS SAINT AMAND POLIAKOFF

9   What Is Non-Negativisable Jouissance?: From Negation to a
Singular Norm   154
AINO-MARJATTA MÄKI

10 Badbeing: What's So Bad about Resistance in the Clinic?   167
IAN PARKER

11 Singularity and the Real that Cannot Be Written: On Lacan's
Use of Frege in His Later Work   173
STIJN VANHEULE

SECTION 4
Spare Parts   189

12 To Create, Perform, Produce Psychology from Scratch:
Negativity in the Work of Wolfgang Giegerich   191
NICHOLAS BALAISIS

13 (Un)Mourning the End of History   199
MARK FEATHERSTONE

14 Trauma, Negativity, and Death Drive in Spielrein, Heidegger,
and Buddhist Thought   207
WANYOUNG KIM

15 Why Positive Thought Must Be Negated in the Analytic
Session: Negative Dialectics as Therapeutic Technique   212
JOEL MICHAEL CROMBEZ

16 The *Hau* Must Be Returned: The Exile of the Dead and
Its Effects on the Western Imaginary   218
JULIETTE TOCINO-SMITH

Index   *225*

Editor Biographies

Duane Rousselle, PhD, is a practicing Lacanian psychoanalyst. He is also a visiting assistant professor at the Indian Institute of Technology in Guwahati, visiting associate professor of sociology at the University Colleges of Dublin and Cork, and Nazarbayev University. Some of his recent publications include *Post-anarchism and Psychoanalysis: Seminars on Politics and Society* (2023); *Real Love: Essays on Psychoanalysis, Politics, & Religion* (2021); *Gender, Sexuality & Subjectivity* (Routledge Focus on Mental Health series; 2020); *Jacques Lacan and American Sociology* (2019); *Post-Anarchism: A Reader* (2011); and *After Post-Anarchism* (2012).

Mark Gerard Murphy, PhD, is an editor for the political journal and blog *Taiwan Insight* and a visiting lecturer at St. Mary's University, Scotland, Gillis Centre, convening courses on ethics, philosophy, and mystical theology/spirituality. His research interests include the relationship between psychoanalysis and mystical theology. He has published in the *Journal for Cultural and Religious Theory* and has a forthcoming book titled *Ethics of Hiddenness and Psychoanalytic Theory* (2024).

Contributors

Nicholas Balaisis (RP, PhD) is a psychotherapist in private practice west of Toronto, Canada. He is also a lecturer in media and communication arts at the University of Waterloo. He is the author of a book-length study on Cuban film and media in the "late socialist" period (*Imperfect Aesthetics*, 2016).

Sergio Benvenuto is a psychoanalyst in Rome, president of the Institute for Advanced Studies in Psychoanalysis (ISAP), and a scientific researcher at the Institute of Sciences and Technologies of Cognition at the Italian Council for Scientific Research (CNR) in Rome. He is professor emeritus in psychoanalysis at the International Institute of Psychology of Depth/University of Nice in Kiev. He is also the founder and editor of *EJP, European Journal of Psychoanalysis*, published both online and in print.

Leon S. Brenner (PhD) is a research fellow at the International Psychoanalytic University (IPU) in Berlin, Germany, and the Hans Kilian und Lotte Köhler Centrum (KKC) at Rühr University in Bochum, Germany. His work draws from the Freudian and Lacanian traditions of psychoanalysis, and his interest lies in the understanding of the relationship between culture and psychopathology. He is the author of *The Autistic Subject: On the Threshold of Language* (2020), and practices psychoanalysis in Berlin, Germany.

Joel Michael Crombez is an assistant professor of sociology at Kennesaw State University. His research is in the tradition of critical theory and lies at the intersection of political economy, technology, and mental health. Recent work includes the book *Anxiety, Modern Society, and the Critical Method: Toward a Theory and Practice of Critical Socioanalysis* (2022) and policy-oriented recommendations on the future of Artificial Intelligence and the humanities for the European Union. Having lived and worked across North and South America, he now resides with his wife in the Atlanta metro area.

Mark Featherstone is a professor of social and political theory at Keele University, UK. He is the author of *Tocqueville's Virus: Utopia and Dystopia in Western Social and Political Theory* (Routledge 2007) and *Planet Utopia: Utopia, Dystopia, and the Global Imaginary* (Routledge 2017), and the editor of *The Sociology of Debt* (2019) and *Writing the Body Politic: A John O'Neill Reader* (Routledge 2019). He is also editor of *Cultural Politics* (Duke University Press).

Wanyoung Kim is a philosopher, translator, and psychoanalyst-in-training. She completed her PhD in philosophy, art, and social thought in 2018 at the European Graduate School, and a master of arts degree in philosophy from the New School for Social Research in 2016. Wanyoung's most recent publication was *Cosmophenomenology: The Alterity and Harmony of Consciousness as Quantum Energy* (2019). She is currently completing a master of science degree in clinical psychology at Capella University.

Aino-Marjatta Mäki is a psychoanalyst and researcher from London and Helsinki. She is a member of the London Society of the New Lacanian School and part of the editorial board of the *Psychoanalytical Notebooks*. She is finishing her PhD thesis at the Centre for Research in Modern European Philosophy (Kingston University) on the question of therapy for contemporary psychoanalysis.

Todd McGowan teaches theory and film at the University of Vermont. He is the author of *Universality and Identity Politics*, *The Racist Fantasy*, *Only a Joke Can Save Us*, and other works. He is the co-editor (with Slavoj Žižek and Adrian Johnston) of the Diaeresis series at Northwestern University Press and the editor of the Film Theory in Practice Series at Bloomsbury. He is also the cohost of the *Why Theory* podcast.

Ian Parker is a practicing psychoanalyst in Manchester, UK, and co-author, with David Pavón-Cuéllar, of *Psychoanalysis and Revolution: Critical Psychology for Liberation Movements* (2021).

Cyrus Saint Amand Poliakoff is a psychoanalyst and editor practicing in Brooklyn, New York. He is a member of the Lacanian Compass, New Lacanian School, and World Association of Psychoanalysis. He is the editor in chief of *The Lacanian Review* and the editor in chief of *Lacanian Press*, the publishing house of Lacanian Compass.

Simone A. Medina Polo is a philosopher and interdisciplinary artist based out of Edmonton, Alberta, Canada. Currently affiliated with the Global Centre for Advanced Studies, Simone is a researcher studying through the Certificate in Psychoanalysis and she holds a BA in philosophy from Concordia University of Edmonton. Under the creative moniker pseudo-antigone, Simone deploys contemporary electronic and pop music to explore the voice and instrumental intensity as an expression of transgender embodiment that concerns itself with the partial object and matrixial aesthetic encounters. Under that same moniker, Simone publishes clandestine essays on the internet such as "On the Simulation of the Principle of Political Reality," "Matrixial Compassions," "The Dialectic of Love and Power," and "Absolute Antigone."

Ellie Ragland is the author of six solo books, two edited books, three co-edited books, and more than 100 articles. From 1974 on, her work focuses on Jacques Lacan and Jacques-Alain Miller. She retired from the University of Missouri as an emerita professor of English and an honorary professor of French. She holds the title Frederick A. Middlebush Chair. Ragland is also a member of the New Lacanian School and the World Association of Psychoanalysis. She is also a practicing psychoanalyst.

Juliette Tocino-Smith is an anthropologist at University College, London. She meanders around the world in search of extraordinary urban essences.

Stijn Vanheule is a clinical psychologist and professor of psychoanalysis and clinical psychology at Ghent University, Belgium. He is also a privately practicing psychoanalyst and a member of the New Lacanian School for Psychoanalysis. He is the author of more than 200 papers in academic journals and of several books, including *The Subject of Psychosis: A Lacanian Perspective*; *Diagnosis, the DSM – A Critical Review and Psychiatric Diagnosis Revisited: From DSM to Clinical Case Formulation*; and *Why Psychosis Is Not So Crazy*. With Derek Hook and Calum Neill, he edited the book series *Reading Lacan's Écrits*.

Colin Wright is an associate professor of critical theory at the University of Nottingham, UK, where he is also Head of the Department of Cultural, Media and Visual Studies. He has a psychoanalytic practice in Nottingham and is in formation with the London Society of the New Lacanian School. He is the author or editor of *Badiou in Jamaica: The Politics of Conflict* (2013), *Perversion Now!* (2017), and *Returning to Lacan's Seminar XVII* (2022). He is also working on a monograph – of which the chapter in this volume provides a glimpse – entitled *Toxic Positivity: A Lacanian Critique of Happiness and Wellbeing*.

Acknowledgements

We would like to thank the *European Journal of Psychoanalysis* for permission to republish a version of Mark Gerard Murphy's "Apophatic Psychoanalysis: The Plenitude of the Negative." It first appeared in the "What's So Negative About Psychoanalysis?" series, edited by Duane Rousselle. See: www.journal-psychoanalysis.eu/discourses/whats-so-negative-about-psychoanalysis/.

We also thank the journal *Filozofski Vestnik* for permission to translate and reprint Stijn Vanheule's "Singularnost in realno, ki ga ne moremo zapisati: Frege pri poznem Lacanu," *Filozofski Vestnik*, 35(1): pp. 131–147.

Introduction

Duane Rousselle

This book was inspired by our confusion. It seemed to us that the concept of negativity in psychoanalysis was being used too casually within some of the popular online literature. Yet, perhaps it was even worse: what was in fact positive was being referred to as negative, and what was negative was sometimes referred to as positive. For example, we have witnessed the growth of psychoanalytic theories of "constitutive negativity" at the same time that the Freudian and Lacanian psychoanalytic schools were increasing their reach, particularly within the anglophone world. Clinical experience necessitates that we interrogate some of these theories: what from the theorists of "constitutive negativity" has been said about the positive, that is, non-negativizable, domain of jouissance?

Theories of negativity and death drive had become routinized within philosophical expositions of Freudian and Lacanian psychoanalysis. And upon further inspection, they seemed to us to be concealing, by implication, something resolutely positive. Hence, some of my own work has aimed to expose a range of contemporary practices involved in the perpetuation of *faux* criticality, or what I've elsewhere referred to as "false negatives," "false holes," or "false twists" (see Rousselle, 2022, 2023). It therefore became important for us to explore this further by collecting together essays from today's leading theorists and clinicians.

The book is cut into four sections.

The first section aims to provide readers with extended introductions to essential topics of negativity within the Freudian and Lacanian clinical registers. The section opens with our longest chapter by Ellie Ragland, who is perhaps today's leading psychoanalytic theorist in the anglophone world. She provides readers with a historical and conceptual introduction to some of the most essential coordinates within the Lacanian field. The introduction forms the basis for our book because it demonstrates the *difference* of Lacanian psychoanalysis, particularly on the question of negative transference, resistance, and madness. Sergio Benvenuto's chapter provides readers with a rigorous deep reading of the concept of "negation" within key texts from Freud. This chapter is also extended because it allows readers to get a sense of the key concepts and nuances to "negativity" within the Freudian field.

The second section offers readers more casual assessments of questions having to do with drive and desire for their social, theological, and philosophical implications. The section begins with a provocative text from Colin Wright that examines the neoliberal emphasis on happiness and toxic positivity. The next chapter, from Todd McGowan, examines the ethical space opened by disruptions of the death drive, with fun examples from popular culture (such as the television show *Mad Men*). Simone A. Medina Polo develops Alenka Zupančič's depiction of death drive as a fundamental concept of psychoanalysis in relation to philosophical themes of tragedy and comedy. Mark Gerard Murphy's groundbreaking chapter proposes a late reading of Julian Norwich at the intersection of apophatic theology and the late teaching of Jacques Lacan.

The third section focuses on some important clinical implications for negativity in psychoanalysis. The first chapter, from a leading autism specialist, Leon S. Brenner, offers a nuanced reading of negation in Freudian psychoanalysis and its clinical implications for working with autism. Cyrus Saint Amand Poliakoff extracts from some of his analysands a notion of "spiraling," which he presents in relation to the topological structure of the torus. Aino-Marjatta Mäki's chapter presents us with a rigorous and extraordinary reading of the concept of "non-negativisable jouissance." The next chapter, from Ian Parker, explores the concept of "badbeing" within the clinic, and the question of resistance across various registers within the clinic (as well as its implications for politics). Finally, Stijn Vanheule, whose clinical work on psychosis has been pivotal, explores the concept of negativity at the intersection of Lacanian psychoanalysis and Frege's philosophical work.

The final section of our book, titled "Spare Parts," aims to showcase work that explores the negative in ways that are not always reducible to Freudian or Lacanian psychoanalytic clinical work or theory, but which, in each their own way, offer some insights into the topic of negativity. We borrow the expression "spare part" from Lacan (and picked up by Jacques-Alain Miller), who used it to describe the detachable object of desire. For example, Nicholas Balaisis provides an illuminating reading of negativity in the work of Wolfgang Giegerich. Mark Featherstone provides an interesting political history of so-called "post-modern America," with a Freudian tinge. Wanyoung Kim provides some coordinates for thinking about trauma, negativity, and death in the work of Sabina Spielrein, Heidegger, and Buddhism. We can see an attempt to explore "negative dialectics" as a therapeutic technique aimed at confronting instances of "positive thought" within analytic sessions with Joel Michael Crombez's chapter. Finally, Juliette Tocino-Smith examines the "Othering of death" and "hau" (a spirit of unreturned gifts) from an anthropological and sociological discourse, which has led to the rise of a denial of mortality.

We hope that this book will help to orient future discussions on negativity in psychoanalysis.

References

Rousselle, Duane. (2022) "The Deep Positivity of False Negativity in Seven Saturated Signifiers," *European Journal of Psychoanalysis*. As Retrieved on May 9th, 2023 from <www.journal-psychoanalysis.eu/articles/the-deep-positivity-of-false-negativity-in-seven-saturated-signifiers-or-psychoanalysis-and-new-love/>

Rousselle, Duane. (2023) "Escaping the Meta-Verse," *Sublation Magazine*. As Retrieved on May 9th, 2023 from <www.sublationmag.com/post/escaping-the-meta-verse>

Section 1

Foundations

Chapter 1

Who Is Transferring What to Whom? Resistance to Lacan

Ellie Ragland

Preamble

Lacan's theory of transference (Seminar, Book VIII, 1960–61) was being translated by Bruce Fink at that time. It has, since, appeared with Norton in 1988 (New York and London) as *Transference*. The radical newness that was spoken of at Amherst concerned Lacan's concept of knowledge: the theory that we transfer our feelings, expectations, and speech onto another (an analyst or another person) because we think they know something about who we are and who we should become. The Freudian concept of the analyst has been that she can offer a perspective on reality that is true and a guarantee of how one is to act or change. Lacan argued, rather, that the analyst does not have the correct reality paradigm to help an analysand with his or her impasses in knowledge and desire. But, he maintained, the phenomenon itself (including the fact that it includes feelings of love and hate) tells us more about an unstable base for knowledge in being, than it does about who has the correct theory. The analyst's role, then, is to sit in as a silent cause for a desire and knowledge that only the patient knows and that he or she can speak only in the (logical) time it takes to unravel repressed traumata, drop harmful personae, and make new identifications to live by. I would suggest that the truth of the Lacanian Real appears both in analysis and outside it, in the logical time of the moment of seeing, the time for understanding, and the moment of concluding (Ragland, 1988; Lacan, 1977a).

Introduction

I am aware that the question in the title of this chapter may seem naive to some and purely rhetorical to others. But Lacan posed it in the *Discourse of Roma* in 1953, the year from which he dates his official teaching (2006a: 197–268). Whoever revives this question in 1985 or 1998 in North America may well suppose the answer to be obvious. Lacan contradicted the American view in which doctors themselves are idealized, where the analysand is automatically seen as *transferring* her child-like feelings to the adult analyst. Lacan said that at the beginning of an analysis, the analysand often supposes that she is the subject who knows.

DOI: 10.4324/9781003375920-2

Confronting an analyst for the first time, it is not unusual to hear the patient say the everyday dictum: I know *myself*, or *I* myself know, therefore, I do not need an analysis. I'm fine, I'm happy: "I AM what I SAY: Contemporary Denials of the Unconscious" was presented at the 52nd Study Days of the School of the Freudian Cause in Paris, France.[1]

At the point of having an unsolvable problem, many who have started an analysis at someone's suggestion stop: self-confident, self-sufficient individuals have no need of analysis. They just want a quick fix by way of medications, short-term therapy, self-help groups, or the like. James Jackson Putnam, a Harvard neurology professor, underwent a short analysis with Freud. At age 63, in 1909, Putnam had gone to hear Freud speak. They began a correspondence in German and Putnam decided to go to Vienna to be analyzed by him. After his analysis ended, he insisted, against Freud's strong protests, that medicine/psychiatry be the base of psychoanalytic practice in America (Hale, 1971). In his first session with Freud, Putnam, a rigid, idealistic Bostonian, had told Freud he felt guilty for not having done enough for psychoanalysis or even for civilization in the USA. In fact, any American who wanted an analysis had to go abroad to do so.

In 1911, Putnam founded the American Psychoanalytic Association (APA), following Freud's example of founding the International Psychoanalytic Association (IPA) in 1910. Psychoanalysis and psychiatry have been joined together in the USA since 1911. Today, America is the only country in the world that requires medical licensure as a necessity for practicing psychoanalysis. Lawsuits have been brought against the IPA and the APA by American psychologists who have demanded the right to practice their expertise without a medical degree. These legal efforts have paid off and psychologists, counselors, social workers have won the right to practice without medical training. Yet, they must seek out a psychiatrist or psychiatric nurse to prescribe the necessary medications for their patients. Putnam's identity remained that of a medical doctor with psychoanalytic training (Miller, 1988; Ragland, 1988: 88–104). Putnam had done a three-year analysis with Freud in Vienna: because of that, Freud designated him to introduce psychoanalysis to the USA. Lacan, like Freud, was trained as a psychiatrist. Both of them went on to develop psychoanalysis beyond medicine, as a practice outside chemistry, biology, and neuroscience. Unlike them, Putnam privileged the *supposed* certainty of medicine over the uncertainty of the unconscious. He was the model for what has become the standard American treatment for those seeking help for psychological problems – somatization over unrecognized knowledge.

Knowing nothing of the history of psychoanalysis in the USA, many individuals seek help for their mental distress. They want to know how to handle their lives, how to get "a hold on" things as Tom Svolos says (2020). In the USA today, the usual treatment for those challenged by problems they cannot solve is to try to change their *behavior* or teach them to *adapt* to "reality." With this goal in mind, the "helpers" join hands with a psychiatrist or psychiatric nurse. If someone begins an analysis, sooner or later, they will look to the clinician onto whom the *transfer* hopes, ideal ego projections, love, and suffering. The analyst/caregiver gradually becomes idealized and is seen as the one whose expert knowledge will find the correct answers for the patient. The Neo-Freudian standard practice in North American clinical practice today reinforces the patient's illusions. Practitioners view the one who has come for help as weak. And they see themselves as strong. The clinician's expertise becomes the criterion of care. She is *supposed* to know the answers for what will help the patient. Should the analyst reciprocate any feelings toward the patient, she is guilty of countertransference. Freud invented the notions of transference and countertransference, the latter said to be an obstacle to analytic work (*SE*, vol. XI, 1910, vol. XII, 1911–1).

Countertransference indicated to Freud that an analyst should be analyzed anew. Lacan did not agree. If the analysis is not a two-body involvement, a dialectic between analyst and analysand constructed to help her in her quest for knowledge and insight, she will remain adrift, drowning in her sea of "emotional" pain. Lacan's critique of the clinic that developed in Freud's wake addresses principally ego psychology, which sometimes dovetails with object relations theories and practice. Although Lacan gave no account of the "uses" of the countertransference in object relations theories and praxes, he, nonetheless, developed a thorough-going rethinking of the concept of the "object" as understood by these analysts. His thinking here can be found in myriad places, such as the brief correspondence he had with Donald Winnicott. They maintained a friendship for many years and tried to arrange exchange lectures, a venture that failed. It has been called a missed encounter.[2] In his early *Seminars*, Lacan discussed object relations theories and the uses made of various concepts of the "object" in the countertransference. His thinking is incipient in his letter to Winnicott and is elaborated in the greatest depth in two of his *Seminars* on "the object" (Lacan, 1967, 2020b). The focus of my article on transference and resistance is on Lacan's view of the theories and practice of ego psychology, not his theories concerning "the object" or object relations. (*Seminars* IV and XIII are just two of the 26 Lacan gave from 1950 to 1980. A list of Lacan's *Seminars* can be found on "Lacan's Seminars"/Wikipedia/Chronological/Internet.)

Knowledge and Negative Transference

The Lacanian analyst places herself in the difficult position of encouraging a "negative" transference to help an analysand become acquainted with his own unconscious structure. The silence of the analyst in Lacanian practice enables the analysand to gradually hear and see himself. From this place, he will gradually become able to name his Desire, apart from the desires others have for him. Lacan's model goes in the opposite direction from the ego-psychology paradigm. American Neo-Freudians use the supposed *reality* of transference love to help the patient *remake* his ego, to reform it on the model of the analyst's supposedly healthy, reality-based ego. The Lacanian model argues that transference love is an Imaginary misrecognition of the other and, as such, *blocks* the analysand's unconscious truth, leaving him the slave of his Other's Desire. When the Lacanian analyst does not return the love the patient offers him, he creates a kind of "true love," which is not the everyday love of Imaginary misrecognition.

The Lacanian analyst, therefore, presumes to inscribe himself *in the action* of the transference, with the goal of helping the analysand see his ego as his own object. This analyst does not want to understand the patient, feel his sorrows, or give him a soft shoulder to cry on. Not only is the patient already enslaved by an Other's Desire, but her body is also marked by the Real of the signifiers that *speak her*. Miller outlines this theory in his development of Freud's and Lacan's notions of the source of unconscious knowledge as coming from a *parl-être, the speaking being* (Miller, 2011). She is unaware that an Other's language *speaks her* and enslaves her to her Desire. The Other – the outside world – has begun to structure a person's identity, even before birth, in the sense that she will be born into an environment where she is wanted or not. From the start, her unconscious subjectivity is alien, created by others (Lacan, 2019). From Lacan's perspective, the analysand's suffering comes from her living in a state of unconscious subjugation and alienation, spoken by the Real of signifiers she did not invent. When the analyst takes a patient's transference literally – positive or negative – he will erroneously think that it is aimed at him. He will believe that he should respond to the patient's demands. If the analyst thinks he has the answer to the hysteric's demand for love, for example, or the obsessional's search for answers, or thinks he serves as a stand-in for better parents, the analysand will remain imprisoned.

Lacan's campaign against ego psychology manifests itself throughout his teaching. He opposed the idea that there is a *whole* self that serves as an agent of strength, synthesis, mastery, integration, and adaptation to realistic norms. Lacan perceived ego-psychology analysts as pushing their analysands toward an ideal of health that is nothing more than a regurgitation of cultural group norms. In his early essays, Lacan accused the psychoanalytic establishment of having rendered Freud's revolutionary discoveries banal. By prizing technique above the meaning of the unconscious, such analysts believed that Freud's rules alone provided direct access to truth (Lacan, 1988b). Insofar as these rules have evolved into a ceremonial formalism, any questioning of the Neo-Freudian canon amounts to heresy. Lacan alleged that Freud's miraculous structures had been reduced to the nonconceptual, nonintellectual conformism of social suggestion and psychological superstition (Lacan, 1982: 39).

Lacan's aversion, particularly, to psychoanalytic practice in the United States can be attributed in part to cultural differences in intellectual formation. Since the 17th century, pragmatism and empiricism have reigned supreme in Anglo-American scientific investigations. Sir Francis Bacon founded the scientific method by arguing that truthful knowledge is obtained through observation and inductive reasoning where it is weighed and measured by controlled experiments (Bacon, 1620). John Locke, the father of cognitive psychology, maintained that at birth the human mind is a blank slate and should be studied in terms of the *experiences* written on it: those studies should be based on a medical model of natural science (Locke, 1690). The French academy has given primacy, rather, to philosophical and theoretical conceptualizations from, at least, the time of René Descartes. The question of whether God existed as the source of knowledge was not of concern to him. He simply assumed God's existence. But as a philosopher and mathematician, he said "*I* THINK, therefore *I* AM." Conscious thinking and being were equivalents: *cogito ergo sum* (Descartes, 2018). Unlike Descartes and the British empiricists, Lacan was not concerned with thrashing out the relative merits of induction or deduction. Some have suggested that Lacan's epistemology can be reduced to a deductive methodology.

While Lacan's "empirical" data are not those of *quantifiable* studies, they are "scientific" in the sense that the word *science* means "to know." Adhering to Freud, Lacan developed Freud's thinking on the phenomena that govern evanescent occurrences such as dreams, fantasies, desire, all pointing to an unconscious part of the "mind" that gives it a subjective structure, rather than an objective one. He based his rereading of Freud on mathematics, linguistics, and multiple fields of investigation that study the human and its knowledge. Given his training as a medical doctor, it stands to reason that he would incorporate knowledge such as that gained from Jacques Monod, who had won a Nobel prize in 1965 for his work in physiology and medicine. In his teaching, Lacan took account of Monod's revolutionary thinking about biological theories on perception, mathematical symbolism, ethnological realities, animal behavior, genetics, DNA, the Real of psychic pain (1997). Insofar as today's *scientific* studies are done in a laboratory-controlled system and conducted relatively quickly, even if they are repeated later to ascertain possible errors, the idea of *readily available* knowledge is a prototype of American thinking. If one questions the everyday American, even the highly educated ones, about the cause of a given behavior or "dis-order," they readily answer that the scientists know the answer: studies show, they say, that scientists know more every day because of their discoveries concerning the human organism: DNA, genes, neurons, cells of the brain that controls the nervous system, and more. Or, if these answers do not seem certain enough, scientists themselves say that they will not know the answers to questions about the body and mind; they will not know the answers in their lifetimes.

For most Americans, progress is linear and based on the discoveries of the next superior biological model. Whatever the question, the reigning ideology is that the *master* discourses of science will find the right answer. If empirical data seem fuzzy, the dominant view is that the next test will find the right answer. In other words, such "thought" assumes that the body simply *thinks itself.* Miller has called one *resistance* to Lacan in the USA, the desire for quick and easy data, measurable and fixed solutions, practical answers, a quick fix, in short, Slavoj Žižek (2015). Nancy Gillespie and Marie Christina Aguirre have called the USA "the home of ego psychology" (2018: 107): science = ego = body = knowledge. Yet, in a sense, the criticism that Lacan aimed at the American establishment could be more correctly aimed at 19th-century Austria, where psychoanalysis was born, or in England where it fled during World War II. Freud himself contributed to the image of the analyst as an objective, scientific observer who regarded the patient's behavior and speech as an object of study *outside* the analyst. One might even call Freud's "scientism" an Anglo-Austrian neo-positivism in the wake of Darwinian evolutionary materialism. Indeed, Freud *was* influenced by Darwin. Like his daughter Anna after him, he increasingly stressed the defensive properties of the ego and proposed that its synthesizing and adaptive functions can gradually access reality (Anna Freud, 1993). In 1937, Heinz Hartmann, also Viennese, went further afield than Freud or his daughter. The ego is autonomous, he said, a conflict-free zone. It has no unconscious base and can, thus, be treated by a direct kind of communication, by what he named ego psychology (King, 2013).

Lacan did not attack Freud's implicit Darwinism so much as the general Anglo-American belief in the concept of an objectifiable reality ego that assumes its knowledge to be true and accurate. Lacan unflaggingly insisted that the human subject is neither unified nor finally unifiable. Because Lacan delimited consciousness, making consciousness and language themselves defenses against unconscious knowledge, he is not generally understood by ego psychologists who place the defenses in the conscious ego itself. The Lacanian subject *(je/I-moi/ego)* is not unified in consciousness. Although the ego *seems* intrinsically unified, it unravels in dreams, psychoses, fantasy, and other psychic manifestations such as jokes and slips of the tongue. The Freudian ego projects itself into consciousness as the principle of individuality, personality, and the base of emotion and affect. Lacan demonstrated that because the ego emanates from the unconscious – the split off part of its knowledge base – it must continually verify itself through the very means of its occultation: through the conscious knowledge one spouts to others through the seemingly arbitrary mechanism of language.

The Lacanian ego functions by the logic of this paradox: it is there and not there. The very structure by which it exists means that the ego cannot "see or hear" itself. Following Freud's late thinking, Lacan retained the concept of a split in the ego *(Ichspaltung)*. But he differed from Freud radically by conceiving of the split as a mental function that is operative in every human subject's life. Indeed, the split is not manifested in the psychoses in the way that Freud had proposed it was. Lacan depicts the psychotic ego as full blown. It only becomes disorganized, obviously split, when a challenge comes to it from the Symbolic order. Challenges that threaten this ego concern its identity in relation to the father function, its identity as a social person apart from the mother. Late in his life, Freud returned to the ideas of biology as *causative* of mental structure. He argued that a split in personality is a "split" from reality that occurs in a psychotic event that is caused by quantitative biological organic factors. He found one explanation for this strange phenomenon in the idea that the ego has a cortical surface that breaks (Freud, 1938: 139–143).

Identification: Structure, Topology

Where Freud returned to biology, Lacan went forward to topology. The Lacanian ego is separate from its existence as a physical organism with the inherited traits given by genetic DNA microcellular structure (Crick, Watson, & Wilkins,

1953). Not surprisingly, given the *human* tendency to reduce its mind and body to its organic structure – if a religious explanation for life is missing – Richard Dawkins came along in a post-religion era. He wrote a book claiming that genes structure everything: the brain, muscles, the body, personality, emotions, paradoxes in nature, and much more (Dawkins, 1976).

In today's America, one commonly hears people, even the most learned, say that genes cause homosexuality, bad moods, all diseases, everything: whatever it is, some gene in one's ancestry tree will validate it. I have heard the highest-level medical doctors say that they are *sure* scientists could isolate the causative gene of a disease if they could go far enough back in family history. If a gene is not the root cause of a disease or a personality trait, then the linkage of the gene to a brain neuron will explain the cause of a phenomenon, so say scientists and the general public who spout their views. Biology is mind and body. Truth and knowledge are sought in the data given by empirical researchers. In *Neurologie Versus Psychanalyse*, Hervé Castanet bases his contentions against the world of neuroscience on Jacques-Alain Miller's course of 2007–08, *Nullibileté – Tout le monde est fou* (11/14/2007–05/28/2008/Course given in the Lacanian Orientation, unpublished). In that course, Miller argued that the concept of the *neuro* has created a new Real, something beyond body and mind, beyond language and identification (Castanet, Paris: Navarin, 2022: 165, currently being translated into English for Routledge by Julia Richardson). I would say of this new Real that it is, strangely, to be located not just within the physical organism but in the theological logic that imputes answers to questions of existence to a God who knows all.

Freud did not depart from his neurophysiological training as Lacan did. Given his training as a medical psychiatrist, Lacan was, of course, concerned to know the true causes that structure human "being" and knowing. Of course, he took account of genetics and neuroscience in his teaching. Speaking at the most basic level, no one could say that eye color, hair color, body features, or Huntington's Chorea, for example, are not genetically caused. But when *normal discourse* argues that homosexuality or musical talent are caused by genes within the family lineage, one might look, rather, at the phenomenon of identification (Lacan, 1961–1962). Lacan separated the Real of the physical body's *needs* (food, air, sleep) from the mirror moment when a baby sees its *image* for the first time and brings together its disunified body with this image that serves as a prototype for the sense of having/being a unified body. Calling the body an envelope or a sack containing its organs, Lacan taught that the image of its unity is a false harmony.

The ego ignores the division by language and the control exercised by the drives. Instead of deducing the mind from genes or neurons, this Imaginary event constitutes the origin of the mind in an image, and ego. Mirror stage logic has it that the body equals the ego/"I Am Me," a narcissistic image. Although the body is only a sack of skin that holds its internal organs, the guarantee of wholeness comes from the baby's identifying its image with that of the other holding it before the mirror stage: I am *me* and I am *one* with the other. The symbiosis of mirror logic starts between 6 and 18 months of age. This event is revolutionary for the baby. He builds his ego on the mistaken idea that being is seeing, that he and the other, the external prop, are one. The first *dits maternels* (maternal sayings) provide him with a way to make sense of the world as he shows in baby speech, especially in the happy announcement before the mirror – "Me/Mommy"!

Given the scientific uncertainty about which senses are innate, we can say, at least, that reflexes are considered innate. No studies have shown that the brain or the body organizes the first images, sounds, touches, and drives that constitute an infant's pre-mirror stage perception. We know that they are unstable, floating, and chaotic. In reference to pre-mirror stage fragmentation, which functions like metonymy, by thing-to-thing contiguity, the mirror image functions as a substitute, a *primary* metaphor that joins body, being, and image, in a sense of totalization. During the first 18 months of her life, the baby has discovered her nose, her feet, her toes, and her fingers, and has been given nursery rhyme names for them in a language Lacan called *lalangue*. It is the first language of pure jouissance. At around 18 months of age, formal language begins to emerge in the infant's use of images, *symbols*, and words to substitute one thing for another. The outside Other prompts the child to speak as *I*, not *me*. At approximately this age, the child is encouraged to not be one with her mother anymore. The Father, an outside Other, a third term, enjoins her to accept separation from her mother to whom she is not-all in any case. This *secondary* metaphor is what Lacan called the law of the Name-of-the-Father, which teaches the infant "no," gives her ever clearer boundaries (Ragland, 1986: 196–266).

Departing from Freud, Lacan said that the ego is *constructed* not by biology or neurophysiology but by a child's taking in words *from*, and identifications *with*, outside others. Freud never truly exited from biology. He said at the end of his life that much more had to be learned about the brain before final conclusions could be made about the nature of the mind. Lacan was interested in Freud who resisted the science of his day. Following Freud, who postulated the idea of an *Ich Ideal* and an *Ideal Ich*, terms that he used indeterminately, Lacan reformulated these concepts. Freud characterized the *ego ideal* as the agency that sublimates the unconscious sexual and aggressive id. It shows its face in conscious life as one would want oneself to be. His *ideal ego* is housed in the unconscious superego and is the perfect image of one's sexuality (Freud, 1914: 67–100).[3] Whereas Freud was revolutionary in inventing a three-part model of the mind, ego–id–superego, Lacan turned it into four parts that work differently depending on which structure one is talking about. Early on, Lacan split both the narcissistic ego and the speaking subject, but not between a superego and an id, agencies that he did not retain. He proposed, rather, the ego ideal/ideal ego/speaking subject/Other). He depicted the unconscious *ideal ego* as being formed by identification with *ego ideals* – the outside others of the child's world – that structure its identity and perception.

This is an antithetical view to those of geneticists and neuroscientists who locate everything *inside* the physical organism. He advanced the theory that the way these primary ego ideals offer language (Symbolic), images (Imaginary), and treat the realities of the body (Real) build the child's ego as linguistic, narcissistic, and passionate. The first *outside* others give the child a sense of *inner* self, of narcissistic self-love that becomes the base from which an ego launches transference love into the world by identification. The *ideal ego*, which projects itself to others, is an *unconscious* part of the ego, not of Freud's superego. It is patterned on the specific others the ego has come to idealize. Paradoxically, the ideal ego is a secondary structure that projects itself into conscious life as a constellation of the unconscious. It was formed in a (false) certainty that its words and perceptions are objective and true, not subjective as they are in fact. Lacan promoted the idea that one assumes that the Imaginary ideal ego she *projects* onto the world is identical with itself, while it is but a narcissistic formation, a fiction linked to her mirror-stage formation of her ego. The formations that create the life of the mind as a kind of inner life are the opposite of innate. In life, paradoxically, one must identify with outside others in the world for affirmation and support of an unconscious Imaginary construction.

I'll give a personal example: I once played a trick on friends at a dinner party. I told them that I knew a secret each husband had. They said, "Oh yeah, What?" I said that each of them thought his wife knew the truth about people. They were stunned. Each one said, "but my wife does:" ego. The status of the speaking subject is uncertain (the doubting *I*). The ego and the Other speak the *I*, who must await validation of its certainties from others. Yet, the mere idea that an unconscious part of the mind speaks the conscious subject would be called a myth by most, a *spectral* notion of the mind. In the *game* of everyday life, the ego usually wins, and truth remains hidden from sight. This is quite a different theory regarding Lacan's teaching from the popular misconception that the Lacanian "subject" is in a state of permanent fragmentation. The "whole" ego dominates the contest: "I'm better than you." Stuart Schneiderman, despite his being the only returning American to have been analyzed by Lacan (Pamela Tytell went to Italy), wrote to me that I must not make a mistake about Lacan's ego. It was/is whole, he said (Ragland, 1986: 355). Perhaps the American thinking about the ego led Schneiderman to forsake practicing as a Lacanian analyst in favor of practicing as a life coach, someone who trains egos.

The picture of the ego as whole has led clinicians to analyze what they call "defenses," which Freud placed in the conscious ego's typical patterns (Freud, 1894). He called these defenses psychotic in 1894. His revolution in turning the normal mind into three parts did not happen until 1914. Not questioning the ego, except to think of it as a conscious "self," analysts apply their *conceptions* of health to their patients, in attempting to remodel the patient's defenses on their ego. The patient's ego "defenses" are taken by the analyst to be unobjective and a distortion of *reality* (Ragland, 1986: 6). Lacan calls this ego psychology a *surface* approach that muddles psychic truth and reality, thereby allowing the unwary analyst to take the postulates she does not question to be objective viewpoints. This kind of knowledge and certainty was described by Lacan as a *university discourse*, a discourse of license and certification (Lacan, 1972–1973/1998, 1969–1970/2007).

The analysand becomes a victim of the *analyst's* self-illusions and is unaware that Freud's discovery did not situate truth or reality in the analyst or in technique but placed "truth" itself in question (Lacan, 1965–1966/1989). Lacan claimed that in the wake of Freud, who took science itself as his object of study, typical Neo-Freudians conceive of an analytic cure as objective. The analyst, unwittingly, imposes her own Desires and symptoms on the analysand, thereby infusing him with an imagined "reality" that is supposed to make him healthy, capable of adapting and changing his behavior (Lacan, 1956–1957/2020: 261). Such a procedure is meant to "strengthen" a weak ego. What occurs, from a Lacanian standpoint, is a deepening of the patient's alienation from the truth of her being. The patient's ego is a structure that has already been created as alienated by the Other's Desire and its discourse, which imposes her words (S), needs (R), and wants (I) on her child. The analyst who subjugates his analysand to his ideals merely pushes her ego further into the abyss that has led to her subjugation in the first place. Treating the ego by such a discourse does nothing to change the repetitions of her history.

Resistance and Repetition

Current Anglo-American psychoanalytic theory, in addition to retheorizing Freud's concept of the transference (*Ubertragung*), has focused a lot of attention on the analysis of a patient's resistance (*Widerstand*). Indeed, the theory of *ego resistance* has been a cornerstone of psychoanalysis since Freud's day: partisan practitioners see the patient's *ego as a resisting bundle of defenses*. By pointing them out, they become the copy to be imitated. Freud conceived of psychodynamic psychology to treat libidinal energy caused by the brain. Today's practitioners who believe that the ego is the seat of the mind do not look for an unconscious, only for mechanisms of resistance. Freud named these defenses as projection, denial, sublimation, displacement, repression, rationalization, regression, humor, acting out, introjection, and 15 more. It is not surprising that the concept of resistance has a *negative* connotation in standard analytic speech. Transference is said to offer a *positive* affective means by which a patient can overcome his resistance to knowing his truth. Freud, nonetheless, said that the transference occurs through a "false" love the patient feels for his doctor.

He called it a misalliance, a false connection (Freud & Breuer, 1895/1955). In treatment, the analyst says the analysand is resisting when she fails to attain a new level of behavior or understanding. She is resisting her own wishes and drives, resisting what some analysts have called the *hic und nunc* of (objective) reality. Freud thought dreams were *repressing* unfulfilled wishes (Freud, 1900–1901). Today's Neo-Freudian analyst believes he, like Freud, can *interpret* the patient's dreams and in that way begin a "liquidation" of her ego defenses. Interpretations are thought to give the patients *insight*, a step in the progression of cure, a step by which ego-oriented analysts try to rid the patient of her resisting ego, rid her of the defenses that keep her "weak" ego from being whole and healthy. "Insight" is supposed to restore a whole ego that has been broken and damaged by bad parents. Although the concepts of id and superego are still relevant in analysis, they play little role in the clinical world where the ego is king, and adaptation and behavior are the stake.

By contrast, Lacan's elevation of the subject of the unconscious over conscious-ness sheds new light on the phenomenon of resistance itself. A person's uncon-scious insists *in* speech and in meaning. It plays its role there as invisible, as speech that means more than it says, that denies that there is any hidden meaning to the words spoken. The absent unconscious speaks an unacknowledged discourse that prefers to *repeat* itself in language and behavior, rather than know itself (Lacan, 1964/1977a). The repetitious phenomenon of everyday life is true of everyone, not only of people with obvious problems but of clinicians as well. The idea is to get the patient to quit repeating "bad" behavior. Certain about their "know how," psychological professionals resist their patient's truth, and often their own. It may come as a surprise to some that Lacan called Freud's interpretation of the *content* of his patients' speech a resistance, Freud's own. Freud erred, Lacan said, in calling almost all human speech-acts defense mechanisms. If the ego mediates between superego ideals and dangerous sexual and aggressive thoughts, as Freud thought, then education of the potentially realistic ego becomes necessary.

In Freud's thought, if resistance comes from the patient's ego repressing uncon-scious drives and unquestioned ideals that she does not want to integrate into con-sciousness, into reality, then she must be re-educated. Freud used transference as a discourse of the analyst as master, as the analyst working against what he saw as his patients' resistance to his interpretation of their unconscious wishes: Freud said wishes and repression; Lacan said desire and jouissance. But Freud, the expert on sexuality, drew back, in the face of abusive sexual acts recounted by his patients. He dropped his seduction theory at the insistence of friends and colleagues and decided, rather, to attribute acts of sexual abuse to his patients' fantasies. He implicitly denied the widespread phenomenon of familial sexual abuse. He found no perpetrators – only sexual patients unable to unveil their fantasies. It would be unwelcome to admirers of Freud to accept his complicity in the failure of Dora's treatment. She had caused Herr K.'s sexual advances, he said. She had spurred him on. Is it any wonder that Dora left Freud after three months of treatment? She felt *lost*. She was lost in a forest in one of her dreams during her analysis. On finding her way out of the forest, on finding her home, she discovered that her father was dead. Indeed, the figure of a dead father, typified the men aligned against her. Freud was *supposed* to be her ally. Freud misinterpreted Dora's resistance to Herr K.'s sexual advances. He felt that she was resisting what he had hoped would be a positive transference love. These things helped Dora find the will to confront the K. family and her own and to unveil their lies.

After leaving Freud, she revealed the sexual deceptions hidden behind the pre-tenses of the adults around her. Frau K. was pretending to be Herr Bauer's nurse. The K. family had moved some distance to the new Bauer residence so that, in theory, Frau K. could continue being Herr Bauer's nurse. Since Herr K.'s wife was in a sexual relationship with Dora's father, Herr K., as a kind of revenge against his wife as well as an attraction to a beautiful young girl, pursued Dora. He arranged occasions for them to be alone together so he could try to seduce her. He bought her gifts that her father insisted she accept. Dora's father took her to Freud for analytic treatment when she upset the family applecart by finally slapping Herr K. when he tried to kiss her and at the same time denigrated his wife. Dora must have felt doubly confused. He was saying that he desired her sexually and that his wife gave him nothing: was he interested in her or his wife? Freud misconstrued Dora's sexual confusions. At age 18, her sexual identity was in flux. She found the naked women's bodies that Frau K. showed her in a picture book interesting. She had no interest in the boy of her age who was pursuing her. Herr K. was not a solution for her either. He was married to her father's mistress, and he was old, although "comely," as Freud pointed out. Who was she sexually? She was trying to figure that out within the world around her. Freud erred in telling Dora that her *resistance* to Herr K.'s kiss was *abnormal* for a (sexual) girl of age 18 (Freud, 1901a). He thought physical problems, her cough and her aphonia, might be contributing to *her* problems, to her Dora's refusal to adapt to her family situation.

Doctors could find no physical reason for her cough. Lacan suggested that her cough showed an identification with her father who was suffering from lung disease (Lacan, 1958). Freud was not particularly interested in Dora's physical symptoms, but he was fascinated by her sexuality. The cause of her neurosis, he suggested, was a mental *conflict* that indicated that bisexuality was at the root of her problems as revealed by the pleasure she took in looking at pictures of naked women with Frau K. and her mentioning Frau K.'s beautiful white body. Lacan pointed out that Freud's *interpretation* of Dora's words was Freud's idea of her, not a true picture of her at all. Freud, like the ego psychologists who followed him, supposed that he had given Dora an objective, realistic picture of herself in her treatment. He erred, like today's empiricists, in placing himself outside, posing as a rational, separate, objective, scientific observer. As a young psychiatric medical student, Freud had been Jean-Martin Charcot's pupil. For a time, he found his master in Charcot, who presented his case studies by *observing* his patients – mostly women – naked. Charcot found this pose to be necessary for his diagnosis of their symptoms. He thought that by looking at the outside body, the external part, he would find the key to some inner organic disturbance. If D. M. Bourneville, a left-wing socialist and practicing alienist, another of Charcot's pupils, had not caught his ear, he would never have labeled many of the women who were sent to his clinic as hysterics, rather than psychotics ("alienated").

Prior to Bourneville's influence, Charcot had resisted the idea of thinking beyond the medical paradigm of his day. Under Bourneville's influence, he took the idea of hypnosis from F. A. Mesmer who thought animal magnetism, an invisible fluid, could run between a doctor and patient if she were in a state of hypnosis: if she were semi-conscious, he would be able to diagnose a medical disease. Charcot adopted the method of mesmerizing to induce hysteria in patients for the purpose of diagnosis. He thought that once they were sedated, semi-conscious, he would be able to detect the neurological root of hysteria. If not for Bourneville, he would have continued to adhere to the reigning doctrine: dramatic, emotional, traumatized women were psychotics, mentally disabled, demonically possessed, and epileptic (Brais, 1993). Charcot's influence marked the history of diagnosis in that Freud was the first in the centuries of labeling hysteria to find its cause as psychological, not physiological. He called it a neurosis, by which he meant the psychic return of repressed memories. The label *hysteria* has been applied to emotional, dramatic women since the discovery of the Kahun papyrus in Egypt where the word *hystera*, meaning the womb or uterus, was said to describe a nervous disease caused because the woman's womb was suffering from starvation or displacement (Ragland, 2024).

Unlike Freud, Lacan had no unified systematic theory of defenses (Ballestin, 2021). Ballestin argues that Lacan's Teaching – his oral seminars and his *écrits*, which are transcriptions of his written-up speeches and other texts – offers a knowledge that constitutes a new Symbolic order. His opus is both a testimonial to Freud and a resistance to stopping where Freud did. Ballestin points out that in his thinking, Lacan went from theories of the ego to that of discourse where he refined Roman Jakobson's discourse theory (Lacan, 1972–1973/1998, 1969–1970/2007). After discourse, Lacan developed the topology that he had begun with in 1953 in the "Rome Discourse." He began to present his theory of ego formation in 1936 at Marienbad, where he gave the first version of his mirror stage article, which he refused to publish. In 1949, he gave a subsequent version of it at Zurich (Lacan, 1949). In 1953, he began to interrogate Freud's followers on questions of technique and ego psychology (Lacan, 1955; and in *S*. II, Lacan, 1954–1955). Freud's followers, including those today who do not know how to acknowledge him, seek to validate the ego of his second topography from 1923–25 (Freud, 1923). In his second theory of the mind where he lays out its tripartite structure, he depicts it as a triumph over his first topography (Freud, 1900/1953).[4]

In the history article, Freud attributed the idea of an unconscious part of the mind to the neurologist H. Bernheim (1899). In "The Unconscious," Freud described two kinds of unconscious processes: the *latent* one of everyday life in which one thinks things to himself, things like "gotta do this, *do dit do dat*" (Dutch)/intentions, inferences. Freud recognized the latent state as the one evoked in hypnosis, a state Charcot used to induce hysteria. The other unconscious is repressed, not latent conscious thoughts, but pressed-under buried material that conscious life has segregated from its knowledge base because it tells truths of the Real that are impossible to bear, to hear. What agencies *manifest* these unconscious elements Freud asked himself. He invented the notions of the ego, the superego, and the id to carry both aspects of the unconscious: ego, superego, id. Freud's representational picture of the mind contained a reality principle, an idealizing and judging element, and a sexual and aggressive component. With this picture, he confidently launched his second topography.

Lacan relocated Freud's agencies. Resistance became an Imaginary function of the *ego*. He located its base in the unconscious ideal ego, which has an idea of itself as perfect (superego/Imaginary). The id stirs up resistance to the ego since it is the sexual and aggressive component of the mind (Real). Resistance, thus seen, is not a function of conscious ego defenses as ego psychologists believe it to be. Lacan's picture is, rather, that the ego reveals its *truth* as being: I *am me* denying my aggressive and sexual narcissism. The ego is a different constellation from the speaking subject – "*I* say" – with its pretense and puffery (Lacan, 1964/1977c: 148, 246; Lacan, 1957–1958/2017). In the popular psychological clinics of today's America, talking tends to be eschewed in favor of somatization. All too frequently, the only help a suffering person will get is a drug prescription and a DSM label. The clinical worker (increasingly, psychiatric nurses) will change the medication dosage of a patient whom she has *seen* for a five-to-ten-minute session or has *heard* on the phone but never met. These sessions occur once every four months, and in the time it takes to write a prescription. Psychological helpers are often found in behavioral institutes where they measure a patient's problems by the amount and kinds of drugs they give them. A typical session goes like this: "How are you feeling? We'll raise this dosage by 5 milligrams but lower the other two." Not only do they not want to hear a patient's story, nor are they interested in her hearing it. They do not have time. They have so many patients, and time is money. They do perk up if a patient says she is feeling worse than when they had previously talked.

The question of which medicines are to be changed and of how many milligrams of each is immediately addressed. Of course, many psychologists, social workers, counselors, and life coaches do listen and try to respond. Yet, even if they grasp something of the difficulties a patient has and want to help, they are bound by American law to turn to the psychiatric clinic where medical prescriptions are lotted out. The doctors (shrinks) make money. The pharmaceutical companies make money. The everyday caregivers usually do, although life coaches are said to be among the most highly paid professionals in the USA. In today's America, psychiatry is *resistance* incarnate. Putnam, with the ego pride that came from his being an American medical doctor, set up the psychoanalytic profession as a psychiatric clinic. Charcot, who stepped out of the bounds of medicine to help his patients, was superior to Putnam in helping patients. In contemporary America, many medical doctors earn salaries on a par with wealthy businessmen, unlike medical doctors in the rest of the world.

There Is No Unconscious Here

Lacan called today's American, so-called *mental health* clinics a place where a one-body psychology is practiced. Together, a licensed clinician and a medical person practice a kind of seeming two-body psychology, the treatment Lacan promoted. But in America, neither of the bodies (neither the care giver nor the drug prescriber) is the patient. The fastest growing class of mental health workers in the USA is that of life coaches. Although there are no federal or state requirements for anyone to operate as a coach, they are advised to take out malpractice insurance and encouraged to seek certificates from the many business companies who will grant them a certificate for a hefty fee. In these clinics, the practitioner's ego is supported by the power he gets from being certified. He speaks a *master* discourse supported by *university* credentials (Lacan, 1972–1973/1998, 1969–1970/2007). His prestige is enhanced by his association with medicine. Although it is difficult in any part of the world to get people to pay for their mental health, Lacanian analysts welcome suffering people. They practice sliding scale payments so that their doors are open to most people. American medicine, insurance companies, and pharmaceutical producers have no interest in Freud or Lacan, and certainly not in the idea that an unconscious part of the mind/body is in play in causing a patient's symptoms. These practitioners, usually not psychoanalysts, give medications without knowing or caring about a patient's life story.

They give them without knowing anything. The only requirement is that the patient pay. The *DSM* is a billing manual, following on from the International Classification of Diseases (ICD), which was founded to pay the families of soldiers who had gone missing in wartime. Money and power rule the game in America, and businesses have joined hands with the "health" workers whom they advertise as providing a wellness clinic where "clients," as in a business relationship, can find health: seven hours of sleep a night must be accompanied by a scheduled routine in which a certain amount of time is spent in physical exercise and diets are handed out to anyone concerned with his mental health. Businesses hold gourmet dinners in expensive restaurants that advertise them to clients with problems. Of course, there is a $50 entry fee for the client at the restaurant door: adaptation, behaviorism, "self-analysis," neurocognitive disorder. There is no unconscious here. One certification offered to life coaches is to tell future "clients" that their specialty is "self-analysis."

American short sessions cannot in anyway be tallied with Lacan's practice of short sessions where the stakes are to speak the truth(s) of the Real, not the lies of the Imaginary and the Symbolic: to speak the *bien dire* of the unconscious, not that of rhetoric (Ragland, 2015: 170). In 1963, Lacan was exiled from membership in the International Psychoanalytic Association, the Association founded by Freud in 1910. The reason given for the expulsion was what they called his deviant practices, his use of short sessions. The IPA had the rule that analytic sessions must last from 45 to 50 minutes. Although they said that their rule was unbendable, orthodox, some concerns about Lacan's unorthodox teaching and its growing popularity were in the wings. Lacan had developed the practice of variable length sessions, lasting from 10 minutes to long sessions. Starting in 1953, members of the IPA had begun to quarrel with Lacan over his short sessions and his theories. This resulted in Lacan and several followers breaking with the Parisian Society of Psychoanalysis (SPP) and founding a new society called the French Society (SFP). In 1963, with the strong protests of Sasha Nacht, they removed the membership status, not only of Lacan, but of all his followers who belonged to the French Society of Psychoanalysis.

René Laforgue and others had founded the Parisian Society of Psychoanalysis in 1926 on the advice of Freud to whom Laforgue had sent Marie Bonaparte for analysis and training. At the time of Lacan's 1963 "excommunication" and that of his followers, the IPA quickly relented concerning the status of all former members, except for Lacan. Membership was returned to his followers on the grounds that Lacan be struck from each one's list of training analysts. Five members stayed with him. The others dropped any relationship to his teaching and practices (Johnston, 2022/2013). As a former analysand of the Lacanian clinic, I can say that analytic sessions are repeated up to three to five times a day and as many times a week as an analysand can spend in time and money, given the analyst's calendar. If distress should arise for a patient in the interim, these analysts see them on Saturdays. And telephone calls are accepted without fees being asked for.

American analysts have, in general, dismissed the theories and practice of Lacan. There is a pretense at studying Lacan in some institutes where the teachers who are acceptable have no current standing in the Lacan world. Yet, despite the ascendance of ego psychology in the USA, Freud has been trounced here. For 20 years, Otto Rank (1884–1939) was one of Freud's pupils. He contradicted Freud on every part of his theory and practice. The fact that Freud accommodated Rank on every point led followers to say that his relationship with Rank proved that he was not the dictatorial master some had described him to be. Finally, in exasperation, Freud's students forced him to abandon Rank. Yet, paradoxically, Rank has triumphed over Freud in America. Not only do psychiatrists use the short sessions Rank recommended, but psychotherapists do as well. In his writings about psychoanalysis and in his practice, Rank promoted ever shorter sessions and ever decreasing frequency. The patient's speech was not to be heeded. Rank assured mental health care workers that a cure should arise quickly because of their keen insight and vision. He invented the term "psychotherapy" to describe a clinical learning and unlearning experience that should be focused on *feelings*, not speech. Patient learning (and unlearning) occurs *quickly* as if the patient were coming out of a *birth trauma*.

Although it is thought that he had invented the idea of a birth trauma, the notion was first suggested by Freud in a note he added in 1909 to volume IV of the *SE* (Freud, 1900–1901). There, Freud, ever seeking a physical explanation for the cause of psychic trauma, suggested that the experience of birth itself is the first human experience of anxiety because of the necessary separation from the mother's womb. It is the prototype of all future affects of anxiety, he suggested. He went as far as to suggest that birth is the biological/psychological nucleus of the unconscious, which remembers being asphyxiated in the vaginal canal. Furthermore, he suggested, it is the original experience of separation that lingers in the thorny relations between the sexes and the prototype of castration anxiety. In 1924, Rank's theory of *The Trauma of Birth* was published (Chelmsford: the Courier Corporation). He then visited the USA in 1929 and proclaimed to the IPA that Freud's concept of *neurosis* was wrong: to tell an individual she is neurotic is the equivalent of telling her to "self-destruct." If a person has emotional problems, she is not neurotic. She has simply failed to be *creative*. Furthermore, rather than focus on individual cases, Rank promoted what he called *action* learning and *group* problem-solving: get rid of your old ego, he said. Separate yourself from yourself, just as you separated from your mother at birth. Patients must pursue *care* by using their *heart muscle*.

It is not surprising, given that the name of the mental health game in America is a quick fix, the quicker the better, that Rank's idea of a *learning coach* has taken hold. Life coaches flourish. The only training required of them is their say-so: I understand people! And they are paid well. They have become the necessary equivalent of a swimming coach or an exercise therapist (Rank, 1978/1936, 2011). In *Seminar* X Lacan adhered to early Freud by continuing with the idea that birth lies at the root of anxiety (Lacan, 1962–1963/2014). The first loss is not of the breast, Lacan said, but of the placenta. Contemporary empirical scientists have taken up the question of whether or not there is a birth trauma. Their answer is that there is *no trauma* because the 23 individuals they asked said they had no memory of it. How could a person remember the impact of birth on his body or mind when no human remembers his first cry, but no one doubts that the cry happened. It is the first sign of life, the moment of showing that the infant can breathe.

Although Lacan did not see himself as a revolutionary, his thesis is revolutionary. He presented the truth that conscious language is itself a defense against unconscious knowledge and, moreover, that affects do not arise from repression, but translate the language of the unconscious (Lacan, 1962–1963/2014). There are no *repressed* emotions, Lacan proposed, just representations that attach themselves to the latest ideas. In *Seminar XX*, affects are adrift and unmoored and seek an anchoring idea. There Lacan said, "I speak with my body, and I do so unbeknownst to myself" (1973: 119). Miller chose the theme of "The Unconscious and the Speaking Body" for the Xth conference of the World Association of Psychoanalysis, held at Rio de Janeiro, Brazil, in 2016. But, before he said "speaking body," Lacan clarified his early ideas where he had developed the theory that the mind is structured *like* a language, like metaphor and metonymy which work together, like primary and secondary thought. In the 1960s, Lacan described speaking subjects/egos as "speaking beings" (Imaginary and Symbolic) who refer their words to the image or the imago.

Discourse and Truth

In *Seminar* XI, he taught that representations of the Symbolic are attached to unconscious signifiers that repeat. There is a moment, he said, when the speaking *being* becomes a speaking *body*. In *Seminar* XVII (1969–70), before he was to say, "speaking body," he had developed the proposition that the unconscious dwells within four coherent discourse structures, a discourse being that which makes a social link between subjects, intersubjectivity. In Lacan's teaching there is no discourse structure for the psychotic who does not make a social link. Where most subjects find a "no," a *limit* in language, the psychotic encounters a hole, a void. A neurotic subject speaks in a four-part structure, there being no whole subject or ego in his way of thinking. The four discourse structures he invented are formations where elements that he symbolized as mathemes are held together in a topological way, in which four elements are held together like the Borromean structure by the Real (the object *a* as surplus jouissance), the Symbolic (S1), the Imaginary (S2), the Real ($ and *a*) (the $). The subject of speech, alternately, S1, S2, $, *a*, display the logic of the Symptom, the knot, which has the properties of the three orders.

The discourse of the social can exist because the subject has separated mentally from the (m)Other of the mirror-stage in the name-of-the-father who breaks the illusionary sense of Oneness that marks the first sense of identity a person has. This "necessary" separation guarantees the speaking subject a place in the Symbolic.

The separation begins for most children at approximately 18 months of age (Ragland, 1986). In psychosis, separation/castration has not been inscribed in the child's knowledge base. There is, then, no possibility that the subject can speak from a place of difference, within a dialectic of self and other. In psychosis, one could say that there is a malfunction in Oedipal identification. The child identifies with the mother and forecloses the father: whatever the person's gender, the psychotic remains identified with the feminine (Lacan's *pousse-à-la-femme*), psychosis being the result of no "no" having enabled a split in the Imaginary symbiosis between the (m)Other and child. In psychosis no masculine phallic logic of difference has insinuated itself (Ragland, 1997). This logic is paradoxical because the psychotic person identifies herself as the mother's phallus, as being ALL to her. Still, this logic stays on the Imaginary side, plagued by a difficulty in organizing the Real of the drives because the masculine Symbol for difference is lacking. The operation of metaphor in speech is made possible by the father function that introduces the possibility of metaphor, of transference, as the logic of substitution over the metonymy of the sameness and contiguity. The role of the father is to introduce anchoring points of limit (an *I*) into the signifying flow of endless metonymy (ego). In psychosis the *I* of speech is not divided, nor is the ego. This being speaks as pure ego, as his ideal ego, which is one with his ego ideal(s). The psychotic person's unconscious lies dormant, failing to impose the logic of metaphor on his speech.

Lacan's *dialectical* discourse structures necessarily exclude psychotic speech. At the place of the *subject* one finds an *agent* (cf. Kenneth Burke) of speech who operates as an Imaginary *ego* (master/S1), a Symbolic professor (S2), a Symbolic/ Imaginary hysteric ($), and a subscriber to the Real (*a*/analyst). In the place of the *other* to whom his speech is addressed, the master imposes his knowledge (S2); the academic takes the other as the cause of his jouissance (*a*); the hysteric seeks the other as a master (S1); the analyst addresses his patient's lack ($). The knowledge *produced* by the subject in addressing an-other is what has been learned from others through speech and transference (other/Other). The master *produces* his knowledge as jouissance gained from dominating the other's discourse (*a*); the academic produces his knowledge by depending on the student's lack of knowledge ($); the hysteric accumulates her knowledge by taking it in from the masters (S2) who speak a discourse of power and opinion (S1). The academic speaks as an expert in the field for which he has trained. The *hysteric* speaks from her division as subject, from her lack ($). The analyst speaks for the *cause* of his patient's jouissance, by remaining mostly silent (*a*).

The topological places are spaces where distance can be measured in open or closed sets within a neighborhood of interconnectivity and intersubjectivity, but not by a metric number. The places are all sites of distinct kinds of power: opinion (S1), knowledge (S2), being as lack ($), and the truth of being as cause(*a*).

These are alternately represented by a *master* signifier whose words come from a discourse of certainty (S1), an *academic* whose knowledge comes from library/lab/book/knowing (S2), a *hysteric* who lives from knowing the truth of castration ($), an analyst who sits in to enable his patient to find her *cause* in jouissance. The *master* directs his words to the *other* who is meant to accept them as the sum and substance of her knowledge (S2). *Academics* aim their command of book knowledge at the students whom they wish to seduce by their brilliance (*a*). The *hysteric* seeks to attach herself to a master who will fill her lack with his certainty and ego (S1). The *analyst* strives to make it possible for his patient to speak her desire and experience a full measure of jouissance ($). Subject division ($/lack) dwells in the place of (repressed) *truth* in the *master* discourse and shows that behind the bluster and certainty of the ego convictions by which he tries to control the other, his assurance is precarious.

In the *academic* discourse, *truth* is found in the master signifiers that underlie his speech, drenched as they are in the narcissism that goes with the prestige of his training, the post he gets as a job, the money, and titles he earns as a scientist, professor, businessman, computer expert, web technician, and more (S1). In the *hysteric* discourse, *truth* is the jouissance she obtains from seeing the masters' flaws and castrations and from the paradoxical pleasure she gets from subverting them (*a*). In the analyst's discourse, *truth* resides in his accumulation of knowledge (S2) gleaned from his various masters, including masters of jouissance. The *analyst* uses his knowledge on behalf of his patient, not himself, except indirectly. The elements (S1, S2, $, *a*) change place from discourse to discourse, each matheme moving its position, as if within a circle. The discourses shift from the one of master's ego confidence, to the academic's reliance on Symbolic order training, to the hysteric's comprehension that everyone is lacking, to the humble cause of supporting the other's desire by the analyst.

Lacan showed the changes in subject position as one moves from a resistance to the unconscious by the master, and an ascendance of the unconscious as the agent in the hysteric's and analyst's discourses ($, *a*). Individuals, of course, change discourse modes, depending on their profession, their social engagements, their relations with others of the world. One speaks to another as a master, a professor, a hysteric, or an analyst. But the basic structures of the subject/ego remain intact for each speaker, hiding and revealing the *truth* of her being and body. Lacan advised the patient not to expect certainty or objectivity from her analyst. Even though he situated knowledge in the place of truth in the analyst's discourse, what the analyst knows is only the sum of what he has learned, which is, above all, subjective and prone to his jouissance because his knowledge is marked by his passions, his ignorance, his drives, and his symptoms. Nonetheless, he is not an ego psychologist or a doctor with pills. The four elements in the discourse structures show what has structured each speaking being from the Real (*a*/the drives), the Symbolic (language and law), and from the Imaginary (ego). These orders are held together by the Symptom that tells the story of the subject's experience of the *law* of the father as it shapes the mother's desire. Jacques-Alain Miller has said recently that we can only hope for knowledge, not truth. Living we can bear, knowing is not what anyone wants. Knowledge sits in the place of the receiver/*other* in the master discourse. It is the *agent* of speech in academic discourse. It is the product of *assimilated knowledge* in the hysteric's discourse. It resides in the place of *truth* in the analyst's discourse.

Lacan never dismissed the truth. He claimed, against the tradition of Western philosophies and religions, that truth is not beautiful and is not necessarily beneficial to know. It is not universal either, but radically singular for each subject who pursues it. With the four discourses he invented, Lacan demonstrated eloquently and elegantly that the conscious and the unconscious are interwoven, and intertwined. In his quest for speaking "surely," Lacan maintained that truth and knowledge cannot be separated from one another. Bogdan Wolf has recently called the Lacanian idea that *truth* resides in knowledge, nonsense. Truth, he says, is a matter of mere signifiers with no inherent meaning, no truth (Fink, 2015: 99). If nothing else, one might ask Wolf if signifiers do not speak the ego? Signifiers create the unconscious in a *differential* logic in which words represent themselves to one another, by the principle of word-to-word (metonymy, S1), which are only anchored in the quilting moments of meeting with a signified (metaphor). A subject's signifiers only take on a full meaning in a *combinatory* when they hook themselves to their unconscious signifieds that function as concept, condensation (S2/metaphor). These signifiers/signifieds speak to us as beings and bodies of meaning and truth. They come from the *outside* (other/Other) to give shape to our *inner*-most "self" where the I and ego are joined in the time of a *twist* that links inner and outer by the Symbolic addition of a father's name principle to the happy ego. This third term hooks the Real to the Imaginary and produces a coherent syntax.

Lacan said that we stumble over truth (Lacan, 1990). *Meaning* is not where we expect it to be, in a logical framework. It takes up residence, rather, in the *non-sense* that gambles between the Symbolic and Imaginary and produces a Real material concreteness in language. Non-sense plays an enigmatic peek-a-boo game that conceals and reveals our sense of its true meaning in our efforts to grasp exactly what others are saying *to* us and *about* us. When my daughter was young, I picked her up, pro-forma, from day-care. She was sobbing. I asked her what was wrong, and she said that Shaundra, her best friend, had *stolen* her song. Shaundra was singing "Old MacDonald's Farm" and it was *her* song. Lacan taught that at the level of syntax, language is shaped in small sentences of *lalangue* which functions circularly as its own object. Such language does not bear messages to communicate. Instead, it carries the freight of the subject's/ego's jouissance. In developing this logic, Lacan contradicted Aristotle's principle of contradiction: that something *cannot be* both false and true. Lacan said that meaning and truth do not stop not writing each other.

In adhering to Freud, Lacan developed the category of the modal logic of the *impossible*, which functions by a double *negation*. Like Freud, he was a modern-day Sophist (Cassin, 2020, ch. 4, pp. 59–92). Wolf points to Miller's reformulation of Lacan, to his saying that truth is a mirage (Wolf, 2018: 23). Lacan, of course, said this, one or more times. Miller also quotes Lacan from *Seminar* VII, saying "truth [is] the little sister of jouissance . . ." (1969–70, ch. 4). Wolf quotes Miller as saying there is no truth, only knowledge, which life cannot stand (2015: 160). Miller said that truth is not what anyone wants to hear. In 2016, Miller published an essay entitled "Truth Is Coupled with Meaning" (2018). Like Lacan and Freud, he reformulates his axioms, arriving at certain fixed formulas and examining them over time. In "Lacan Clinician," Miller spoke of Lacan *against* Lacan (2022). At this conference, Miller presented the dialectical Lacan, a *true* master speaking to and against himself, a thinker in the lineage of Plato who created Socrates whom Lacan called the masculine prototype of a hysteric: "I know this, but what do *I* know?" (Ragland, 1989, pp. 725–755).

One can understand Lacan's discourse structures more easily by noting the dialectic regarding four different elements that mark the way a subject uses language: places of agency (*I*), other (ego), production (knowledge), truth (object *a*). Lacan situates the object *a* – which designates a surplus enjoyment – in different places in each of the four discourses. He borrowed the concept of a *surplus value* from Marx who created communism by drawing attention to the *excess* suffering that occurs in society when the lower-class worker produces a commodity to sell. The buyer consumes the product without heeding the value in it that goes above and beyond any money paid for the worker's labor (Marx, 1959). Lacan used the idea of a surplus value to indicate an excess in enjoyment that marks ego gain. An instance of the buyer's ignorance of surplus value can be seen in the case, for example, when someone buys a can of peas in a market without thinking that the juice in the can may contain bits of the worker's sweat as well as the liquid from the peas. In his discourses the *a* moves from the source of motivation for the master's discourse whose pleasure from *controlling* others. In the university discourse, the *a* is the student who allows herself to be *seduced* by the professor's expertise. The hysteric's pleasure comes from her *subversion* of the certainty of speaking subjects.

The analyst's pleasure derives from his ability to use his knowledge in the *service* of another's suffering. Speaking an ego discourse of *resistance*, the master know-it-all does not acknowledge the fault ($) in her own "wise" opinions (S1) which mark her as "self-confident." Sadly, she gains her superiority from treating another, who allows it, like chattel. In the master discourse, Lacan situated the object *a* under the other whom he implicitly commands to obey him by accepting *his words* as *the sum of her* knowledge. He *uses his* speech as a weapon of mastery. The academic's *pleasure* stems from his coaxing the other (the student) to give in to his point of view. He resists the student's questions ($) that are posed in a bid for a place within the dialectic. The hysteric's *pleasure* comes from seeing, and sometimes pointing out, the flaws in the other/Other ($). The analyst uses the totality of his knowledge to get the *pleasure* that comes from defending his patient's jouissance.

Within Lacan's discourse structures, neither the analyst nor hysteric resists knowledge of the unconscious. To become a Lacanian analyst an individual undergoes an analysis to change her relation to the other(s)/Other who have structured her knowledge as alien, as theirs. By gaining "insight," she eclipses her ego resistances to truth, her certainties that *she knows*. The Lacanian analyst instigates a true transference, not an ego dominated one, by offering his silence in the time it takes for her to separate desire and create a new subjectivity. Lacan said that hysterics would make the best analysts because subversion is the name of the game for them – taking apart, analyzing, criticizing, taking lack as their base for knowing.

Lacan finalized his discourse schema, addressed to Roman Jakobson, in *Seminar* XX during the years 1972–1973 (ch. 2). He sought to answer Jakobson's implicit question about the relationship between the addresser and addressee. He sought to give Jakobson a logic that was personal, moving, and did not fall back into the staticity of the ego. In the *master* discourse of power, speech alone acts as the signifier that speaks on its own terms, eschewing any disruption or input by the other.

Amy, the master ego in town, talks about her friend who had breast cancer and I say that the misfortunate disease had happened to me long ago, but one can recover from it as I did. Roger says: "Be quiet. *Amy's talking* about *her* friend." When the master falters for a moment on some piece of knowledge, he says that he will look it up, but that the most recent discoveries of scientists *say it all* – DNA, the brain. *They learn* something new every day, he says. He's not you like the psychotic person is. He is them, a universal *we*. It is not surprising that knowledge dwells in the place of the other in the master discourse, not as a dialectic between the subject and other, but as the master's knowledge, which depends upon the other's guarantee to help him foreclose knowing anything about his unconscious absent/present knowledge base. In seeking to foreclose any interplay of discourse, he sends his discourse of *opinion*, informed in any way at all, to the other to *consume*. If the other asks a question or tries to dialogue with him, he says: I'm tired of talking. I'm too busy to talk. There's nothing left to say. Yeah, I've got it. That doesn't interest me. Or he pronounces a banality such as "forgive, *but not* forget" – end of discussion. The master *cuts* off the other's discourse, silences her with "whatever," looks away, looks at his watch – oops, it's time to go. If she tries to talk further, he turns to someone else, to the one whom he *supposes* has a mastery as great as his, perhaps greater.

In the *university* discourse where book knowledge dwells as the agent of power in speech, she delivers her discourse of acquired knowledge *seductively*, carefully foreclosing his question. In the other's place she sees someone to be convinced and persuaded, someone to bolster her ego. In the hysteric's discourse, the divided subject is the agent ($) of speech. In this place, Lacan locates the power of lack, of knowing she is not-all (Socrates). She looks to the other as a master of knowledge and his certainty serves as her guide. The S2 appears for the first time in the hysteric's discourse as *unconscious* knowledge that has been produced by what she has learned from her master(s). But beware. Her knowledge is threaded with the Real. When she asks a question ($ → S1), she may be trying to win the master's love, to attract his gaze, but, unwittingly, she subverts his certainty. The paradox of her life is that she wants a master but sees his castration.

Dora: What Is a Woman?

The hysteric's prototype was Freud's Dora, Ida Bauer, whom he treated for a "small hysteria" during 11 weeks in 1900–01. Her father had been treated by Freud before his marriage for the effects that syphilis had imposed on his psychic and physical health. Dora was a problem child. Not only was she beset with physical maladies, but at age 16 she became reclusive and threatened suicide. Her family had her treated by electroshock, which did not help. Dora had first become upset when Herr K tried to seduce her in a store when she was 14. When she was sixteen the Bauer and K family were together at the Bauer summer house on a lake. Herr K took her for a walk by the lake and tried to kiss her. She slapped him and later accused him, in the presence of her father, of making illicit sexual advances to her. He denied it and said that she had fantasized the idea. In fact, he said, she had tried to seduce him. Dora's father believed Herr K. He took her to Freud for treatment, but nothing happened.

During the next two years, Dora continued to accuse Herr K. of being sexually improper. When she was 17 her father took her back to Freud, because her continued accusations of Herr K. were creating a family drama. Freud reported her as being 18, older and more sexually aware in his mind. She told Freud that Herr K. had kissed her when she was 14 and pressed his erect member against her body. When she was 16, he had denigrated his wife at the time he tried to kiss her. I get nothing from her, implicitly saying that she *should* give him what his wife denied him. At the same time, he was having an affair with his children's governess. Dora ran away from him and asked a stranger for directions to her house. The stranger told her it was a two-and-a-half-hour walk, so she returned to Herr K. in despair. She had let sleeping dogs lie in her family scene since childhood by submitting to the family fiction that Frau K. was his nurse only. As long as Herr K. stayed away from her she abetted her father in his secret affair with Frau K. As a man of upper-middle-class prestige and money, a textile merchant, he had made every possible move to have Frau K. with him. He was sexually impotent, and Frau K. gave him the illusion of being potent again by performing fellatio on him. When Dora refused to "shut up," her father took her to Freud, not to be helped, but to be silenced.

Freud was eager to have Dora as a patient. He thought he could advance his reputation in the Viennese Psychoanalytic Society by curing her and, thus, satisfying her father who had the arrangement with Herr K. of "you take my daughter, I'll take your wife." Freud also wanted to add her case to *The Interpretation Dreams* volume published in 1900. Before he published her case study as a "Fragment of Hysteria" in 1905, he had entitled it "Dreams and Hysteria." During her three months with him, she had two dreams. One of them was a recurring dream of fleeing her *burning* house with her father who had woken her from bed to run for her life. Freud gave two interpretations of the first dream. In a literal sense, he said the fire referred to her brother's playing with matches. He also gave his standard *psychosexual* development interpretation. She had dreamt about fire as a wish fulfillment, as a distorted symbol of her repressed memories of childhood masturbation.

From today's perspective, it is difficult to imagine Freud's relegating that dream to her childhood when sexual *passion* was the name of her adolescent life game. In the second dream, she was lost in a town and seeking directions to the train station, which everyone told her was only five minutes away. She ended up in a forest where she asked a stranger where the train station was, and he said two and a half hours away. She wandered out of the forest and found a Bahnhof and found a train. When she arrived at her apartment, she saw a letter from her mother that announced that she hadn't wanted to trouble her by telling her father was ill, but she had to let her know he had died and wanted her to return home. She left immediately, but when she reached the family home, everyone had already left for the cemetery. She was alone and opened a book. Freud interpreted her finding the Bahnhof as her trying to find a place for her female genitalia. He made the same kind of sexual interpretation of her first dream in which her mother's efforts to retrieve her jewelry box was Dora's displacement of her own obsession with holding onto her virginity. Herr K. had given her a jewelry box a year earlier so the symbol reference was valid in Freud's view. Her mother's effort to save a vanity box despite the fire was Dora accusing her father of failing to protect her virginity, her point of vanity. She left Freud when his interpretations of her life difficulties were too far afield for her to accept. She had told him about standing in front of Raphael's Sistine Madonna, staring at it in rapt silence for hours. He told her what was wrong with her that that fascination revealed her problems. She was refusing Herr K. because she was frigid and disgusted by men rather than aroused by them. Her fascination with the Sistine Madonna proved his point. A Madonna is a virgin mother, frigid. He made his point about her identification with being a frigid virgin by telling her that she was seeking refuge from sex by caring for the K. children.

Dora had enough. She left Freud. He was just another dead father, one of the men who had joined hands in trying to buy her silence and sexual complicity. She had also had enough of Frau K. who joined the fathers by leaving Dora to care for her children so that she could continue her liaison with Dora's father.

However, Dora's departure from Freud was not absolute. She had been deeply dissatisfied with his interpretations of her actions regarding the sexual complications in her life. He told her that she was secretly in love with her father and Herr K. and was jealous of Frau K. Moreover, she was projecting her angry feelings at Herr K. onto him, instead of onto Herr K. It is surprising that Freud said this given that her father had brought her to him to shut up about Herr K., to stop her efforts at vengeance. Her father told Freud he wanted Dora to be "reasonable." When she discontinued treatment with him, he said she was seeking vengeance on Herr K. through leaving him. But she returned to see him quickly. She was happy and triumphant and eager to get even with him for having failed to help her. She came to tell him that she had gotten the two families together and exposed their clandestine sexuality, dismantling the familial falsity. Freud did not grasp that at age 18, she was disinterested in the married older man who was trying to seduce her.

Perhaps she was fascinated with Madonna because she seemed to possess a secret, the secret of a calm *mother* holding her baby, her gift. Her young life was a search to answer the question Lacan found at the root of hysteria: What is a woman? One can tell in his essay about Dora that he was so plagued by his failure with her that he reformulated his manner of thinking about and practicing psychoanalysis. He realized that psychoanalysis was not about diagnosis or interpretation, but about the *transference* relation between the doctor and patient, about psychodynamic analysis.

Psychodynamic practice is strong in American psychoanalysis today. The doctor sees himself as an empathetic caregiver who offers good advice to his patient, thereby helping her with self/other relations. But there is no unconscious there. Lacan took up Freud's idea of a two-body practice of analysis, but, rather than see it as a dynamic between the patient and doctor, he saw the analyst as a mostly silent guide to help his patient recognize her unconscious desire and to uncover the truth behind it. For me, unlike many feminist commentators, there is still a question about whether Freud helped Dora. He did not relegate her to the garbage bin of history that had marked the treatment of hysteria for centuries. He listened to her story but did not agree with her interpretation of it. He did, however, make her angry enough to put an end to the family complicity that had enslaved her for 18 years. By tracing Dora's life, Marge Thorell tells Dora's story after she left Freud.

When she came to Freud she was suffering from physical ailments – a persistent cough and aponia, ailments medical doctors could not explain. At first, he thought her physical problems might be contributing to her neurosis. But her departure from him and her *confrontation with both families*, unexplainedly, gave her relief from her physical symptoms. She said she had "cured" herself. She soon married a would-be musician and gave birth to one son. Fearing for their child's life as a Jew, she and her Jewish husband converted to Christianity. Her father had been reduced to penury at the end of WWI when Austria lost its power. In order to survive, Dora (Ida) and Frau K. (Zelenka) got together and started a small business teaching rich Viennese ladies how to play bridge. She insisted that her gifted son learn music and the languages that would enable him to leave Austria at the right moment. She stayed close with her brother Otto who became the leader of the Austrian Socialist party. Since she was Jewish, she was fortunate to have survived Hitler's invasion of Vienna. She eventually moved by way of France and Casablanca to the US where she rejoined her son. He had become the famous maestro of the San Francisco Opera House. He was praised throughout the opera world for having discovered some of the world's greatest voices, such as Pavrotti (Adler, 2022).

American Mental Health Clinics

In the analyst's discourse, the matheme S2 stands for the unconscious knowledge that makes up his *truth*. His knowledge is made up of the Real of his drives, the language of his Symbolic, the ego fantasies that inform his Imaginary, and, finally, of the Symptom that knots the orders together, and has properties of all of them, and subtends his *actions* as an analyst (Lacan, 1974b). The *other* the analyst targets unveils the complexity of the patient's division between the Other who has constituted his desire, which he tries to represent in his speech cast in the mold of the egos who have made his own an unconscious singular formation with narcissistic images of perfection. Since the ego typically resists knowing anything about its division, the Lacanian would-be analyst is *trained* to let his patient know that, despite the transference phenomenon, she should not remodel her ego on the analyst's. The Lacanian analytic process operates by hystericizing the patient's speech where she *represents* her ego. The analyst's silence hystericizes any subject who is not psychotic and should not be used carefully with a psychotic person who, despite his solid certainty, is fragile because his Symbolic order is always at risk. When the analyst's silence leads the patient to confront her division as both subject and ego, she becomes tentative, unsure. Her knowledge is supported only by the master signifiers that guarantee her that what she knows is correct, that she is *who* she thinks she is. Yet, to speak is a risk for normal/neurotic individuals because their ego is always decentered, and they must use language carefully to defend and protect it. The patient uses language to seek reinforcement of herself/ego control. If she loses ground in a speech act that interprets a situation, she quickly seeks others to assure her that her perceptions are correct.

In the American mental health clinic, the patient expects an immediate fix for her difficulties. If she does not get it, she leaves that "helper" and finds someone who will give her meds based on one or two interviews. Eight sessions are now standard practice in the American psychiatric clinic before medications are refilled automatically by the medical person's assistant who calls the pharmacy to say that the doctor or nurse has approved the refill. The patient has come to the analyst to get answers about why she is having problems. The American clinic of mental health has the answers. It calls itself a Health and Wellness clinic. Helpers tell the patient she must learn how to manage stress and to that end, they offer her not only medications but also diet sheets and study sheets that she can fill out at home. These self-help feedback forms are intended to teach her how to *control* her *behavior*, how to take care of herself without outside assistance, other than the exercise gyms, the painting workshops, and the like, that are listed on the forms. The helper has an undisclosed telephone number.

The Lacanian analyst offers no such "help." He does not even prescribe medications except in cases of dire distress when he will contact a Lacanian psychiatrist. He leads his patient to question her suppositions about who and what she is. She must tell him because he does not know. The patient will not be able to replace her (decentered) ego with his ego that he imagines itself to be whole and healthy. She will not be asked to manage herself through techniques that speak the superego dicta of the Other who has subjugated her being and desire in the first place. In the American mental health clinic, the patient is always in the position of the slave confronted by a combination of the master discourse and the university discourses. There's no unconscious there. The American Wellness Clinic resists knowledge of a patient's suffering, quickly somatizing the patient's effort to talk.

In couples therapy, the mental health worker plays the blame game of deciding if the husband or wife is causing their difficulties. In group therapy, the group members get to decide who among them has a problem, who is not adapting well. A Lacanian analyst could well see such a clinic as psychotic, as foreclosing the Symbolic order principle of accepting difference. The mental health worker's resistance to hearing about his patient's problems and his refusal to engage in a transference is "invisible" proof of an unconscious topology at work in being. In the subject/ego *structure* that Lacan called *topology itself*, the Real of the drives overlaps with the language of the Symbolic and the ego of the Imaginary. These orders shape each person's knowledge and being in a toric figure, like the handle on a coffee cup. Inside is outside and outside is inside. Lacan diverged from modern thinking about how the mind is formed. His topological picture of the mind/ego is not linear or chronological. It is spherical. Each part shapes the other and simultaneously connects it and differentiates it (Greenshields, 2017). The (new) Imaginary that Lacan saw at the end of analysis ascends over the patient's ordinary speech and relates to new forms, to new identifications. She speaks in a new way. Mortifying, repetitive identifications of the past are buried. The people one knows will seem old, inappropriate. The patient will do new things, such as create a new landscape for her house, organize her house by framing it in color. In unanalyzed speech, ego narcissism speaks the master discourse of its jouissance. Speech and ego are co-equivalents of an *ignorant* discourse that rules and resists any temptation to compromise.

Chomsky and Language

The phenomenon of resistance, in Lacan's view, is not just simple passivity, nor just grandiosity. Nor is it just a dogmatic adhesion to the known. Rather, resistance takes on a cosmic meaning: that of the *necessity* of maintaining a sense of "self" unity above despite everything. The ego projects its alien ideals – given it by another – its narcissism, onto the egos of others addressed (or not) and battles for superiority in a fight that must be won despite everything else. The other's very existence arouses a combative instinct for jealous people and must be demolished. The sorrow for this dominating ego is that she must wait for verification of her "truth(s)" from the outside world. Individuals (speaking subjects, enjoying egos) fight the fundamental human reality that uncertainty, ambivalence, jealousy, fear, even hate, come from this paradox: The conscious subject thinks she is speaking from a knowledge base (professional, intuitive, experiential, mature wisdom), but her speech is governed by an ego division that she denies to the death. She is always at risk of confronting an-other whom she might not be able to control.

To complicate "reality" further for this master ego, her speech is drawn from an unconscious Other of which she is unaware. Some phenomena that arise from the split between the ego (ego ideals and ideal ego) and the subject (Other and speech) are the reality of fantasies, daydreams, night dreams, nightmares, talking to oneself. These "facts" are *deposited* from the start of life by way of an infant's reception of sound, image, touch, sense. Elements of the outside world impose themselves on a physical organism and structure it for meaning from birth – and possibly even before – as a subject of language and identifications.

Some of Noam Chomsky's students came up with the idea of testing newborns to see if they listened to the mother's voice in particular or if it didn't matter to them who was speaking. In their empirical study, they claimed that a newborn baby attends only to its mother's voice and turns away when someone else is speaking (Ragland, 1986). The baby they describe hears its mother's voice in the womb. Their claim makes sense of the admonition pregnant women give others: "Ssshhh, the baby's sleeping." "Talk softly or you'll wake her up." The baby sees its fingers (images) but has no idea what they are. The (m)Other names them: "here is thumbkin . . . , here is pointer . . . , here is tall man . . . , here is old man . . . here is pinky . . .", as she does with the toes, the nose, the chin, the bottom, and all other body parts. There is no *innate* biological language that is hardwired into the brain and its cells at birth as Noam Chomsky claims. The brain does not tell a new baby what its body parts are. It is a mass of muscle and cells onto which knowledge from the outside world is imposed because it is plastic. It can be, and is, structured from the outside. It is structured by language.

Chomsky argues that language resides in the linkage of genes to neural synapses, which the brain possesses at birth. For Chomsky, the brain is a universal *machine* made up of mind/body/genes/neurons/cells/membranes/language. Any brain can learn any language because its innate capacity only strengthens with age. Language and the brain are one and the same: everything is created by biology. Lacan said that for Chomsky, language seems like an organ that he can get ahold of. And Chomsky called Lacan an effete charlatan whom he "disses" for posturing and a lack of arguments (Lacan & Miller, 2022). No matter how hard Chomsky looks to neuroscience to argue that language is a universal grammar that is hardwired into our brains at birth, he cannot explain dreams, schizophrenic speech, hallucinations, delusions, fantasies, or autistic language or talking to yourself. Nor can he explain to his students why a tribe they found in Brazil has *no single element* of what he has calls a universal grammar (Chomsky, 2002).

When questioned on these language phenomena, Chomsky falls back on his idea of an ideal community of ideal speakers who can perform competently. Chomsky is unlike the psychiatrist, Martin Harrow, from the University of Illinois at Chicago. Harrow has received multiple awards for his work on thought disorder and schizophrenic speech. Years ago, Marty asked me to give him Lacan's theory of language and gave me M & Ms to reward me for an anticipated compliance. He also promised to footnote me in an article if I would assist him. He thought maybe Lacan's ideas could help him understand the examples of schizophrenic speech that lined the shelves of his office. I refused to provide him with any of Lacan's theories. He was going to footnote me, he said, not Lacan. I directed him to texts of Lacan which had become available in English, not many at the time. Unlike Chomsky, Harrow had a question, a desire to know more, a desire to win a big grant if he could answer a question that still stumps American psychiatrists: What causes schizophrenic speech? Chomsky says he has read Lacan and Žižek and so he knows they are poseurs. If he actually read Lacan, would he find a way to think anew about how language is structured? Or is his ego hardwired into his master discourse? Lacan demonstrated that language is not structured by the brain, but, rather, that the brain is structured by language.

Lacan's Other is the register of culture, unconscious language traces, and desire. Although its power over each subject is absolute, it is inconsistent from the moment of birth. The knowledge it gives is particular, and, thus, partial. The Other produces its desire and language and mirroring through a process of structuring the Real, the Symbolic, and the Imaginary. It gives meaning to stimuli, not through genes, but through teaching each new person one by one. Outside others *feed* the human baby fragmentary signifiers to give it speech. Yet, as fate would have it, the price the infant pays for receiving language is that of being subjugated to an Other's desire and discourse. An acquaintance of mine, a genius who is said to have invented Microsoft before Bill Gates, claims that he invented himself. When pushed on his dictum, he says that his parents were happy he was born because they had an RH blood factor that complicated his birth. He was their only child, which was a disappointment to his father. Even though he was a boy and an only child, they didn't pay much attention to him, he said. His father was disappointed because he was not athletic and his mother's gaze was drawn to the wrestler, Gorgeous George. He was raised by a distant mother and an overbearing grandmother who prevented him from having a relationship with his father. But he found father's name signifiers in astrology, star gazing, newsprint, and technology and through these fields affirmed himself. He was not aware that in disclosing this information, he was telling a bit of the story of *how* he was invented.

In 1955, Lacan introduced the four-way pattern by which he forged an entry into topology with his dialectic of subject/ego/other/Other as depicted in his Schema L (Lacan, 1954–1955, 2006: 40). Lacan said he chose the L because it resembled the Greek word for lambda, the 11th letter in the alphabet, meaning wavelength. One cannot help but note that it is also the first letter of his last name.

Extimacy

Lacan saw language itself as resistant to knowledge. Resistance, in his view, is not just a pathological clinging to neurosis (inertia) as American psychoanalysts believe. Resistance is the human *incapacity* to recognize the gaps between being (I), wanting (R), and speaking (S). Primary other/Other meanings condition secondary meaning in a syncopated logic from birth on (Lacan, 2007b). When a new baby arrives in a family, one suddenly remembers not only the toe-counting game but also melodies from childhood. One hums to the new baby, almost instantly, saying, "there, there, hush," making calming sounds. Images, sounds, the Real of the body coalesce from the start of life: "This little piggy went to market, this little piggy stayed home, this little piggy had roast beef, this little piggy had none, this little piggy cried wee wee wee all the way home." Lacan created the word "extimacy" (*extimité*) to describe the joining of outside to inside. The spaces combine to create a central *intimate exteriority* at the heart of human beings. He called the Thing that dwells at the interstices of inside and outside the object *a*. At the center where inside and outside meet, they embrace *and* resist one another (Lacan, 2007: 167). As early as 1953, in the "Rome Discourse," Lacan turned to topology. He presented the logic of the Möbius strip to explain the paradoxical human phenomenon of being/thinking, inside/outside (Lacan, 1962; Ragland, 2015). *I* speech provides a mechanism for a person to either *submit* to or *avoid* the other in human relations. In moments of identificatory truth, the *I* confronts its own divisions: inside/outside – introjection/projection.

Although individuals think their identity is theirs, somehow innate, it is alien. Perhaps, this is why so many people think that the body creates itself. The idea of an alien aspect to being is threatening. The external aspect of Otherness as distant, not me myself, is, paradoxically, the necessary base for being and speaking. By reinterpreting Freud's notion that the ego is only split in fetishism and psychosis, Lacan demonstrated that in its structure the human is split between ego, speech, desire, and drive. They are irreducible to one another. The four-part structure of being/speaking can never be healed. In psychosis, the mirror stage ego governs speech, giving a tenuous hold on speech to this person. The basis of any Lacanian transference is the *logical time* it takes to account for her subjectivity when she is in the position of questioning her division as a subject ($) and ego. This question is not posed by the psychotic person for whom the ego and *I* are one, ensuring that there will be no dialectic in her thought. Most people have the possibility of imputing a "subject" to their unconscious repressed knowledge.

Others who are not psychotic resist the source of their subjectivity and deny that this knowledge means more than it says. The man who told me that he had invented himself said to me recently that he had met some hermits who lived alone and had no need of an-other. I had said to him that in "Group Psychology and the Analysis of the Ego," Freud had written, in thinking about the concept of a group, that everyone has an-other. We are born of an-other, to another (Lacan, 2015: 67–143). I did not say it to my friend, but I thought that hermits choose to live alone, often in religious solitude, contemplating God. But hermits are *human* animals (Ragland, 2015: ch. 1). Someone has given the hermits language, the notion of otherness, the idea of befriending the animals that surround them, or the words they use to pray to God. Hermits are far luckier than those newborns who never receive language but are stashed in a garbage can at birth. Instances in which humans have not been given any speech are rare. Even autistic beings, without an Imaginary, range in their capacity for speech from one word to the category of *savant*.

Lacan got the attention of his listeners when he declared that resistance comes from the analyst, not from the analysand. The one who seeks help is in trouble, in pain. The patient's symptoms may not be just psychological: *physical* symptoms often speak loudly of *psychic* stress. One of seven inventors of Emergency Medicine said to me recently, "I didn't understand the article you gave me on neuroscience and psychoanalysis." "I get it that they are bowing to Freud as having the

superior model of mind/body, but they used too many scientific technical terms."
"Oh well, as we used to say to each other in medicine, the psyche and the soma
are intricately inter-woven."[5] Lacan thought the analyst/analysand relation must
be interwoven if the analyst is going to help the patient reduce her suffering. Paradoxically, this is best accomplished by the analyst's silence, not by his talking and
interpreting, but by his opening a space in which the analysand can listen to herself.
In 1953, in the "Rome Discourse," Lacan said, humorously, that the patient being
treated by ego psychologists – those offering a model of health as behaviorists,
psychiatrists, or "self-help" doctors – might as well be a desk. The desk would be
an ideal patient. Never having had an ego, it would not mind substituting someone
else's for its own (Lacan, 2020: 135–136). In this scenario, the patient would just
sit in the analyst's chamber, like a block of wood, getting superior advice on reality,
behavior, health, medications: and No Help.

We're All Mad

Another kind of resistance is to be found in the kind of patient who feels fine and is
convinced that she is well-analyzed, having been in analysis or therapy for much of
her life. One such patient (*patienter/pathos/suffering*) said to the *Lacanian* analyst
in her first session with him that she was very happy, blissfully married, and blessed
by a child. She did not know why she was in his office. It was true that she admired
Lacan's work, and wrote about him, but marriage had given her life's solution. She
talked for a few months anyway, happily recounting dreams. At one point she began
to have dreams about her husband's behavior. She mentioned that she had hospital-
ized him in a mental (psych)ward for what doctors had not diagnosed but for which
they had given him strong medications. It also turned out that there had been a hos-
pitalization in his past, an event that she had not known about when she married him.

She recounted to her analyst the instance of his second break with her. Instead
of hospitalizing him, she had talked him through the episode. Her husband, in
an atypical fear, had been anticipating a major conference to which he had been
invited as the keynote speaker. Suddenly, he questioned whether he should go. He
would face hierarchically superior people, men of the race that had killed his father
in WWII when he was four years old. How could he, having lost tenure, face his
Symbolic order superiors within the framework of the Academy? Suddenly, his
perplexity was gone. He stood up in the bathtub like a lightning bolt and told her
he would not go to the conference. He confessed, happily, that he had never let on
to her, but he was Jesus Christ. He did not need to go to the conference: as Christ
he was already famous. He was *not* joking. When he looked in the mirror, he was
horrified. He saw his body as having come apart. He pointed to the ceiling, saying
to her that surely, she could see that his shoulders were in separate corners next to
the ceiling. She calmed him by telling him to look in the mirror again. His body
was normal, like everyone's.

Gathering some fragmentary signifiers, he talked to her for two nights and half
of the next day, using the language of war to *construct* a *delusory* bomb site from

which to bomb his mother's castle (she had lived in an actual castle). He made loud exploding sounds and hit his head with his fists for two days, saying the bombs were killing his mother. He calmed down within three days and went to the conference where he became voiceless when it was his time to speak to the enemy. In the paradox that inside/outside creates, her husband had started German lessons shortly after his father was killed. He wanted to learn the language of the enemy so as to confront and conquer his "inner" enemy. He became an expert in all things German, and eventually became able to live there. After living all over the world, always avoiding Germany. Finally his writing ensured him a place in their literary history, so he went there to live.

Over time, after having imparted these memories and dreams about her husband to her analyst, the patient learned about psychosis. She had thought that her husband was a male hysteric, an esoteric genius. Eventually, she became able to divorce him. Other repressed memories, such as the details of her then ex-husband's violence and psychotic breaks, came to her after she had finished analysis. She recently told me that she is surprised at the turn the Lacanian world has taken in describing everybody as mad. In Caracas, toward the end of his life, Lacan had quoted Lewis Carroll in saying "We're all mad here." My friend's experience with "madness" did not resemble the light-hearted/dark-hearted humor on madness recounted in *Alice in Wonderland*. "We're all mad" is a dark, ironic, existentialist expression. It does not describe actual psychosis. In Carroll's novel, Alice is lost and does not know which way to go. She asks the Cat which direction she should take. He told her that it was normal to be lost: "Oh you can't help that, we're all mad here. I'm mad, you're mad." "How do you know I'm mad?" asked Alice. "You must be, or you wouldn't have come here." With his ironic grin, the Cat tells her, "We're all *mad-e* here, all fabricated." She goes on to the Mad Hatter who tells her life is simple. She should just surround herself with people who make her smile and then she will find *Wonderland*. In the beginning of the novel, before she met the Cat, the Caterpillar had asked her the key question about human existence: "Who am I?" (Carroll, 1865).

Jacques-Alain Miller theorized and introduced the epistemic category of ordinary psychosis in the 1990s (Miller, 1999). He retains Lacan's conclusion that the father's name signifier – the law of "no"– which gives a young child the injunction to separate from the first other of primary care, is missing in psychosis. The injunction to difference over sameness has been mentally *foreclosed*. With the concept of the father function, Lacan asserted that the rejection of this signifier early in life, is a *resistance* to the Symbolic realm of life, a resistance to the logic of metaphor (substitution/condensation). This foundational rejection is the core of an unstructured identity that is unbound and, thus, functions in language and thought as a limitless flow of metonymy where boundaries seem limitless and spurious at best (Jakobson's contiguity/Freud's displacement).

Gilles Deleuze and Félix Guattari celebrated schizophrenia and treated it at La Borde Hospital in France where they refused to recognize it for the tragic illness that it is. They treated it with its own deficit, a lack of boundaries and law. Capitalism, not foreclosure, causes schizophrenia, they argued. They published their book in 1972 after 1956 when Lacan had first pinpointed foreclosure of the father signifier as the deficit that causes psychosis. Life is a tragedy for a schizophrenic person, not a place of endless creative freedom, as Deleuze and Guattari declared (Deleuze & Guattari, 1972). With the concept of foreclosure, Lacan gave a name to the defense mechanism Freud discovered at the root of psychosis: *Verwerfung* (Lacan, 1993; Redmond, 2013; (Re)-Turn: A Journal of Lacanian Studies, 2003). The "law" of "no" prohibits the infant and mother from being *all* to each other. The father's duty of saying "no" makes it possible for a mother to signal difference to her child and facilitates the larger task of enabling the mother to *cut* (topological) the child from being her fantasy object *a*, the phallus she lacks. The second castration allows the child to separate from his mother's body and become a *subject* of the Symbolic. Lacan learned this from Maud Mannoni's clinical work and developed the theory in *Seminar* (Lacan, 1962).

The time of the cut is not developmental, however, but occurs in what Lacan called logical time. The cut describes the mother as mentally separating from her child whom she takes as a Real object. It is essential for her child's well-being that she allow him to create his own *separate* objects, the objects being an *Ur-lining* of the Real (Lacan, 2006: 671–702; Ragland, 2015: ch. 3). This cut is not just one among the many that mark any life with their comings and goings. It is the mother's response to the law of the father within the triad: mother/baby/father. The father function is the first castration that breaks the infant's mirror-stage illusion that he is one with the mother. By promoting difference, the father lays the groundwork for the final castration (cut) whereby the mother separates herself from her Imaginary ego identifications with her child and from her attachment to him in the Real of the drives. This is a different theory from the one which maintains that the castration that separates the child from its mother is carried out by the Real father of sexuality.

The Sinthome

My interest is, rather, in Lacan's promotion of the Symbolic importance of the father function. The Real culprit in the mother/child bond is the mother. The Symbolic father empowers the mother to let go of the fulfillment the child gives her. He delimits the Real of the drives between mother and child. The master signifier – the father's name – finds its complement in the phallic signifier that denotes difference (Ragland, 2004). The father function gives its final order to being (I), thinking (S), enjoying (R) by its role in tying the orders together. In psychosis, the three spheres exist apart from each other. No knot unites them. The operation of knotting, paradoxically, allows the processes of difference and sameness to combine and differentiate: the Imaginary speaks the language of the ego, while the Symbolic uses language to enable law to subsist.

The Real carries the weight of the drives. If the father's name has been foreclosed in the Symbolic, then no union with the other as separate (I), no limit to speech (S), and drive (R) is possible. In a moment of encountering his lack in the Symbolic, the psychotic ego encounters the void in the Real. In psychosis the three spheres float as three separate spaces, unknotted and not cohering. Each bears the weight of the isolation of sameness because no dialectic of one with the other/Other is possible: only imperative and command. There is no lack, no difference there. The psychotic *resistance* to society, to the other, is profound. Apathy reigns. When the knot functions to unify the orders, a society is fortunate because there is a principle of difference at its base. The failure of the father's name function is so widespread in contemporary Western cultures that Miller has proposed that a generalized foreclosure of the father function marks these societies (Miller, 2022). The Borromean knot combines the properties of sameness (I), difference (S), and drive (R). The Symptom combines the three dimensions in a logic of *difference* and sameness, which allows them, paradoxically, to cohere. Lacan postulated three jouissance(s) that link the orders. Between the Imaginary and Real, Lacan situated the jouissance of the Other that dwells just outside language on the side of desire and the unconscious. He placed language as a formal function of the father who acts as the principle of difference, thereby imposing a dialectic on speech, between the Real and Symbolic. Between the Imaginary and the Symbolic, he located the concept of meaning (*jouis-sens*) that arises from the sense one has of oneself as castrated, lacking. At the center of these three spheres, he presented the object *a* as cause and goal of being, language, and the drives (Lacan, 1974).

Lacan named the knot the *Sinthome*, playing on the old French spelling of the word "symptom" and the name of St. Thomas of Aquinas (1225–74) who was the patron saint of learning, universities, and scholars (Lacan, 2016). The purpose of the knot, a fourth aspect of the Borromean trinity, is to ensure that the three spheres, as abstract as their relations might seem, depend on each other, hold together. Topologically speaking, the role of the knot is to delimit the space(s), to separate them (father's name/S), yet hold them together (mirror stage/I) and organize the drives (R). The motto of the Borromean knot, a symbol taken from the Borromean family's coat of arms, is "strength in unity: one through difference."

Lacan used the Borromean structure to depict his understanding of how the mind (S), body (I), and drives (R) work together. He emphasized the use of language (S), over the Imaginary speech of the "talking cure" ("how are you *feeling* today, honey?"). Lacan had no interest in playing such Imaginary games. His aim was to help the patient break up the ego speech between her ideal self-image and the others who had constructed it. He focused on the ego-to-ego complicity in her life games. His goal was to allow her to reveal the Real of the Desire hiding her truth from her. The path to psychic health that is pursued in a Lacanian clinic requires that the analyst and patient work together to disturb the patient's Imaginary (ego) fictions that are tied to the Real of her deadly, repetitious jouissance. Such an opening to truth can occur when both the analyst and the analysand allow an intervention of the Symbolic into the totalized speech of each. The American analyst, *and* his patient, speak an Imaginary language of denial that retains Imaginary ideals that Freud sought to destroy by his archeology of the mind. Unlike Freud, the Lacanian analyst does not want her patient to dwell in/on her past, but to re-create her identity, her subjectivity and, thereby, speak anew and speak truly. The Symbolic means of analysis, speech, give the patient the possibility of creating a new anchoring *place*. If she does not hear a "no" to her continuing ego repetitions and resistances, her ego walls will lock her into a refusal to live with freedom: she would rather die with certainty than examine her motives. Those who have left the (m)Other of their first transference, have broken the primordial bond, prove that if the father function is operative, they can live beyond their identity closures. A true analysis enables the patient to welcome difference and accept the other/Other as Real and Symbolic, not Imaginary.

Difference spells out the logic of what Roman Jakobson called the principle of metaphor: one thing or word is *substituted* for another (Jakobson & Halle, 1956; Ragland-Sullivan, 1989). The operation of substitution in metaphor is inoperative in a mental structure makes a linguistic sense out of what Freud called displacement. In psychotic speech, things do not stand in for one another. They collide with each other: words function by the law of metonymy in a word-to-word, object-to-object fashion. Jakobson, and Lacan following him, called this the operation of contiguity. But psychosis is not the purest form of *resistance* to the social and to conscious life that can be found in psychic structure: autism. We have no reason to develop Lacan's theories on autism here, but we will say that for Lacanians, the most radical foreclosure in existence is autism. The psychotic person does not usually seek an analysis, for his ego is closed to the other/Other except insofar as he believes that he and she are One. He operates from the mirror-stage mentality of symbiosis as the basis of his relations with others.

The psychotic husband of one of my patients helped her edit a book she had written. When she finished the preface, she showed him the glowing praise she had given him for his editing skills. He was perplexed for a moment and then said to her: you can't put my name in the preface, my name must go on the cover because I wrote the book. He knew nothing of his wife's field of study, knew nothing about the subject she was writing on. The book was in no way a collaborative project. His editing skills were keen and for that his wife was grateful and thanked him magnanimously in print. But she was stupefied when he declared that he had written her book. She knew nothing about the structure of psychosis, nothing about the mirror logic of pure undifferentiated symbiosis. Psychotic "structure" is a nondifferential structure. In Lacanian math, using natural numbers, one might say that the psychotic person can count to two, thereby mistaking himself and his mother as a set, a unity. But he cannot count to three which would let him know that he and his mother are not one, but two, separate. It takes a third person, a third term, to break an infant's illusion that he and his mother are one (Ragland, 2015).

In mirror logic, the failure to have inscribed father principle means that the ego will resist the Symbolic, resist the demands and requests of others. The ideas of others count only as long as he claims they are his. I would go so far as to suggest that *psychotic* language offers a kind of empirical proof that language and identification structure the brain, not the reverse. *Behavior* demonstrates eloquently that it cannot reveal a subject's truth, any more than his ego can. Rats responding to a flash of light or rats becoming violent when the bell that signals their food does not arrive, tells us nothing about humans. Rats do not speak and do not have an ego. Because he has not been castrated, has remained attached to the primary maternal bond, the psychotic doesn't function as a subject ($). He *is Ego*. Because the jouissance(s) of language, meaning and the Other, do not link his spaces, he is left to make each order function on its own.

A Language of Psychosis

In his early writings, and particularly from 1945 on, Lacan often referred to the "subject" by an S (ES/Freud's ID). In these writings, he emphasized the idea that the subject is the sum of his physiological and psychological needs, of all that defines him as a "person." In the 1960s he focused on the idea that the signifier creates the subject by referring him to another signifier that represents him in a particular way. As such, the subject is created as an effect of language. Lacan did not use the barred $ to describe psychotic mentation. In his Schema L, Lacan draws the four-part structure of the ego ideal/ideal ego/Other/speaking *I*. Insofar as language transports the ego, one can describe the psychotic subject as full, an ego not divided by the S1 of conscious language into an S2 of unconscious knowledge. Psychotic speech is not subjective, but objective, spoken by an ego that supposes itself to be full. When Lacan talked about the speaking subject, rather than the ego, he called "full" speech true speech and "empty" speech a discourse of lies ("Rome Discourse," 1953).

Lacan did not depict psychotic speech on the Schema L where he demonstrated subject division (castration) as uncertainty. He symbolized that ($) by a dotted line. The gaps in the line appear at the point where the Other intersects with the ego and its speech, demonstrating a conscious/unconscious split in normal/neurotic subjects. Because he has foreclosed the signifier for difference from the (m)Other, the psychotic person encounters a hole hollowed out in the Symbolic when someone opposes his totalized ego. He has no basis from which to debate, and often resorts to various acts of violence. Having no grounds from which to account for the difference between himself and the other, his logic is that of mirror identity: you or me, not you and me. While most subjects identify with others through traits of similarity, the psychotic goes beyond this metaphorical logic and takes the *other as being himself*, not *like* himself. A patient of mine recounted her husband's psychotic break when he was challenged on the signifier for a "good enough" father: when he did not get a first at Oxford, he went to Harvard, which he considered second rate. His French professor at Harvard refused to read "Roland's Song" in Old French and reminded him that he was not at Oxford, the world's premier University; he became agitated and soon became violent and disordered in his speech and behavior. He was taken to a mental hospital in a straitjacket. The "no" that he could not bear concerned both the professor's refusal to read in the *original* language (the mirror stage) and the loss of the signifier, Oxford, which he had interpreted as a "good enough" father's name. His mental/ego spaces collapsed into one another, forming a closed circle, not a dialectizable one.

Psychotic speech is founded on the belief that the *other is me*. Although it might seem like it, the psychotic ego does not speak a master discourse, but a discourse that is purely Imaginary. In the master discourse of seeming certainty, the subject *is divided* between the signifier and signified that shape language as a dialectic. Typically, the master dismisses any idea that there is an unconscious part of his mind, relying, rather, on his certainty that what he calls correct opinions come from the "fact" that his perceptions are true. Yet, the master is divided/castrated ($) in the place of truth that underlies his discourse of power (S1). When he accidentally lets uncertainties escape, he quickly hides the sign of insecurity with his blustering ego. Not only does he demand that the other confirm what he says (yeah, you're *right*!), but she must also admit that he has the best sources for looking up anything. Yet, unlike the certainty of psychotic speech, there is a dialectic at play in the master discourse. The psychotic ensures total control of the other by telling her what to say and how and when. When she speaks in her style, he tells her she is speaking wrong, he tells her, with no uncertainty, how to speak, what to say and when. The master seeks to control the other, lest she see his flaws. There is no dialogue with a psychotic person. Nothing is transferred except his mirror-stage certainty. His efforts at control go far beyond the master's demand that the other submit to his words and gaze. Such acceptance by the other answers his narcissistic bid for ego worship and approval.

Today's popular discourse attributes "madness" to all. In Caracas, toward the end of his life, Lacan cited the Cheshire Cat from *Alice in Wonderland*: "We're all mad here" (July 1980). Lacan said the Cat's four words. In the novel, the Cat continued, telling Alice who had tumbled down a hole into a strange world that the best direction was to "Go see the hatter or the hare, both of whom are mad." Alice replied, "But I don't want to go among mad people." Miller's 2007–08 Course, entitled *"Tout le monde est fou,"* is a caption being used throughout the Lacanian world today (*The Lacanian Orientation*, unpublished). In 1932, Lacan published his doctoral dissertation on the case of Aimée, his patient in a mental hospital. Lacan found an unbridled narcissism and *paranoia* underlying Aimée's fear that a famous actress, who she claimed had stolen *her* identity, was seeking to harm her son. Lacan was not content with this early theory as the explanation of the cause of psychosis, and in his "return" to Freud, combined all of Freud's theories about the cause of psychosis. Lacan paid particular attention to Freud's analysis of Judge Daniel Paul Schrebers' *Memoirs of My Nervous Illness* where he recounted his experiences of schizophrenic breaks and his subsequent hospitalizations (Schreber, 2000). Based on this material, he developed a new theory of the cause of psychosis, different from his understanding of the Aimée case.

After reading Schreber's *Memoirs*, Freud proposed that his psychosis was caused by his repression of a sexual desire for his father and brother (Freud, 1911). Lacan moved away from Freud's diagnosis of repressed sexuality and proposed that the *cause* of psychosis, not only in Schreber's case but in general, was a malfunction of the unconscious concerning language and identity (Lacan, 1993: 445–448). Lacan was the first doctor to offer the idea that the *cause* of psychosis is rooted in something other than biology. He changed not only the meaning of the word "psychosis," but the face of psychoanalysis.

Karl F. coined the word "psychosis" in 1941 to abbreviate the words 'psyche" and "neurosis." With this term he gave a name to what was considered a disease of the nervous system or some other part of the physical organism. The word "mad" was used as early as 1100 and the term 'insane" became standard in the 16th century. Canstatt's term was revolutionary because psychotic ("mad") people had been tortured, shunned, locked up for life, and burned as witches throughout the centuries. Alongside the medical diagnoses of insanity as having its roots in a defective, "cracked" body was the religious belief that strange, crazy behavior was an illness of the soul, a sign of demon possession. In 1953 Jean Oury bought a castle and turned it into a hospital for the mentally ill. Lacan supported his efforts to provide dignity to psychotic patients by offering them social acceptance and, even, equal status among all others, including their doctors. After the appearance of *Anti-Oedipus* in 1972, Lacan finally resisted their crazy theories and practices, their romanticization of schizophrenia (Deleuze & Guattari, 1972). What is not revealed in the book is the harsh treatment they gave their patients by viewing them as machines to be controlled.

In his *Seminar* of 1955–56, Lacan read Freud to find there a mechanism sufficient to explain the cause of psychosis. As early as 1894, Freud proposed that in psychosis, as well as certain manifestations of neurosis, the ego detaches itself from an incompatible idea and the affect that accompanies it. He throws it out (*verwefen*), yet in doing so, he accidentally breaks with reality (Freud, 1893–1899). Lacan focused on the concept of *Verwerfung* which he translated as foreclosure, a term he borrowed from the French legal system meaning to chase somebody or something out. With his concept he answered a question that had plagued the mental health world for an exceptionally long time: Is there a difference between neurosis and psychosis? There is a massive and global difference between them, Lacan taught. The root cause of psychosis rests on the exclusion (foreclosure) of a term for a father, a third term, which intervenes to break up the symbiosis between the baby and the other of primary care. Lacan showed that the function of difference is foundational in building a normal/neurotic subjectivity.

The theory that only a continuous attachment between mother and child can establish a healthy being was first presented by John Bowlby in 1958 (Bowlby, 1958: 350–373). The necessity of a foundational law-of-the-father's-name is a distinction that the American DSM system has never entertained (American Psychiatric Association, 1980). *DSM* III removed the diagnoses of "neurosis" and "hysteria" and replaced them, as well as others, with a *vast* catalogue of names and labels, dis-orders (1980). There is no logic other than an Imaginary one in the system. Going in the opposite direction from Lacan, American psychiatrists, and psychoanalysts cling to the notion of a "borderline personality disorder," the most difficult one to treat, they say. The category was introduced in 1938 by the American analyst, Adolph Stern. This classification claims that neurosis and psychosis are similar, while there are some distinctions. Lacan made sense of psychosis in

1955 by uncovering the mechanism that causes the lack of structure. But there is no *discourse of madness* in his teaching. He wrote his four discourse structures to describe four modes of speech that "make a social link": the master, the academic, the hysteric, the analyst. There is no *mad* language in Lacan. We are all a little "mad," the Cheshire Cat said, ironically, thus expressing an existential realization of the darkness of life. But there is a *language of psychosis* (Ragland, 2016).

Liar's Paradox

Freud maintained that primary-process thought is made up of wisps of incipient fantasy, sounds, images, and the drives of the Real. This thought is chaotic, like metonymy in language, It flows without an anchor. Such thought gives a *negative* logic to time, the logic of a lack of control, a resistance to "reality." Yet, conscious thinking is built, paradoxically, upon memories from the past, memories that *repeat* learned "behavior" in the present. The past *structures* a person's actions and speech through transference, projection, resistance, denial, and repression. These are a few of the defense mechanisms proposed by Freud. In primary and secondary processes, one encounters an intertwined logic: conscious perception cannot be separated from unconscious knowledge. Freud demonstrated the following paradox: thinking and feeling are neither true and objective, nor false and subjective. They are contradictory, both true and false. Adhering to Freud's thinking here, Lacan accepted the idea that a non-contradictory/contradictory logic governs thinking and speaking. True is false, but false is also true. Such thinking has been classified by logicians as the *Liar's Paradox.*

As early as the 4th century BC, Eubulides of Miletus, a Greek philosopher, had engraved on his tombstone the *words* of his conclusion to one of seven puzzles in logic he had proposed. His final words were a response to Aristotle's proposition that classical logic can function in only one way in relation to negation (384–322 BC). He argued that a sentence cannot be both contradictory and true (*Metaphysics*, Book IV, c. 3, p. 1005, lines 6–34). Eubulides, even in death, answered Aristotle by way of the liar's paradox puzzle: a man says he is lying. Is this true or false? The paradox is both true and false. If he is not lying, the sentence is false. If he is lying, the sentence is true. The sentence is both true and false. The words, "the liar's paradox is both true and false," were Eubulides's last contribution to classical logic, and marked its end. He introduced the truth-functional logic of contradiction into philosophy. Historians surmise that the problematical paradox existed long before Eubulides's day, in papyruses that have been lost to the decay of time (*Internet Encyclopedia of Philosophy*).

Freud, centuries later, advanced the same logic in understanding the function of negation in thought: something can be both false and true. He believed that "representations" were somehow involved in the mysterious negational factor at the base of mind. Compelled by the paradoxical nature of psychoanalysis where something can be false in one's conscious conception of it, but true in the unconscious mind, he turned to the study of re-presentations. The word first meant "likeness, image, show, exhibit, on behalf of an original, stand in for." In 1895 Freud proposed that a rigorous study of the brain systems would one day explain the phenomenon of representation (Freud, 1954). *Mens*/mind-*tal*/language = *mental*. Yet, he was unable to solve the problem. He decided that representation is a thought construct that works mentally but is independent of perception. Later, he proposed that it is a third function in dream language, added to condensation and displacement. He does not know how, but it translates images into language that later becomes the speech that drives the "talking cure" (*SE*, vol. IV, 1900).

Aristotle explained representations as pictures, *imitations* of beautiful forms that somehow pierce into their inner beauty. For Aristotle, form speaks for itself. For Eubulides, a sentence can describe the true nature of man who is both true and false. Unlike Aristotle who was satisfied by thinking that an effect was its own cause, or logicians who stop at the paradoxes of a descriptive sentence, Freud kept seeking to localize representations in their contradictory mental nature. He concluded that, if they are to be found, they will reside in three areas: the id, the superego, and the ego. While the first two are composed of unconscious memories and thoughts, the ego mediates between these agencies in conscious reality. Although he had proposed that *body* phenomena are rooted in the cerebral cortex, he opposed Theodor Meynert's argument that the source of body and mind are to be located in the nerve cells (Bechterew, 2015). Forty-eight years after Meynert's book on brain diseases, where he claimed that insanity can be *located* in the forebrain, Lacan showed how representations can be localized *by* and reappear *in* language (Symbolic), images (Imaginary), and drives (Real) to structure what is generally thought of as unoccupied and limitless, that is, space (Miller, 2003).

Freud's search for an answer to the riddles of the source of the mind in biology reflected the absence of general linguistics in his day, thus forestalling any research by him into the history of language or the origins of a word. Stranded in biology for a while, dreams led him to conclude that representations re-appear in a mnemic form that establishes them psychically. Yet, strangely, they cannot be traced back to their origins in the history of a life. The first representations are thoughts that translate images and appear in a primary form as drives (Freud, 1901). They appear in everyday conscious life as *affects* that, paradoxically, inform human behavior from unconscious beliefs. While listening to one of his patients recount a dream, Freud suddenly paid attention to the words spoken: "you ask [yourself/himself] who this person in the dream can be." [Patient says:] "it's not my mother" (Freud, 1923: 233). The logic at work in these words concerns the phenomenon of recognition: re-cognition, re-petition, re-turn, re-present, re-member, primary/secondary, *Bejahung* (taking in)/*Ausstosung* (spitting out). Although he was unaware of it, the patient had told a *contradictory truth* that Freud heard. The figure in the dream cannot be *she*, the patient said. But it is *her*. Freud understood that the negation was his patient's way of telling a difficult, hidden truth. We do not know what the patient dreamt about his mother. Freud does not tell us.

Lacan advanced Freud's grasp of the contradictory logic that conjoins language (Symbolic) and image (Imaginary) and drive (Real). In adhering to Freud's insight, Lacan said that the negation of an unconscious truth depicts a *modal* logic that structures the human mind. To explain such a phenomenon, Lacan borrowed many figures from *topology*, the field of mathematics that was introduced by J. B. Listing in 1837. Listing is also credited with having discovered the properties of the Möbius strip at approximately the same time as Möbius who introduced the "figure-8" as one example of a non-orientable surface (The Editors of Encyclopedia Britannica, 2023). Henri Poincaré is usually said to have marked the definitive introduction of topology into mathematics by his publication of *Analysis Situs*. His finding that a situs (site) is a point was revolutionary (Charpentier, Ghys, & Lesne, 2010). Poincaré's mathematics rethought the difficult idea that a linkage of spaces can change, but at the same time retain their original properties.

Topology Is Structure

Topologists work with objects that represent spaces in a contiguity of circles that are contained within material. We can point to figures like the Möbius strip, or a doughnut hole. These figures are devoid of the two-dimensional geometrical notions of space. Topological spaces are sets whose elements are points. They can be stretched and contracted, like rubber, but cannot be broken. When we look back in the history of mathematics, the idea of a topology – a logic of space – that could analyze sites or points was suggested as early as the 17th century by G. Leibniz. In 1735 L. Euler introduced a topological idea in his graph theory. He demonstrated a solution to the "Königsberg bridge problem": How can one define a relative position without regard to distance? Closeness can be defined, Euler said, but it is not measurable by a numeric. In his logic of circles, one is faced with a "hole" truth. Lacan took this notion as the basis for his claim that if a key signifier is missing in the Symbolic sphere of language – a father's name – a subject who confronts this reality in a life situation, encounters a hole, a void that causes disorder, collapse of his mental structures: the Imaginary, the Symbolic, the Real.

The knot that usually holds these orders together is missing, nonfunctional. Such breaks with apparent reality can occur when a person is fired from his job, or when he confronts the possibility of being a leader (father), a position for which he feels incapable, as was the case with Schreiber when the senior judges in his field of law wanted to elevate him to a position above them, a position of difference from them for which he had no signifying base in his knowledge system. Working with the mathematical phenomena of circles and holes is called "rubber-sheet geometry." Its functions are qualitative, not quantitative as in geometry. Topology depicts a moving/unmoving logic at play in mind, body, and speech. Lacan took the Möbius strip to demonstrate that the *twist* in the figure is not arbitrary. It links two dimensions, otherwise thought of as contradictory: inside and outside are contiguous (Lafont, 1986). The Real (drives) joins the Imaginary (body/ego) to language (Symbolic) by the partial drives – oral, anal, invocatory, scopic – drives that *link* the mind/body frontiers where the psychic is inseparable from the mental (Lacan, 2006a). These drives are both of and not of the body. Their linkage of the Real and Imaginary has the logic of topology: inside and outside cohere in a twist created by the insepara-bility of drive from "word" (*parole*).

The Möbius figure depicts the structure of language, Lacan asserted, while the other topological objects – the torus, the cross-cap, the Klein bottle – convey the relation of jouissance to the inside and outside of the speaking body (Ragland & Milovanovic, 2004). Lacan recognized the logic of Freud's patient's dream about his mother. Freud had realized that his patient's negation revealed that his con-scious speech was denying his unconscious truth. Lacan went beyond his medi-cal training in psychiatry as early as 1932. At the time he diagnosed the cause of Aimée's psychosis, Lacan comprehended that Freud had realized that the mind is not the brain, that biology will never provide the answers that demonstrate how conscious and unconscious language combine in speech and thought (Ragland, 2015). In 1900 Freud had already put together the intertwined relationship of lan-guage to dream thought. In trying to understand the *twist* that joined Freud's pri-mary process thought to secondary process, one enters Lacan's topological time. In 1945, Lacan understood that we see the meaning of problematic *events* in our lives in logical moments: the first moment of comprehending is structured by the gaze. It is the moment of *seeing*.

The second moment is the time it takes to *understand* the events. After seeing a problem and then understanding it, one faces the moment of *concluding*, deducing what to do about it. Lacan developed this logic in 1945 and delivered it in a paper in which he presented the logical problem of temporal tension: three prisoners are faced with the self/other problem, the intersubjective problem of transference and resistance, love, and hate. In order to ascertain who was the smartest of his prison-ers in regard to human relations, the warden made up a riddle as a test. The prisoner who solved it first would be freed. In the paper, Lacan explained that there is a function of time that has a past/present/future logic wrapped into moments of tem-porality that are not probabilistic (inference), nor clock time, nor calendar time, but concern, rather, the kind of logic people use to determine problems in their lives. The three prisoners were confronted with the problem of who should leave the cell first. The warden had given them a problem that could not be solved by looking, nor by language, but by determining who has the *correct* answer to a conundrum (Lacan, 1988a).

Lacan proposed a temporal logic that was new to the history of thought about time. He confronted his listeners with a topological picture of how mentality func-tions: we live our lives in logical time, through the intertwined orders of the Real (the drives/the organism), the Symbolic (language/culture), and the Imaginary (ego/body) in relation to the *Sinthome* that functions as the knot that joins the three orders together in a Borromean style. Lacan called this knot the "father's name" signifier. The correct answer to give the warden – who represented the father's name for them – was the first prisoner to realize that the three men were *equals*, that they all had the color white pinned to their backs, that they all could go free. The warden had not tried to trick them by mixing up invisible colors that would prove which one's mentality was superior. Lacan's use of mathematical topology depicted this paradox: there can be no conscious mind without an unconscious language to tell it what to think. Until the end of his teaching, Lacan said that *topology is structure.*

It *Is* Mother!

The three orders of the drive (R), language (S), and the ego/body (I) work together in relation to three types of jouissance that bind each order to the other in a spatial logic that has the shape of a Borromean knot (Ragland, 2015). In talking of the body, Lacan said that the Symbolic body is the scientific one that is mechanized and digitalized. It is medicalized and its organs carefully named. The Imaginary body is an ideal, phenomenological, a fantasy, a delusion. The Real enjoying body inserts itself tentatively, fragilely.

Lacan followed Freud's affirmation that a dream statement *cannot not* be true. Eschewing the centuries of work done by logicians since the time of Aristotle's optimism regarding how easily true can be distinguished from false, the psychoanalytic logicians went straight to the place of truth. Lacan developed Freud's one-time statement that there is a true center to the human being: the kernel of our being. Lacan called this space the non-excluded middle. In his Borromean structure, Lacan named this place the site of the object as the *cause* of the drives that he labeled the Ur-lining of the Real in "The Subversion . . ." (1960). Freud spoke only once in his entire work about *das Kern unseres Wesens* in *The Interpretation of Dreams* (1901). Here he was speaking about the negation that links primary and secondary process thought by repression and other unconscious motivations he had found at work in dreams: you say it is *not* that, *but it is* that.

Alenka Zupancic has written decisively about Freud's paper on negation. Her interest lies in his interpretation of his patient's "not-mother" dream. For her there are many logical explanations for any negation: non-contradiction, not non-contradiction, excluded middle, intuitionist, and others. Her favorite theory is that of Alain Badiou who argues that there are three types of negation: classical, intuitionist, and paraconsistent (Zupancic, 2008). Badiou thinks the best kind of negation to choose is the weak intuitionist one wherein almost anything is *possible.* A negation depends upon the intensity and degree of the statement under consideration, he says. It *might* be mother in the dream; it might not. Everyone has a mother, so it could be any mother. Everyone is both with and without a mother (Zupancic, 2012). Lacan went for a darker logic than Badiou and Zupancic. "It," *das Ding, is* mother.[6]

Freud's patient said simply it is not mother, pure denial. Freud heard something else there; it cannot not be mother. His patient's denial opened up Lacan's category of the modal category of the *impossible*, which states the possibility that the negations are true: the impossible, he said, is "what does not stop not stopping to write itself" (Lacan, 1998). It is the category of the Real, the impossible to bear: the forbidden, the taboo, the unthinkable. Lacan asked his audience once, regarding the jouissance that marked their life pursuits, if they could bear the life they had

(Lacan, 2007b). The impossible is the category of the paradoxical logic of it *cannot not* be true: it *is* true. Many commentators on Lacan have dismissed his category of the impossible. Others have said that his order of the Real defines a true impossible, that it is simply the idea of nature in a raw state, in a state of inaccessibility.

The dream statement regarding "mother" is not contradictory, they say, but ungraspable. I agree with Freud and Lacan. We have to grasp the Real, the impossible: what Hitler did to the Jews; what mothers and grandmothers do to their daughters in many countries throughout the world today – perform genital mutilations on them, sometimes shortly after birth, to make sure they get a good bride price for them later. In the contradictory logic that Lacan named the Real, there is no heaven, only a grimace. Freud heard the truth-functional logic of negation as it operated in his patient's words about his dream. Lacan proposed early on in his teaching that speech/language structures the unconscious, the drives, imagined others. It is the only means by which unconscious truth reenters everyday life in logical time. The category of the unthinkable Real carries the weight of jouissance into language. By naming the unconscious as a part of the mind, not of the human organism *per se*, Freud gave witness to the fact that something in the mind is not ordinary. He *named* what fortune tellers, soothsayers, witchdoctors, poets, gurus, medical doctors, scientists, astronomers, and others have said throughout time and space: something out of the *ordinary* thinks. It tells the future and, strangely, the past, at the same time. It tells of joy and pain. And it is not Chomsky's brain that stands alone on its own.

Lacan's theory of the Symptom addressed both psychic and physical distress. The ego tries to dismiss distress by mitigating *substitutes*, metaphorical others who pretend to love us, who talk to us, give us medications, organize our social lives, somatize us, go walking with us. Metaphorical structure works by substation, by giving temporary meanings and a rhythm to everyday life. In the American psychiatric clinic, pills are substituted for speech.

Lalangue and Primary Process Thought

In his "return to Freud," Lacan went back to Freud's early work on *language representations* in *Aphasia*. In this article Freud showed that he had already moved out of biology. He challenged neuroscientific thinking by advancing the thesis that the cause of aphasia was not cortical, but psycho-dynamic (Freud, 1893–1899). In trying to make sense of his recognition that the mind is structured by something other than biology, Lacan turned to Ferdinand de Saussure and Roman Jakobson. Using theories from both linguists, he argued that the unconscious is structured *like* a language. It functions by the logic of signifiers and signifieds that are carried by the laws of metaphor and metonymy. These basic laws of language organize the words that make up the material of the unconscious and compose a jouissance language from the start of life: *lalangue/lallation* (de Saussure, 2011; Lacan, 1997). In the 1970s Lacan said that language is not only a system of signs and speech but also its own object.

It is *lalangue*, the language of jouissance, spoken to the youngest infant. And Lacan marked this concept by calling language *lalangue*, both the language of primary maternal sayings (*dits*) and the language of the drives and jouissance. The earliest meanings are spoken well before the moment of the mirror stage which occurs between 6 and 18 months. Early speech provides the human infant's first mode of thinking, helps him interpret the drives: Is he listened to, kept dry and clean, fed? I would equate Lacan's notion of the *dits maternels* with Freud's idea that primary process thought is based on the images and sounds of its world. This language is concrete and material. Lacan taught that the very existence of a speaking subject depends upon the imposition of language onto (into) him. It is first deposited by the outside (m)Other. Even before speech is directed at her, an infant's sense of existence starts with a response to his first *cry*: it is answered quickly by the midwife, doctor, or mother (or sometimes not answered at all).

Lacan's picture of the early interplay between speech, images, and drives is a radically different theory of how language is acquired than the contemporary psychological and biological theories that suppose there to be no acquisition of language at all. Proponents of the "mind is the physical organism" theory declare that infants are born with residual innate tools of language located in the brain's subcortex. In the 1970s, Lacan advanced the idea that, paradoxically, we do not use language primarily for the purpose of communication. We use it to carry jouissance. Although such theories may sound far afield from Freud, Lacan reconceptualized Freud's theories of the drives, the libido, and the id in terms of what he called jouissance. Lacan announced his *return* to Freud in 1955 (*S.* II) and he maintained that return throughout his teachings.

Whereas Freud postulated a superego in the structure of mind, Lacan introduced a father figure who says "no" to the infant's symbiosis with the other of primary care. He called this separation *castration*, thereby removing the concept of castration from the realm of biology, away from the Real of organs of which Freud spoke. He invented what would mistakenly be conceived of as a "developmental" theory of structural stages. They focused on the infant's separation from the primary (m) Other and the acceptance of the father's "no." In trying to answer Lacan's question about whether his students could count to the logic of six, I proposed in 1984 that human thinking unfolds in terms of natural numbers, going from the mirror stage number two – symbiosis – to number three, with identification with difference and law (Ragland-Sullivan, 1989; for a mathematical set-theory account of Lacan's thinking about counting from 0 to 6, cf. Morel, 2019: 149–160).[7]

Human thinking *is* subjective reality. An infant escapes from the mirror structure of symbiosis (metonymy) by the process of metaphorization (Miller, 1993). Freud said that the primary process of thinking works in dreams by *displacement* (*SE*, vols. IV, and V, 1900–1901). Unlike metaphorical substitutions, metonymy relates words by *contiguity*. Freud's condensation is metaphor – substitution – and his displacement is metonymy. In dreams, and in conscious thought, things and words are displaced and substituted for one another. These primary and secondary processes depend on one another. I hear in Lacan the suggestion that metonymy functions in language like primary process thought: it shows language as destabilized (mirror stage) while metaphor stabilizes it (father's name). Slowly, by the process of naming, and then, accepting the formal language of the Other, of society, the child stabilizes her frantic cries, the metonymy of her existence.

The structure of metaphor enables secondary process thought. It substitutes one thing for another and, thereby, gives a solidity to an infant's early thinking by *resisting* the chaos and fragmentation that mark the beginning of thought as Real (drives), Symbolic (language), and Imaginary (images). The infant cries and you give her a pacifier, thus calming her instinct to find comfort by taking in food. She stays on at the breast long after she has satisfied her need for food. Being held is a fundamental need. Bobby Fischer, one-time world chess champion, went completely mad. He was given shelter in Iceland. Although he never regained his sanity, he never forgot the basic things that make one human. His dying words were: "the only human thing that counts is touch." Lacan reformulated Freud, by way of Jakobson. Metaphor becomes secondary process thought by the assimilation of a paternal metaphor (Freud, 1953–1974/1895: 283–397; Ragland, 1989: 49–92).

From this perspective, primary process thought would not be *mythical* because it operates by the linguistic logic of metonymy, which is Freud's displacement. One thing is contiguous with another. This free flow of thinking in images and sounds marks the infant's thought process before she stabilizes in the substitutive logic of metaphor. This primary *free* flow of thought is, sadly, what Deleuze and Guattari encouraged in their schizophrenic patients, calling it creativity. Unaware, they were condemning them to the structure that had made them psychotic in the first place. By freeing them from structure, from hierarchy, from family and authority they were denying them the father function which would have stabilized them. In trying to free these suffering people from slavery to authority – the structure of abusive patriarchy – they condemned them to the very logic that had made them "crazy." The structure of the subject, the non-psychotic subject, is divided between signifiers and signifieds ($). These early meanings are signified in the orders of the Real (drives), Symbolic (language), and Imaginary (images). These primary elements of thought are carried by the *laws* of language, metonymy, and metaphor: contiguity and substitution. The Real and Imaginary function by contiguity, while the Symbolic introduces metaphor, substitution.

The phenomenon of transference is on the side of metaphor, substituting the "doctor" for some imaginary (contiguous) authority figure. Resistance functions like metonymy by holding on to the ever-changing contiguities of one's certainties rather than advancing them by accepting a new metaphor, the one that advances the truest picture of human nature. Today's "thinkers" speak by contiguity: the next test, the next "scientific" discovery. They "think" on the side of the feminine, the not-all, the logic of inference: we will never know so we had better cite everybody. The one who comes along with the next complex logic that gives a truer answer (Freud, Lacan) is on the side of metaphor, substituting the new for the old, the masculine logic of having/knowing. Yet, the two laws depend on each other, are necessary to each other in order that there be smooth functioning for an individual subject: the contiguous mother function and the substitutive father principle (Ragland, 2004). The principles of the masculine and feminine are contingent on each other, as are the signifier and the signified, and metaphor and metonymy. But they are not contingent in a binary sense as Jung would have it with his principles of anima and animus.

There can be no secondary thought without a primary one that established it, no possibility of substitution without contiguity, no father's name without a mirror other, no masculine without the feminine it both desires and rejects. These principles are not co-equals, but different, functioning from different logics and with different relations to jouissance. Chomsky's brain has no dialectic. It is an organ standing alone on its own. A literary critic said to me yesterday that the brain causes humans to become sexual in adolescence. I wondered to myself if she knew nothing of childhood sexuality. In diagnosing psychosis, Lacan contended that a specific signifier has been *foreclosed* and, consequently, never builds the dialectical principle that enables one to function smoothly. The rejected signifier is the one for the father's law, his name (be it Daddy, a professor, the attendant at a boy's school, or the church pastor). Lacan's elevation of the Symbolic order (formal language) over the Imaginary one (the body and the narcissistic ego) gives the principle for what regulates the drives of the Real. Because he lacks the father function in mentation, the Symbolic world is unstable for a person who lacks a metaphorical structure at the base of mind. This person is at risk for breaks from the stability of the Symbolic, which might serve as another name for "reality" or society.

Miller has written that one sees *ordinary* psychosis when "good enough father" figures offer individuals enough believable fictions to enable stability to someone with a psychotic structure. It is not a new nosology, not an opening to the concept of "borderline," but a possible way in which psychosis can operate. He offered this theory in three clinical research sessions, following Lacan's lifelong search for the point at which a psychosis can be said to have stabilized (Miller, 1999). Lacan understood that the paternal metaphor (Freud's superego identification with the father, Miller's "good enough father") built a differential structure. The concept of ordinary psychosis demonstrates that some psychotic beings can function in society despite being anchored in primordial bonds, some of the time.

Unconscious truth speaks loudly and clearly at the surface of language. It speaks above and beyond one's conscious sense of what she has said. Freud said, "the truth must be said often." Philippe Lacadée quoted Freud's words and added that one does not have to prove the truth. Rather, one must *speak truly* (quoted by Nathalie George-Lambrichs, Internet, 03/24/23). Perhaps, thinking of some of his patients' endless psychoanalytic sessions, Freud said, "From error to error, one discovers the entire truth" (1923–1925: 1–66). To what resistance in himself must an analyst submit if he suddenly hears within the patient's symptoms, what she *really* desires, perhaps some taboo sexual object. In practice there are incest taboos in many, if not most, contemporary societies (Lévi-Strauss, 1969).

Exogamy

Strauss gave a detailed analysis of the practice of incest in the world. But the exchange of women in marriage means their leaving the primary family bonds. *Exogamy* is widespread today. But *endogamy*, marriage between kin and within social, religious, and ethnic groups, and within castes, still exists in a time when warring tribes have ceased to capture brides because women were scarce, and now that totemic clans have all but disappeared (McLennan, 1865). In fact, Strauss found many cultures where there is no incest taboo. He argued that the cultures that insist on the taboo maintain it as "law" because it fosters society, kinship, and the exchange of goods, as well as stating a prohibition against inbreeding. It has been argued that the move from endogamy to exogamy is evidence of social progress and human freedom.

Whether an individual's psychic structure is psychotic or not, the point is that practice of exogamy demonstrates a cultural acceptance of the Father's Name over the incestuousness of mirror-stage bonding which is a resistance to society and culture. Given that Lacan and Lévi-Strauss were close friends, it is not surprising that Strauss exercised an important influence on his thinking. Traces of Strauss's argument that society structures the mind can be found in Lacan's theory of the Symbolic order. Freud talked about the family romance. Strauss talked about incest. Lacan talked about Freud's *Totem and Taboo* in which the sons bury the incestuous greedy Ur-father and give rise to the bond of the brothers at the base of the social link: the Symbolic, resistance to the Real father (Lacan, 1967, 1998). Although societies have varying incest taboos, in fact, a sexual object is often incestuous, an animal, or what Slavoj Žižek has called the limit of taboos, the child.

Yet, childhood incest is reported frequently by those patients to whom an analyst might listen. For Lacan, the efficacious action of an analysis occurs when the analysand is brought to the point of naming the Desire that insists beyond her awareness. The difficult task facing an analyst is that the "something" to be recognized by the patient does not already exist somewhere. The something, the truth of Desire, is not an entity just waiting to be co-opted. By naming Desire, the subject reframes it. She gives conscious form to unconscious Desire. By letting the certainty of her subjectivity fall, by dropping the Imaginary nature of her fundamental fantasies, her ideals, she creates a *new presence* in her world (Lacan, 1955). Once named, a patient's Desire can be analyzed if she so wishes. Structurally speaking, it will always reveal a "lack" in the Other as it relates to Castration (separation) and the status of the Law of the Name-of-the-Father (order). While all phenomena pass through the filter of the Imaginary, Lacan taught that the Imaginary can be attenuated while the Symbolic organizes the Real.

Liquidation of Transference

Lacan maintained that psychoanalysts who do not understand *resistance* fail to do so because they view the patient as a kind of object under observation. He claimed that this apparent two-body object relations analysis takes its model from bastard forms of phenomenology. It basks in the mirage of consciousness that believes an ego can be a simple object for the other as subject. Such an assumption leads to the claim that one ego can substitute itself for another through transference (Lacan, 1977a). The healthy part of the patient's ego is supposed to identify with – and conform to – the analyst's ego in order that "cure" be achieved by the patient's adapting to reality (Lacan, 1955). Lacan correctly named this aspect of the analyst's ego function "aggressive" (1955). In this kind of analysis, the endpoint – its positive resolution – requires that the patient's ego be identified with the analyst's. What this amounts to in reality is that the patient is encouraged to bid masochistically for approval from a master (1955).

Lacan claimed, perhaps surprisingly, that the only object *genuinely* accessible to the analyst is not a hidden "self" that can be archeologically unearthed, but the *link* between the doctor and patient *qua ego* in its automatic intersubjectivity and in present time (1955). Instead of using this link to "understand" the patient, Lacanian analysts must resist their subjective interpretations of the analysand. The analyst's Desire should be to obtain absolute difference, a Symbolic order phenomenon, the very opposite of Imaginary identification (Lacan, 1977a). The role of the analyst is not to "understand" the patient, but to surprise the liberty which resides in nonsense, to unearth the fantasies that the analysand considers trash, to see how the analysand debates with her *jouissance*, to ascertain to what primitive discourse effects she is subjected. The analyst should restitute what is signified in the unconscious or implied in a discourse. His goal is to banish the Other's jouissance that is symbolized by the patient's own body. And, finally, the analysand may decide not to decide if the "case" should so dictate (Fink, 2013).

Lacan never disagreed with Freud's basic discoveries regarding the unconscious. For example, he fully concurred that without transference there could be no analysis. Certain psychoanalysts have misconstrued Lacan's innovations here. For example, François Roustang misinterpreted Lacan's statements regarding the *liquidation* of a transference (Lacan, 1977a). Roustang's interpretation of Lacan confused the idea of liquidating the transference with Lacan's play on the concept of the *sujet supposé savoir* (Freud, 1980; Pontalis, 1986; Borch-Jacobsen, 1990). Lacan argued that the analyst should aim to maintain a rather continuous transference with the goal of liquidating the analysand's Imaginary projections, which are the narcissistic bond that elevates *ego* fantasies over any knowledge of the Real of unconscious truth. By enabling the analysand to see that her transference with the analyst was based on fiction and illusion, that the Real transference was the *intra*subjective exchange between the analysand's own ego and her *I* conjoined in the absolute Other that "made" him in the first place (Ragland, 1986).

What is to be liquidated, or vaporized, is not transference as a phenomenon, nor the unconscious, but the presupposition of a unified relationship between analyst and analysand. By clinging to an Imaginary identification with the analyst, the analysand remains blocked by the other, the analyst, from hearing the knowledge contained in her own Other, a Desire that has laid down to structure her as a creature of law, or not. When the analyst's actual personhood begins to be grasped by the patient because her ego fantasies are broken up, a paradox occurs: the subject is no longer *subject* to illusion but has assumed knowledge of her own unconscious. She has assumed *subjectivity*, a knowledge that lies beyond the ego. By revealing various pitfalls in transference, not the least of which is the analyst's satisfaction at being recognized, Lacan demonstrated how transference could be used to lead both analyst and analysand beyond narcissistic fixations, to aim the analysand toward knowledge of her Desire, and away from her personhood.

Identification *with* the analyst can never be a final goal since any life is an ever-moving, endlessly unfolding epic of Desire and Law (Lacan, 1977b). The analysis forms one fixed moment in the dialectical writing of the analysand's potential life story. In this way psychoanalysis is an apprenticeship in freedom won through locating the roots of the ego (being) and the I (speaking) in an-Other's Desire (Lacan, 1977b). Unlike Freud who found analysis to often be interminable, Lacan found the end to be necessary, a part of the logic of the process (Freud, 1937). Schneiderman has described the end of analysis as "death's death." It is paid for, he says, with a de-being which, paradoxically, offers the analysand the freedom to live (1980).

In Lacan's view, the standard Neo-Freudian transference goes in the opposite direction from his (*Uberträgung*/carry, pay the cost). Their goal is not to open the analysand to her own occulted Desire and jouissance. Rather, this analysis works by the law of misrecognition (*méconnaissance*). In such a situation, analysands think they are talking directly to the analyst about them-"selves" and solving their problems once and for all. In truth, they are merely rephrasing their identity question to yet one more substitute other. Insofar as people take their perceptions to be objective and true, most analysands miss the *circular* subjectivity of their linear quest. Both patient and doctor constitute each other (1958). In *Seminar* XI Lacan taught that – through transference – the analysand "acts" out of the reality of the unconscious (1977a). In the countertransference, the analyst returns the sum of the prejudices, passions, embarrassments, even insufficient information that character-ize him at any given moment in the dialectical process (Lacan, 1968).

The analyst is above all a human being, in constant flux. However much a patient may not wish to recognize this flux, and however much the analyst may succeed by his steadfastness in creating the illusion of fixity, the facts are otherwise. The analyst is not a fixed point any more than any other person. Standard Neo-Freudian practice aims to help her understand her-"self." Such analysts see the patient's transference as a neurosis, a distortion, a disorder, but a path along which to *re-educate* the patient. The analyst, on the other hand, is not supposed to experience countertransference, unless his or her own neuroses remain unresolved as Freud once said (*S*. VIII). Lacan condemned this static picture of the analyst/analysand interaction as much as he condemned the illusion of an objective realistic therapist and a fantasy-logged patient. Ego analysts and "self" analysts, like their psychiatric prototypes, take their own perceptions as the measure of the *real* and true, even to the point of confusing their conscious intuitions with an unconscious empathy or "listening" (Kohut, 2011).

An analysand usually enters analysis with the idea that the analyst is realistic and objective and "knows" the key to her problems (Lacan, 2006). Lacan iconoclastically subverted the image of the analyst as the one who "knows," but he did not mean by that that the analyst lacks knowledge or analytic tools. He drew attention, rather, to the subject who *thinks* he "knows": the speaking *I* whose *ego* fictions and certainties come from the absolute Other. A Lacanian analyst proceeds by separating this Other "knowledge" (Lacan's matheme/S2) from the conscious attributions of *blame* and *certainty* that dwell at the surface of an analysand's discourse. Such an approach is personal and humble compared with practitioners whose bent is derived from neo-positivistic ideas that pigeonhole and categorize "neurotic" symptoms – now called anxiety disorders by the American DSM V – to the point that a given analyst assumes he "knows" a patient's unconscious from the inception of the analysis, that is, if he believes she has one. How do these clinicians differ from Charcot who thought he could diagnose a woman's symptoms by looking at her naked body. His eye functioned as his mind until Bourneville caught his ear and taught him that looking at the women's uncovered bodies would not tell him what had caused their symptoms: some "outside trigger" or provoking agent had caused their suffering.

For Lacan, the analyst is only a *detective*, not a master of knowledge. He can only aid the patient in finding out about the Other's discourse and Desire. He has no knowledge that will help her. The knowledge is on her side. Today's American scientists run tests and doctors do physical explorations. If they find nothing, they say wait and see. The idea is that the body knows, is its own site of knowledge.

Those clinical practitioners who do listen to their patients seek the truth behind their suffering in their history and archeology. They have their patients recount fantasies and memories. They probe events that lie "beyond" the language barrier, not realizing that everything is already there in speech. Lacan parried this standard theoretical thrust with the contention that psychoanalysis is not a *Wissen* (substantive knowledge), but a dialectical space in which the analyst shows the analysand that he talks badly or ignorantly (1954). "Symptom relief" entails the momentary corrections and completions of a discontinuous epic, not unlike restoring a defaced painting. The restoration gives the patient an identity trajectory with its own internal logic. The analysand wishes to know: Who am I? What should I do? The Lacanian analyst sits in the privileged position of representing the other/Other (i.e., all the interlocutors of the patient's past) without being functionally involved.

Conclusion

I conclude by asking who is transferring what and to whom, and from where? The answer comes back from Lacan's teachings: the patient is transferring his ego, embedded in his speech, distorted like a dream by unrecognized input from the Other. What is being transferred? It is the patient's demand for recognition, for the right to tell her own unconscious story, a story that unfortunately is located in her blind spot. To whom is the analysand transferring? Lacan's answer was to the other who refuses to behave like a *listening* other but preserves the aloofness of the dummy in bridge. The "to whom" the patient is transferring is really her own Other, which created her being and speech in the first place: the "to whom" she is transferring is aped by the Lacanian analyst who acts as a simulacrum. He does not know why she is suffering, nor does she. The truth behind her "problems" is an enigma for her and the analyst. She will only come to hear herself in the time of her seeing, the time for understanding and the moment of concluding. Through her speech, the circularity of her discourse echoes back to her in audible form, without her ever having seen her truth before. Two egos remain intact in the American analytic, therapeutic, psychiatric clinics of today. The patient's unknown knowledge remains untapped, and the "professionals" make money.

Lacan's scenario of what should occur in the analyst's office may seem strange and enigmatic. But this objection has already been ably forestalled by Lacan's mathematical formulations and by the answers embedded in his teachings that have been written. Regarding the difficulty of his teachings, Helena Schultz-Keil of the New York Lacan Study Group wrote to me in 1984:

> [P]rejudice has it that Lacan's teaching is unteachable, obscure. The prejudice reflects in inverted form the fact that the question of what is *teachable in psychoanalysis* was simply not posed before Lacan. Because Lacan attempts to answer that question, his work is precisely not esoteric. It is eminently teachable in that it offers a theory of the analytic situation as such. It lays bare the structures of this situation so that analysts might know from where, for what, and to whom they speak, considering that the analytic mode of operation is *speech* alone.

Author's Notes

I did not publish this article in 1985 because Jacques Derrida and French feminists reigned supreme in the intellectual world of the American Academy. They had left France because Lacan, the supreme European intellectual of their day, had not taken their ideas seriously. Like Paul de Man, and countless others, they left Europe to leave history behind and make their reputations in the USA, a country that did not ask questions about why they had come to the land of golden opportunity. These theorists influenced journals and presses who refused to publish anything on Lacan. Analytic institutes in 1985 were interested in Lacan but wary of his difficult prose and unsure what his practice would mean for the clinic. My work on Lacan became in demand in 1986 when I published the first book on him in the anglophone world. I never thought about that article on transference again. With time and moving, I lost it and did not remember having presented it. However, thanks to the care of the late Marvin Hymann, Etta Saxe, and Bethann Kalt of the Michigan Psychoanalytic Society and the Analytic Academy for the Arts, this article was found and posted on the website of the Academy and *The Journal of Medicine* as well. Both had copyrighted the article while keeping my name as author. With some effort, I retrieved it and the analytic academy sent me a copy to edit. I have revised it from 9 to 38 pages as of April 5, 2023.

To obtain further information about the Winnicott/Lacan relationship, you may contact the F.R. Rodman estate in Los Angeles, California. Rodman was given the Winnicott/Lacan letters by Claire Winnicott after the death of Dr. Winnicott. Dr. Rodman showed me some of the letters and told me in a personal letter how many there were. He sent me a very long one to translate. It has appeared both in French and English, in *Ornicar?* and in *Lacan Study Notes*. For those interested in Object Relations theory, Lacan's *Seminar: The Object Relation* (IV, 1956–1957) is available from Polity Press in NYC. *Seminar* XIII, *The Object of Psychoanalysis* (1966–1967) is available in an unofficial translation by Cormac Gallagher: to obtain Gallagher's translations into English of all Lacan's *Seminars*, you may contact St. Vincent's Univ. Hospital, Med. Dept, Dept. of Psychotherapy, Dublin, Ireland, + 51 3 81 99 29 24. Jacques-Alain Miller, Lacan's son-in-law, has created the World Association of Psychoanalysis and seven Lacanian Schools with one more soon to open in NYC. To these you may add a new Institute called the European University Network. Miller is the official editor of the 26 volumes of Lacan's *Seminars*. Fifteen have appeared in English. From 1980 to 2011 Miller presented Courses on Lacan's teaching. They have not been published in English, although unofficial versions are now being used in Lacanian seminars given in the USA. For further information about these Courses, you may contact the Lacanian Orientation in Paris through Navarin Press. Miller is also the consulting editor of many Lacanian journals in many languages. A complete edition of Lacan's *Écrits* has appeared in English (cf. B. Fink, 2006). Many of Lacan's other publications, such as *Television* and *Other Writings*, have appeared in English. Many have not.

Notes

1 Nov. 19–20, 2022/Cf. *The Lacanian Review Online*.
2 Cf. the transcription of a handwritten letter from Lacan to Winnicott, a letter given to me by F. R. Rodman who inherited Winnicott's Nachlast from Claire Winnicott. Jacques-Alain Miller had my translated letter transcribed by Gloria Gonzales and Russell Grigg and published it in *Ornicar?* (no. 33, 1985, pp. 7–10); to read Winnicott's letter to Lacan, see *Collected Works of D. W. Winnicott,* vol. 6, ch. 3. He thanks Lacan for his "Mirror Stage" article, saying that it had influenced him. Lacan had thanked Winnicott for influencing his thinking regarding what Winnicott called the transitional object.
3 Sigmund Freud's "On Narcissism: An Introduction" was originally published in 1914 and is included in volume XIV of the *Standard Edition*, translated by James Strachey et al. and published by Hogarth Press in London. The *Standard Edition* consists of 24 volumes translated between 1953 and 1974. In addition to "The Ego, the Id, and Other Works" (volume XIX, [1923], 1923–25), Freud published 26 essays between 1927 and 1950. This does not include the 100 papers he wrote on neurobiology before he discovered the unconscious part of the mind, which he refused to publish in the *Standard Edition*.
4 Freud (1900). The pre-conscious. In J. Strachey (Ed. and Trans.), *The standard edition of the complete psychological works of Sigmund Freud* (Vol. IV, pp. 283–289). Hogarth Press; Freud, S. (1909). The interpretation of dreams: Part two. In J. Strachey (Ed. and Trans.), *The standard edition of the complete psychological works of Sigmund Freud*

(Vol. X, pp. 1–627). Hogarth Press; Freud (1914–1916). A history of the psycho-analytic movement. In J. Strachey (Ed. and Trans.), *The standard edition of the complete psychological works of Sigmund Freud* (Vol. XIV, pp. 1–66). Hogarth Press.

5 The @ quote is from Gene, my brother, regarding a new journal called *Neuroscience and Psychoanalysis*, a special issue on Freud and neuroscience, "Psychoanalysis and Neuroscience: The Bridge between Mind and Brain," *Psychology: Frontiers in Psychology*, by F. Cieri and R. Esposito, Aug. 28, 2019; Gene Ragland/Executive Spotlight, Marquis Who's Who, A Lifetime of Achievement, vol. IV, Marquis Who's Who Ventures LLC, p. xi.

6 See F. de Goya's painting on the cover of S. IV/Saturno deverando a su hijo.

7 See Morel, G. (1999). "The Hypothesis of Compacity" in Chapter 1 of Encore: Seminar XX [1972–73]. In E. Ragland (Ed.), *Critical Essays on Jacques Lacan* (pp. 149–160). G. K. Hall & Co.

References

Adler, I. B. (2022). Freud's Dora: A Biography of Ida Bauer. McFarland.

American Psychiatric Association. (1980). Diagnostic and Statistical Manual of Mental Disorders (3rd ed.).

Bacon, F. (1620). Novum Organum Scientiarum. John Brill.

Ballestin, L. (2021). Resistance and revelation: Lacan on defense. European Journal of Psychoanalysis, 7(2).

Bechterew, V. M. (2015). Psychiatry: A Clinical Treatise on Diseases of the Fore-Brain Based Upon a Study of Its Structure, Functions, and Nutrition (1884). Scholar's Choice.

Borch-Jacobsen, M. (1990). The Lacanian Delusion (G. Sims, Trans.). Oxford University Press.

Bowlby, J. (1958). The nature of the child's tie to his mother. The International Journal of Psychoanalysis, 39, 350–373.

Brais, B. (1993). D. M. Bourneville and French Anticlericalism During the Third Republic. In R. Porter (Ed.), Doctor, Politics, and Society: Historical Essays. Brill.

Carroll, L. (1865). Alice's Adventures in Wonderland. Clarendon Press.

Cassin, B. (2020). Jacques the Sophist: Lacan, Logos, and Psychoanalysis. Fordham University Press.

Charpentier, É., Ghys, É., & Lesne, A. (Eds.). (2010). The Scientific Legacy of Poincaré. American Mathematical Society.

Chomsky, N. (2002). On Nature and Language. Cambridge University Press.

Crick, F., Watson, J., & Wilkins, M. (1953). A structure for deoxyribose nucleic acid. Nature, 171(4356), 737–738.

Dawkins, R. (1976). The Selfish Gene. Oxford University Press.

Deleuze, G., & Guattari, F. (1972). Anti-Oedipus: Capitalism and Schizophrenia. University of Minnesota Press.

de Saussure, F. (2011). Course in General Linguistics (W. Baskin, Trans.). Columbia University Press. (Original work published 1916)

Descartes, R. (2018). Discourse on the Method of Rightly Conducting the Reason and Searching for Truth in the Sciences. SMK Books. (Original work published 1637)

The Editors of Encyclopedia Britannica. (2023). History of topology. Encyclopedia Britannica. Retrieved from www.britannica.com/science/topology/History-of-topology

Fink, B. (2013). Against Understanding, Vol. 2: Cases and Commentary in a Lacanian Key. Routledge.

Fink, B. (2015). Lacanian Coordinates: From the Logic of the Signifier to the Paradoxes of Guilt and Desire. Karnac.

Freud, A. (1993). The Ego and the Mechanisms of Defense. Routledge. (Original work published 1936)

Freud, S. (1893–1899). Early Psycho-Analytic Publications. In J. Strachey (Ed. & Trans.), The Standard Edition of the Complete Psychological Works of Sigmund Freud (Vol. III). Hogarth Press.

Freud, S. (1894). The Neuro-Psychoses of Defense. In J. Strachey (Ed. & Trans.), The Standard Edition of the Complete Psychological Works of Sigmund Freud (Vol. III, pp. 43–61). Hogarth Press.

Freud, S. (1900). The Pre-Conscious. In J. Strachey (Ed. & Trans.), The Standard Edition of the Complete Psychological Works of Sigmund Freud (Vol. IV, pp. 283–289). Hogarth Press.

Freud, S. (1901a). Fragment of an Analysis of a Case of Hysteria. In J. Strachey (Ed. & Trans.), The Standard Edition of the Complete Psychological Works of Sigmund Freud (Vol. VII, pp. 1–122). Hogarth Press.

Freud, S. (1901b). The Interpretation of Dreams. In J. Strachey (Ed. & Trans.), The Standard Edition of the Complete Psychological Works of Sigmund Freud (Vols. IV & V). Hogarth Press.

Freud, S. (1911). Case History of Schreber. In J. Strachey (Ed. & Trans.), The Standard Edition of the Complete Psychological Works of Sigmund Freud (Vol. XII, pp. 1911–1913). Hogarth Press.

Freud, S. (1914). On Narcissism: An Introduction. In J. Strachey (Ed. & Trans.), The Standard Edition of the Complete Psychological Works of Sigmund Freud (Vol. XIV, pp. 67–100). Hogarth Press.

Freud, S. (1923–1925). The Ego and the Id. In J. Strachey (Ed. & Trans.), The Standard Edition of the Complete Psychological Works of Sigmund Freud (Vol. XIX, pp. 1–66). Hogarth Press.

Freud, S. (1937). Analysis terminable and interminable. International Journal of Psycho-Analysis, 4 (18), 373–405.

Freud, S. (1938). Splitting of the Ego in the Process of Defence. In J. Strachey (Ed. & Trans.), The Standard Edition of the Complete Psychological Works of Sigmund Freud (Vol. XXIII, pp. 139–143). Hogarth Press. (Original work published 1938)

Freud, S. (1953). Project for a Scientific Psychology. In The Origins of Psycho-Analysis: Letters to Wilhelm Fliess, Drafts, and Notes: 1887–1902 (J. Strachey, Trans., pp. 1895). Basic Books. (Original work published 1895)

Freud, S. (1980). Psychoanalysis Never Lets Go (N. Luchacher, Trans.). The Johns Hopkins University Press.

Freud, S., & Breuer, J. (1895). Studies on Hysteria. In J. Strachey (Ed. & Trans.), The Standard Edition of the Complete Psychological Works of Sigmund Freud (Vol. II, pp. 1–335). Hogarth Press. (Original work published 1955)

Gillespie, N., & Aguirre, M. C. (2018). Delights of the ego. The Lacanian Review, (5), 107.

Greenshields, W. (2017). Writing the Structures of the Subject: Lacan and Topology. Palgrave Macmillan.

Hale, N. G. (1971). Freud and the Americans: The Beginnings of Psychoanalysis in the United States, 1876–1917 (1st ed.). Oxford University Press.

Jakobson, R. J., & Halle, M. (1956). Fundamentals of language. Mouton.

Johnston, A. (2022). Jacques Lacan. In Stanford Encyclopedia of Philosophy. Stanford University. https://plato.stanford.edu/entries/lacan/ (Original work published 2013)

King, P. (2013). L'American Way of Life/Lacan et les débuts de l'Ego Psychology. Lussaud.

Kohut, H. (2011). The Search for the Self: Selected Writings: 1950–78 (Vol. 1). Routledge.

Lacan, J. (1949). The Mirror Stage as Formative of the I Function as Revealed in Psychoanalytic Experience. In B. Fink (Trans.), Écrits: A Selection (pp. 75–81). Norton.

Lacan, J. (1954). Seminar I: Freud's Papers on Technique (J. Forrester, Trans.). Cambridge University Press/Norton.

Lacan, J. (1955). Seminar II: The Ego in Freud's Theory and in the Technique of Psychoanalysis (S. Tomaselli, Trans.). Cambridge University Press/Norton.

Lacan, J. (1958). The Direction of the Treatment and the Principles of Its Power. In B. Fink (Trans.), Écrits: A Selection (pp. 489–582). Norton.

Lacan, J. (1962). The Seminar of Jacques Lacan. Identification 1961–1962. Seminar IX (C. Gallagher, Trans., 1st ed.). Lacan in Ireland. www.lacaninireland.com/web/translations/seminars/

Lacan, J. (1966–1967). Seminar XIII: L'objet de la psychanalyse/On the Object of Psychoanalysis (C. Gallagher, Trans.). Unpublished manuscript.

Lacan, J. (1968). The Language of the Self: The Function of Language in Psychoanalysis ["The Rome Discourse" of 1953] (A. Wilden, Ed. & Trans., pp. xi–xii). The Johns Hopkins University Press.

Lacan, J. (1974a). La troisième. Lettres de l'École freudienne, (16). Rome.

Lacan, J. (1974b). The Seminar of Jacques Lacan. R.S.I. 1974–1975. Seminar XXII. (C. Gallagher, Trans., 1st ed.). Lacan in Ireland. www.lacaninireland.com/web/translations/seminars/

Lacan, J. (1977a). The Four Fundamental Concepts of Psychoanalysis (A. Sheridan, Trans.). Hogarth Press. (Original work published 1964)

Lacan, J. (1977b). Desire and the interpretation of desire in Hamlet (J. Hulbert, Trans.). Yale French Studies, 55/56, pp. 11–52.

Lacan, J. (1982). The Function and Field of Speech and Language in Psychoanalysis. In Écrits: A Selection (A. Sheridan, Trans, p. 39). W.W. Norton & Company. (Original work published 1953)

Lacan, J. (1988a). Logical time and the assertion of anticipated certainty: A new sophism (B. Fink & M. Silver, Trans.). Newsletter of the Freudian Field, 2(2), 4–22.

Lacan, J. (1988b). Seminar I: Freud's Papers on Technique, 1953–54 (J. Forrester, Trans.). Cambridge University Press; Norton. (Original work published 1953–1954)

Lacan, J. (1989). Science and Truth. Newsletter of the Freudian Field, 3(1–2) (B. Fink, Trans.). (Original work published 1965–66).

Lacan, J. (1990). Television. Norton.

Lacan, J. (1993). The Seminars of Jacques Lacan Book III the Psychoses 1955–1956 (J. A. Miller, Ed., R. Grigg, Trans., 1st ed.). Routledge.

Lacan, J. (1997). The Seminar of Jacques Lacan, Book XI: The Four Fundamental Concepts of Psychoanalysis (1964) (A. Sheridan, Trans.). Hogarth Press. (Original work published 1973)

Lacan, J. (1998). The Seminar of Jacques Lacan, Book XX: Encore, on Feminine Sexuality, the Limits of Love and Knowledge (1972–1973) (J.-A. Miller, Ed., B. Fink, Trans.). W. W. Norton & Company. (Original work published 1975)

Lacan, J. (2006a). Ecrits: The First Complete Edition in English (B. Fink, Trans.). W.W. Norton & Company.

Lacan, J. (2006b). The Instance of the Letter in the Unconscious or Reason Since Freud (B. Fink, Trans.). In Écrits (pp. 417–494). W.W. Norton & Company. (Original work published 1957)

Lacan, J. (2006c). The Subversion of the Subject and the Dialectic of Desire in the Freudian Unconscious (1960). In Écrits (B. Fink, Trans., pp. 671–702). W.W. Norton & Company. (Original work published 1959–1960)

Lacan, J. (2007a). The Other Side of Psychoanalysis: The Seminar of Jacques Lacan, Book XVII (R. Grigg, Trans.). W.W. Norton. (Original work published 1969–1970)

Lacan, J. (2007b). The Seminar of Jacques Lacan, Book XVII: The Other Side of Psychoanalysis, 1969–1970. (R. Grigg, Trans.). W. W. Norton & Company. (Original work published 1991)

Lacan, J. (2007c). The Seminars of Jacques Lacan Book VII: The Ethics of Psychoanalysis 1959–1960 (J. A. Miller, Ed., D. Porter, Trans., 1st ed.). Routledge.

Lacan, J. (2014). Anxiety (A. Price, Trans.). Polity. (Original work published 1962–1963)

Lacan, J. (2015). Transference: The Seminar of Jacques Lacan, Book VIII (1st ed.). Polity.

Lacan, J. (2016). The Sinthome: The Seminar of Jacques Lacan. Wiley.

Lacan, J. (2017). The Seminar of Jacques Lacan, Book V: The Formations of the Unconscious (R. Grigg, Trans.). Polity. (Original work published 1957–1958)

Lacan, J. (2019). Seminar VI: Desire and Its Interpretation, 1958–59 (B. Fink, Trans.). Polity. (Original work published 1958–1959)

Lacan, J. (2020a). Ecrits: A Selection. Routledge.

Lacan, J. (2020b). Seminar IV: The Object Relation, 1956–57 (A. Price, Trans.). Polity. (Original work published 1956–1957)

Lacan, J., & Miller, J.-A. (2022). The Lacanian Review 12: American Lacan (M.-H. Brousse & C. S. A. Poliakoff, Eds.). Independently Published.

Lafont, J. (1986). The Ordinary Topology of Jacques Lacan. Points Hors Ligne.

Lévi-Strauss, C. (1969). The Elementary Structures of Kinship [1949]. Beacon Press.

Locke, J. (1690). An Essay Concerning Human Understanding. Thomas Basset.

Marx, K. (1959). Das Kapital: A Critique of Political Economy (Vol. I [1867], Vol. II [1885], & Vol. III [1894]). H. Regnery.

McLennan, J. F. (1865). Primitive Marriage. University of Chicago Press.

Miller, J.-A. (1988). A [Other] and a [Other] in Clinical Structures. In Paris-New York Psychoanalytic Workshop (Ed.), Acts of the Paris-New York Psychoanalytic Workshop (pp. 4–30). Schneiderman Pub.

Miller, J.-A. (1993). The Four Discourses of the Analyst. In M. Fink (Ed.), Écrits: A Selection (pp. 225–246). W. W. Norton & Company. (Original work published 1971)

Miller, J.-A. (1999). La psychose ordinaire. Agalma/Seuil.

Miller, J.-A. (2003). Lacan's Later Teaching. In B. P. Fulks (Trans.), Le lieu et le lien, Course of 2000–01, The Lacanian Orientation (Vol. 21, pp. 43–51). Lacanian Ink.

Miller, J.-A. (2011). L'Un Tout Seul. [Unpublished manuscript, Lacanian Orientation course].

Miller, J.-A. (2022). Generalized Foreclosure; From the Symbolic to the Real (Vol. 55). Lacanian Ink.

Monod, J. (1997). Chance and Necessity: Essay on the Natural Philosophy of Modern Biology. Penguin Books.

Morel, G. (2019). *Sexual Ambiguities*. London: Routledge. https://doi.org/10.4324/9780429480010.

Pontalis, J.-B. (1986). Lacan de l'équivoque à l'impasse. Minuit.

Ragland, E. (1986). Jacques Lacan and the Philosophy of Psychoanalysis. University of Illinois Press.

Ragland, E. (1988). Hamlet, logical time and the structure of obsession. Newsletter of the Freudian Field, 2(1&2, Fall).

Ragland, E. (1989). Plato's symposium and the Lacanian theory of transference: Or, what is love? The South Atlantic Quarterly, 88(4), 725–755.

Ragland, E. (1997). Freud and the construction of the master plot of psychoanalysis. Hypatia, 12(2), 112–141.

Ragland, E. (2004). The Logic of Sexuation: From Aristotle to Lacan. State University of New York Press.

Ragland, E. (2015). Jacques Lacan and The Logic of Structure: Topology and Language in Psychoanalysis. Routledge/Taylor & Francis.

Ragland, E. (2016). Psychotic Language Is Not a Discourse: Discreet Signs of Psychoses. In M. J. Muratore (Ed.), Hermeneutics of Textual Madness: Re-readings (Vol. I, pp. 101–128). Mentalità E Scrittura (Vol. 38). Alain Baudry & Co/Biblioteca Della Ricera.

Ragland, E. (2024). Lacan and Hysteria: The Logic of Paradox. Publisher TBD.

Ragland, E., & Milovanovic, D. (Eds.). (2004). Lacan: Topologically Speaking. Other Press.

Ragland-Sullivan, E. (1989). Seeking the Third Term: Desire, the Phallus, and the Materiality of Language. In R. Feldstein & J. Roof (Eds.), Feminism and Psychoanalysis (pp. 40–64). Cornell University Press.

Rank, O. (1978). Will Therapy: Selections from the Collected Works of Otto Rank, Volumes 1–3 (1929–1931) (J. Taft, Ed.). W. W. Norton & Company. (Original work published 1936)

Rank, O. (2011). Beyond Psychology. Dover Publications.

Redmond, J. D. (2013). Contemporary perspectives on Lacanian theories of psychosis. Frontiers in Psychology, 4, 350. https://doi.org/10.3389/fpsyg.2013.00350

Schneiderman, S., & Ragland-Sullivan, E. (Eds.). (1980). Returning to Freud: Clinical Psychoanalysis in the School of Lacan (pp. 166–167). Yale University Press.

Schreber, D. P. (2000). Memoirs of My Nervous Illness. New York Review of Books.

Svolos, T. (2020). The Aims of Analysis: Miami Seminar on the Late Lacan. Midden Press.

Wolf, B. (2018). More Lacanian Coordinates: On Love, Psychoanalytic Clinic, and the Ends of Analysis. Routledge.

Žižek, S. (2015). Ordinary Psychosis Revisited (Vol. 46). Lacanian Ink.

Zupancic, A. (2008). The three negations. Cardozo Law Review, 5(1), 29–35.

Zupancic, A. (2012). Not-mother: On Freud's verneinung. e-flux Journal, (33). Retrieved from www.e-flux.com/journal/33/68309/not-mother-on-freud-s-verneinung/

Chapter 2

On Sigmund Freud's "Negation"

Sergio Benvenuto

Denying What the Other Knows

In "*Die Verneinung*," Freud (1925) builds upon a clinical stratagem that has since entered the abecedary of many psychoanalysts. Analysands often make statements such as: "I'm sure you'll think I want to say something offensive now, but that is by no means my intention." The analyst should then understand that the analysand *does want to say* something offensive. Or an analysand may say: "You ask who this person in my dream could be. Well, it's not my mother." In this case, of course, it's their mother.

Freud extends the principle of negation, affirming the truth of something to everything subjects *consider furthest from them*: which is actually what is closest to them:

> [The analyst] asks: "what would you consider the most unlikely imaginable thing in that situation? What do you think was furthest from your mind at that time?" If the patient falls into the trap and says what he thinks is most incredible, he almost always makes the right admission.
>
> (Freud 1925, p. 235)[1]

We can derive a great variety of corollaries from this criterion of negation as affirmation. A clinical vignette ascribed to Lacan's practice: a patient of his – who has been doing a face-to-face analysis for some time – tells him in a session, "I dreamt of you suggesting that I should lie down on the couch, and me saying: 'But what's the point now?'" To which Lacan replies, "please lie down, my dear" (Allouch 1998, p. 35).

"Negation" is not the obvious translation of *Verneinung*, which is not *Negation*, *Leugnung*, or even *Verweigerung*, because this instead implies more the notion of refusal. On the one hand, *Verneinung* means *negation* in the logical sense. On the other hand, it also implies what in English would be expressed with *disclaiming*, *disavowal*, and *denial*; a denial that is – above all – rhetorical, as we shall see. We shall use "negation" or "denial,"[2] according to which sense we think prevails over the other in the various occurrences.

DOI: 10.4324/9781003375920-3

So, a subject becomes aware of something but can only accept it with the seal of negation. In classical logic, two negations affirm – "it is not true that it is not raining today" means "it is raining today": [not (not p)] = [p]. Instead, in psychoanalysis, a single negation is apparently enough to affirm.

My comment: everyone will agree that in many cases when we deny something, we are affirming it. A proverbial figure is someone who starts a statement with the premise "I'm not racist" and immediately adds something like "but frankly, I can't stand Jews, gypsies," and so on. And if someone diplomatically states "I really do not believe my opponent meant to say something so stupid," everyone understands that the speaker believes his opponent said something absolutely dumb.

This inconsistency between logical negation and denial in psychoanalysis (and in common discourse) derives from the fact that the "not" Freud speaks of is not a logical *not* (the German *Negation*) but a rhetorical *not* (*Verneinung*). Now, we are in the domain of rhetoric when we try to convince the other not only with logical arguments but when we assume their subjectivity, thoughts, beliefs, desires, and so on. In short, it is when we assume they have certain prejudices. Let's take the statement "I'm tired, but I feel like playing." The "but" is not logical but rhetorical. According to logic, this sentence is merely a conjunction of two propositions: "I'm tired" *and* "I feel like playing."

The "but" is rhetorical because it calls upon the presumed knowledge of the other, of the interlocutor. It is as if I were saying: "I inform you that I'm tired, but, *contrary to what you may think* – which is that someone who's tired is in no mood to play – I'm telling you that, on the contrary, I do feel like playing." We maneuver within the supposed knowledge or supposed desire of the Other (I use, following Lacan, the upper case O here to point out that the reference is not to a specific person but to the Other in general). While logic ignores the knowledge and beliefs – the prejudices – of the interlocutor (of the Other), rhetoric always works with this presumption that the Other knows, thinks, deduces, loves, hates, and so on. So, the denial Freud speaks of is rhetorical, and, in fact, the examples he gives evokes thoughts by the analyst that the analysand supposes. As we shall see, here Freud fails to thematize the fundamental function of the other in the analytic relation, even though his examples and his theory somehow demand it.

Therefore, Freud continues, "[i]n our interpretation, we take the liberty of disregarding the negation and of picking out the subject-matter alone of the association."[3] Now, many would say that, in this case, Freud is taking an excessive liberty. But even many psychoanalysts who bet on the primacy of transference object nowadays: patients actually deny it because they have come to understand the interpretative system of their analysts, having entered their mental system of presuppositions. It is as if they were saying: "I know you'll interpret this figure in my dream as my mother, because this is your decoding system, which I'm very well acquainted with by now. *But I reject this decoding system of yours.*" In the same way, it is as if those who claim they're not racist only to then express racist judgments went on to say: "I know that according to your criteria, I'm plain racist, but I don't think I am, deep down, even if I say things that sound racist to you."

In short, denial – according to these objections – apparently reveals a disapproval on behalf of the analysand regarding the analyst's hermeneutic key.

I think the elaborations by Jacques Lacan essentially take into account this objection to Freud's interpretative "freedom": for Lacan, every denial is ultimately a negation of *the other's* possible discourse. Indeed, he would go on to say that "the unconscious is the discourse of the Other" (Lacan 1999, p. 16). In analysis, through negation, analysands evidently place their analysts in the position of the Other, i.e., of someone who thinks and states things that they, the subjects, *neither* think *nor* believe. So, for Lacan, the unconscious is not something *mine*, but rather something coming from the Other. And it will remain unconscious – i.e., alien to the self, belonging to another – until the subject says, "it is what *You* think, not what *I* think." In other words, it is impossible to erase from the discourse of any subject, within or outside analysis, any reference to the other. Except that some will have the other coincide with a specific other, with the lady or gentleman who upholds certain ideas and tries to engraft them into the subject; instead, Lacan spells the other with an uppercase "O" because he disconnects this Other from all the others who may occupy this position. He can therefore give the other a more fundamental function, that of being the very guarantor of truth. Can this slide be justified?

Freud ultimately says something of which most of us are convinced: that the judgment of others – the *vox populi* – on ourselves is, in a sense, correct. This is a widespread anti-narcissistic assumption: others see us better than we see ourselves. It is the truth of the Other.

If we had more space here, we could show that, despite their complexity and sophistication, Freud's theories are actually largely based on *common knowledge*, on *popular beliefs*. We need only look at the primacy of sexuality in life. Is the overwhelming majority of songs, films, novels, rumors, and of discourses on the analysts couch not about sexuality and love? And if we look at some of Freud's apparently original theories, like dreams as imaginary fulfilments of our desires, is it not what popular culture has always believed? Significantly we say, "I *dream* of retiring" to say "I ardently *desire* to retire." Even the Freudian *Verneinung* is ultimately a "common" idea. Psychoanalytical interpretation is a folkish look at subjectivity.

The Chicken Delusion

In the entry for "(Dé)négation" (Negation) in their *Vocabulaire de la psychanalyse*, Laplanche and Pontalis (1967), with regard to the examples given by Freud, express a scruple Freud later confronted in his paper *Constructions in Analysis* (Freud 1937). When Freud was still alive, his theories were targeted with a great deal of epistemological criticism, which became rampant in more recent decades. Many were already remarking against Freud that analysts arrange things so they will always find a confirmation to what they think; they anticipated the well-known criticism expressed by Karl Popper, who argued that psychoanalysis makes any confutation of its hypotheses impossible. The analyst replies: "when he [the patient] agrees with us, then we are in the right; but when he contradicts us, then it is just a sign of his resistance, so we are still in the right" (Freud 1937, p. 257).[4] In short, "heads I win; tails you lose." For Laplanche and Pontalis this objection also stands with regard to the Freudian thesis of *Verneinung*.

Freud understood that the question of the refutability of analytic theory was crucial to its admittance to the exclusive and fastidious club of the sciences. But, despite the fears of Laplanche and Pontalis, this objection does not apply to the cases cited in "Negation": here it is the analysand who steers self-interpretation while at the same time belying it. The analysand articulates an *excusatio non petita*, an excuse that has not been sought, and we cannot help imagining that this represents an indirect self-accusation of something. It is the analyst who says to the analysand, "YOU spoke the truth."

There's a story about a psychotic who thought he was a grain of wheat. After several years in a clinic, he eventually recovers, is finally discharged and merrily gives everyone his farewells. But after a few hours, he returns to the institution shaking and pale with fear. What happened? He'd walked past a chicken coop and had wondered: "*I* know I'm not a grain of wheat by now. But what about *them*, the chickens? Do they know?"

The story is funny because we realize that our hero, despite the logical soundness of his arguments, has remained psychotic. It is part of a long series of works featuring subjects "cured" of their mental illnesses, but who on the first occasion reveal that their delusions are still flustering them. In this case, we also have a *Verneinung* in the sense of denial: the patient says, "I know I'm *not* a grain of wheat" and claims others may hold this belief – "but the chickens don't know I'm not." By denying his belief and ascribing it to the other (the chickens), the subject indirectly reveals that it still is his belief. In the same way, the analysand who says, "you probably think I loathe you, but that's not the case," ascribes to the other (the analyst) the knowledge of his own negative affect; likewise, the fellow who says, "you probably think I'm racist, but I'm not" ascribes to the other (the politically correct anti-racist) the self-recognition of his own racism. The other acts as a negative mirror: and through this mirror, we disavow and refute what we really are. So, in Freud's example we evoked earlier, the analysand says "*you ask* who this person in my dream may be": he ascribes to the other – the analyst – his own question.

These phenomena are all well-known in analysis, even though the various schools discuss them differently. For example, in such cases, Kleinians speak of projective identification, while Lacan said, "the subject receives his message from the other in inverted form." (I am not saying that Kleinian projective identification and Lacan's inverted message are identical concepts, considering that they are part of quite different theoretical approaches, but both do describe what we are stressing here, albeit in different forms.)

The majority of post-Freudian schools undoubtedly ended up bringing to the forefront what Freud brings to the stage in this article, and elsewhere, but silently, surreptitiously: that the unconscious always expresses itself in relation to others and/or the Other. And that negation is denial of the Other, that it amounts to denying something the Other supposes; but for Freud, the unconscious is precisely this assumption of the Other. And the unconscious remains such until this message remains an assumption of the Other instead of a personal recognition.

Aufhebung

Let's resume our reading of Freud's article. Freud (1925, pp. 235–236) writes:

> Negation is a way of taking cognizance of what is repressed; indeed it is already a lifting [*Aufhebung*] of the repression, though not, of course, an acceptance of what is repressed. We can see how in this the intellectual function is separated from the affective process.[5]

Aufhebung is also a key term of Hegel's dialectics. *Aufhebung* literally means *to lift, to raise up*; the *Aufhebung* of a stone is the lifting of a stone. But the word also means cancellation and revocation: the *Aufhebung* of my journal subscription means that I have ceased to be a subscriber. In English, too, we can say that a ban is lifted, the lockdown is lifted. In German, however, *Aufhebung* also implies preserving what has been removed. Hegel plays on the different senses of the term: synthesis is, for him, an *Aufhebung* of both thesis and antithesis, in the sense that it cancels them while lifting them to a level that preserves them within synthesis. Freud too, when he uses this term, says that by denying what was repressed, repression is lifted, but in a way, it is preserved too. We could translate *Aufhebung* with *lift* in the two senses of the word. For Freud repression is not being able any more to say something that had been utterable; but, thanks to negation, the repressed ceases to be such, because it enters in the speech, but at the price of an "intellectual" negation. The subject speaks the truth by denying it. Denial, Jean Hyppolite says, "is a mode of presenting what one is in the mode of not being it":[6] we reveal what we are by saying we are not that.

In any case, the sign of negation is not exhaustive of every form of denial. Freud (1925, p. 236) notes that:

> We succeed in conquering the negation as well, and in bringing about a full intellectual acceptance of the repressed; but the repressive process (*Vorgang*) itself is not yet removed [*aufgehoben*] by this.[7]

In other words, even the statement of a truth can be its denial. The English translator here translates *aufgehoben* with "removed," whilst further up, he translated *Aufhebung* with "lifting." But translating the noun form and the verb form of the same term with two different words, however, hides the fact that Freud is speaking about a single process – whether we want to call it revocation, suspension, cancellation, to remove or to lift. Essentially, Freud says, it is not enough to remove a "not" to *aufheben* repression, because an excessively "lofty," purely intellectual acceptation of the repressed is always possible. This is because – Freud says with a masterstroke – *intellectuality is in itself denial*. If it remains purely intellectual, any statement is a way to deny or lift (up) what has yet been affirmed.

Most believe they fully understand the opposition between affective and intellectual that Freud suggests here: understanding something with the mind does not *ipso facto* mean understanding it with the heart. But this kind of common sense is not enough to fully appreciate Freud. In fact, he specifies that the intellectual is a "function" (*Funktion*), whereas the affective is a "process" (*Vorgang*). Intellectuality, i.e., articulated thinking, is what was once called a faculty: it serves the useful function of helping human beings to survive and reproduce their genes; a Darwinian would say that intellectuality is adaptive. Instead, affectivity does not serve any evident function according to Freud, it is a *pure process*. Here lies the essential difference between psychoanalysis and Darwinism. For Freud, the unconscious is not adaptive; rather, we can consider it the non-adaptive part of the human mind.

But the statement that intellectuality is essentially denial is hard to swallow. In fact, for Freud, the intellectual function is not merely something other than the affective process; it is not an added dimension that may correct the former: it establishes itself *essentially* as the denial of the affective, hence as the negation of subjective truth. And, as *das Ich* – the Ego of the second topic, which also includes the Id and the Superego – comprises the intellectual function, Lacan's conclusion, for example, of the Ego as a machine for denying truth, as misrecognition, is comprehensible.

A fundamental opposition in Hegelianism is that between intellect and reason. According to Hegelians, the intellect – which always sees absolute contrasts and contrapositions – should be replaced by reasoning, which realizes that contrapositions are apparent, i.e., the result of limited and partial perspectives. By saying that negation is something merely intellectual, Freud seems to refer to a reason that transcends the intellect: to a sort of full affirmation, a concurrence of the self with the self. This overcoming of the split between the self (*ich*) and the world – which is fundamental in German idealism – is also the ideal of psychoanalysis.

In fact, immediately afterwards, Freud admits that, of course, intellectual judgment affirms or denies. So, he sets forth what he calls the psycho-logical origin of the logical faculty of judgment: whether to remove something or not. "Yes" ("it is true") is equivalent to "I don't repress," "no" ("it is false") is equivalent to "I prefer to repress." "A negative judgment [*Verurteilung*] is the intellectual substitute [*Ersatz*] for repression"; indeed, he specifies, a "no" is like a certificate of origin, like "made in Germany."[8] A *no* is the origin of the "intellectual" Ego. Hyppolite points out how *Verurteilung*, which the English translation renders with "negative judgment," is actually a *dé-jugement*, a dis-judgment, a disclaimed judgment. "No" is, therefore, not repression itself; it is its explicit "intellectual" sign. And he adds:

> With the help of the symbol of negation, thinking frees itself from the restrictions of repression and enriches itself with material that is indispensable for its proper functioning (*Leistung*).[9]

A non-obvious development of the previous concept: a "no" is not, therefore, merely a seal or a certificate; it is also what makes thinking, the intellectual function, possible. A no produces the "intellect" in the Hegelian sense. In other words, the symbol of negation is not a by-product of human thinking; it is its condition and ineliminable backdrop: "no" is like the trace of a primal, fundamental separation of the intellectual from the affective, i.e., of the differentiation between thinking and what he would later call compulsion (*Zwang*) or the dominance of the enjoyment-desire principle (*Lustprinzip*).

Lustprinzip has been translated as "pleasure principle," a choice that still causes misunderstandings today. In German, *Lust* has an erotic connotation that we don't find in "pleasure," but above all, it means "desire" and "pleasure," "concupiscence," and "enjoyment."[10] Freud himself had been tempted to use *Lust*, a term from common language, to refer to human desire in its sexual form. Then he chose the erudite Latin term *libido* precisely to avoid the ambiguities of *Lust*.[11] The Germanic word *Lust* has remained in the English language as *lust*. To convey the ambiguity of the German *Lust*, I shall refer to a desire-enjoyment principle and occasionally to a lust principle. As for *Prinzip*, it does not only mean rule or criterion, like when we say someone is "principled." The word actually comes from the Latin *principium*, which was a translation of the Greek *arché*, meaning what was original, what came before, but also that which commands, which has a mastery over something: it meant principle as temporal beginning but also as what has the lead hierarchically. *Prinzip* includes *Prinz*, Prince. We could even translate *Lustprinzip* as "command of desire-enjoyment."[12]

The Original Split

Immediately afterwards, Freud reminds us of a classical philosophical distinction: that between judgment of attribution and judgment of existence. "Socrates is mortal" is a judgment of attribution, "Socrates exists" is a judgment of existence. For him, subjectivity begins with attribution. He overturns common sense, according to which we are led to thinking first of all that we need to recognize that "Socrates exists" and then qualify him as "amiable, intelligent, married, healthy and so on." For Freud, process dominates over function; it is its commander and origin.

In the primary psyche – which Freud conceived of as entirely subject to the command of desire-enjoyment – the attributive judgment is equal to considering something good or bad, useful, or detrimental. Freud considers the oral modality the most primitive; therefore, ascribing a quality is equivalent to "I want to eat it," denying it is equivalent to "I want to spit it out." More generally: the attribution of a quality is equivalent to introducing something within myself, and its denial is equivalent to expelling it from or keeping it outside myself.[13]

Here Freud is evidently talking about an original schism between subjectivity and the real. From this point of view, the latter is not something that is always already given, a feature of the external that every subject faces from birth and has to deal with cognitively. Instead, the real is established correlatively to the subject via a double *process*, active and passive. The original real is *what has been excluded*, what the subject has spat out or thrown up, what it hasn't allowed inside and prevented from becoming a representation (*Vorstellung*) of itself. The dimension Freud calls "affective" is that in which the subject establishes itself as a set of representations in opposition to an "outside" that coincides with what it has excluded. The difference or contrast between the Ego and the real – their "intellectual opposition," Hegel would say – is not then a primitive datum from which to begin, but an acquisition starting from an original differentiation, the "logic" of which is not that of a division between the imaginary and the real, between true and false, but between pleasant and unpleasant, "good" and "bad." In short, for Freud, the original subject is not a cognitive subject: it is instead an *ethical subject*. There exists judging activity *ab initio*, a selective one, not a passive reception, nor a neutral contemplation of the world; for Freud attribution – i.e., appreciation and assessment – come before the recognition of existence. After all, even the word "fact," which comes from the Latin *facere* (to make), implies something that has been *made* – it only remains to be seen whether it was made by humans, by the transcendental Self or by God. We are born as subjects, not when we discriminate between what exists in the world and what doesn't, but when we hedonistically rate what touches us: the original distinction is between what interests us and what doesn't (i.e., the original real – original in our subjective history, but beyond it too – and what doesn't interest us at all, and what manages to interest us only as an evil, i.e., as *what we wished did not concern us*). The radical real disturbs and threatens us. For Freud, the human being is originally prone to illusion, to denying reality. The real is what we originally denied.

One question remains that might seem a captious remark but is not. Here Freud seems to be identifying what we *expel* with what we *keep out*, which is something external. But they're not quite the same thing. To spit something out, we must have put it into our mouths first, we must have tasted it. Tasting has an important role in psychoanalysis. A word for tasting in German, as well as *kosten* or *probieren*, is *prüfen*. Taste-tester is *Prüfer*. If we taste something in our mouths or in our minds, we don't eat it, we don't absorb it: we examine what we might absorb. But the uncertain time of tasting is one during which the thing becomes, at least for a short while, a part of the Ego: it has the time, and the opportunity – Freud would say – for being *represented*. This point, not developed by Freud, would seem important. Because, as we shall see, he would later actually talk about *Prüfung*, tasting, when discussing *Realitätsprüfung*, of reality-testing or reality-tasting.

The real, therefore, has been represented beforehand; it has been interiorized somewhere. In English, Freud's *Vorstellung* was translated as *presentation*, a choice that helps avoid misunderstandings. *Vorstellung* is not full presence through perception, but the state of something re-presenting itself as a representation; a "re-presentation," we could call it.

Vorstellung is composed of *vor*, "in front of," and *Stellung*, "position, place, collocation." It is literally a "positioning oneself in front of." If we were to take heed of the word itself, *Vorstellung*, representation, is something halfway between the passive position (*Stellung*) of perception and the active presentation of thinking and saying. With *Vorstellung* we are not dealing with mere passive effects, but with an activity, albeit not an entirely creative one. Representation – as Heidegger stressed – since Ancient Greek times, has been *noein*, i.e., "the perception that, far from passively receiving the entity, allows itself to be given the present, actively raising its gaze" (Heidegger 1971, p. 295). Perception is passive presentation, but insofar as it becomes representation, it implies something active, even just raising your gaze, wanting to stare.

Archi-Chorismy

For Freud, therefore, originally, what "is bad" is equal to what "does not exist," while what "is good" is equal to what "exists." This idea seems a break with a certain Western rationalist tradition that had always favored human cognitive ability, i.e., our capacity to judge the truth or falsehood of particular representations dispassionately. But it would suffice to remind ourselves that Plato, for whom the true real consists of *idées* or *eíde* (aspects, forms), already placed at the top of these *idées* Good itself (*to agathon*, literally "what is suited to"). Plato's Good is not, of course, Freud's pleasurable (here Freud picks up on Epicurus more than on Plato), but it is still its *idea*-l equivalent. Western metaphysics was marked from its beginnings by an ontological superiority of the Good against the True (and of the Bad against the False, reason why philosophy has often affirmed a substantial coincidence between the bad and the false, between evil and nothingness). This primacy or superiority of the ethical has been seized today by biological philosophy, which distinguishes between the environment and the world: the human species is interested, like all species, in its environment, which is not just the outside world as it is, but whatever is *relevant* to human beings, what determines its survival or reproduction. The environment (*Umwelt*: the-world-around) is what is good or bad in the world for the human being. Here Freud picks up on a coherent line of Western thought, one that Nietzsche had radicalized.

In fact, here, Freud stresses that with these (mythical) pre-intellectual stages, we are dealing with *Lust-Ich*, I-pleasure. For the previously stated reasons, I would translate it as I-desire/enjoyment. And he makes a statement crucial to the understanding of his whole theoretical project:

> What is bad, what is alien to the ego, and what is external, are, at the very beginning (*zumächst*), identical.
>
> (Freud 1915, p. 136)[14]

Freud writes *zumächst* (first of all, firstly), while the English translation reads "to begin with," interpreting in this way his expression as a chronological beginning. But in Freud, precedence is always ambiguous: is it a precedence in the time of life or a genealogical one? So, *firstly*, there's a coincidence between the external world, the bad and what has been expelled from me or kept away from me. This external real is what Fichte would call the non-Ego. My Ego or Self, what I eventually accepted as mine (introjecting it), is not, therefore, part of the world. On the contrary, it sets itself against the world; it opposes it. This "all or nothing" mechanism is described as primitive. Now, we're not simply dealing here with an evolutionary stage of early childhood, soon destined to be overcome as part of a less exclusivist stage: for Freud, a crucial part of who we are never evolves. A part that always remains in this first time or first place, which basically functions based on this fundamental splitting according to which I originally separate not from the world (which, as we shall see, is shaped by the Ego) but from something we can call the real. So, can we conversely affirm that what I've accepted, what is good, what is internal to me and what I recognize as mine are identical? Are they my (ego) Self? Freud doesn't say it, unsurprisingly, because, as we shall see, the Ego is not simply what is good, whole and one's own. There is no symmetry between primitive Ego and world.

Some may be surprised:

> [i]f the ego originally establishes itself as what was accepted, after a first tasting, inside the ego, then this ego precedes its own constitution! In short, in this case, the ego would be even more original than its own establishment, and correspondingly there would be a real that is even more original than that external-world-bad, as it is in this prior, empty, unqualifiable space of the real that the bad thing has to be somehow spat out.

In fact, what seems paradoxical to a developmental psychology – the fact that the ego establishes itself starting from a previous it-self! – is the crux of Freud's project: describing the birth of the psychic not starting from data external to it, from what we know scientifically about the body and the mind, not starting from the reality implied for the subject, but from subjectivity as such. Freud operates like philosophical phenomenology, which turns what we know into an *epoché* – in the sense that it puts in brackets, it suspends, what we know, from the outside, about humans in general. Now, seen from the outside, the psychic certainly belongs to the world, so its genesis can be described and explained causally, starting from something preceding it. Today many invoke the genome, of which the psychic too is a phenotypic expression. Instead, Freud aimed to describe the birth of subjectivity by putting in brackets what we think we know about the biological organism and the mental life linked to it, especially of children. Therefore, his is not a developmental genesis, but a *genealogy* of subjectivity. This is what basically separates psychoanalysis from the cognitive sciences: the latter are interested in the biological history that leads to the adult subjectivity we know, while the former is interested in the history of subjectivity starting from subjectivity itself.

Phenomenological philosophy strives to describe the world starting from subjective intentionality, ignoring what we know about the world to which we belong; in the same way Freud strives to describe our relation to reality starting from what he considers essential: *Lust-Ich*, the subject of desire-enjoyment. His genealogy of subjectivity thus also includes a genesis of cognitive, objective and rational subjectivity.

Freud's genealogy seduced so many philosophers precisely because it dares to describe the very origin of the fundamental correlation between subjectivity and the world: reconstructing, or perhaps, better still, constructing that matrixial separation between subject (*Ich*, "I," as Freud calls it) and the world, from which even every scientific explanation – derived, successive or tardive – is conceivable. Far from wanting to explain scientifically the rise of the scientific approach ("intellectual" Freud calls it), here he seems to attempt a transcendental genesis of scientific objectivity starting from what I would call an *archi-chorismy*, an original split (from *korismos*, separation). An *Urspaltung*. It is the beginning of a fundamental difference, a little like the biblical JHWH, creating the world from chaos by separating the light from the darkness, the skies from the waters: the primary difference between Ego-representations and the real.

This archi-cyorismy of Freud's, however, still assumes an evolutional form, i.e., a mythical one – meaning by "mythical" to give narrative form to a primary process (a genesis is a narrative of how things originated). Archi is derived from *arché*, principle and origin. Freud wants to make certain psycho-logical instances (but ultimately ontological ones) coincide with supposed epochs of development.[15] What commands is also what came first – the *-archia*. Wordsworth said that the child is the father of the man; for Freud, the child is the *arché* of the man, the child is the dominant precedence of humankind.

Therefore, the primacy or primitiveness of the judgment of attribution marks an epoch of archi-corismy that situates itself as a precedent in a supposed history of the individual psyche and in a priority that philosophy calls transcendental. A priority intended as a condition of the possibility of what may happen.

Transitional Space

The emergence of the *real-ego* (*Real-ich*) – a better translation than the reality-ego of the Standard Edition – is connected to the judgment of existence when we have to judge the existence of something represented (*vorgestellten Ding*). This real-ego, which developed from the primitive desire/enjoyment-Ego, is the one capable of reality-tasting (*Realitätsprüfung*) – tasting rather than testing, precisely because it recalls the archi-corismic tasting discussed earlier.

The passage from the original judgment – of introjection or exclusion – to reality-tasting (which is a judgment of existence) actually implies emancipation from the crude thing to its representation or re-presentation (*Vorstellung*).

The introjection/exclusion judgment had split being between good-representations (*I*) and bad-things (not-*I*). Now it's a matter of seeing whether a "thing" present in the Ego as a representation can be *found again* in reality too, something Freud identifies here with perceptive reality. We, therefore, have a new version of the inside/outside opposition: between internal and external:

> What is unreal [*Nichtreale*], merely a presentation and subjective, is only internal; what is real [*Reale*] is also there *outside*.[16]
>
> (Freud 1925, p. 237)

"*Also (auch)* outside": does this mean that the other, namely the real, is inside *too*? But didn't Freud say that "initially" the Ego, the subjective, was only representations, things introjected as representations? We are obviously in a second phase. But in what sense can we now say that the other and the real are *also* inside me?

In fact, what emerges here obliquely is Freud's premise that the other and the real are always represented within Ego. The archi-corismy clearly separates the internal and external, but once separated, the elements – whether internal or external – are not so clearly distinguishable. Because the Ego, insofar as it is made up of the representations of what has been accepted, is always somehow the representation of external things: in other words, the Ego does not have anything of its own, anything purely subjective or irreducibly private, at its core, but is instead a forced construction of the introjections of external "presentations." The Ego is a theater that *also* represents the external world; the Freudian Ego is a drift of the world. Hence this deep ontological uncertainty in the human being as conceived by Freud. After all, the bad-external-real of the archi-corismy is made up of something that was tasted and had therefore been part of the Ego that the Ego had represented to itself. The result is that we find ourselves dealing with a division between elements that are never entirely heterogeneous that can actually change places.

For Freud, therefore, representations are never only and always internal: they are also representations *of* the outside. Every mental image repeats perceptions, presentations; subjectivity is a way of interiorizing the world. It is a being-in-the-world that contrasts with the world, that has a contro-versial (in Latin: the side against) relationship with it, but "I" is unthinkable without its constitutional relationship to the world.

Winnicott (1971) was to talk of transitional phenomena and objects: when the small child becomes attached to objects halfway between the Ego and the non-Ego, like blankets and teddy bears. Thus, defining an ambiguous area – of playful dependence – in which things have a part-of-me side and an outside-of-me side. Now, we can say that for Freud, psychoanalysis always and only deals with this transitional area. After all, analytic work always swings between the two poles that determine this area, without ever directly reaching them. On the one hand, when analysands discuss events, they have experienced, for example, being attacked by someone, analysts will tend to say, "what happens to you is something you partly produce yourself; the hating other reinforces whatever hateful representation you may have." This is because analysis basically aims at interiorizing what the discourse of analysands situates outside themselves; it aims at seeing passive suffering as the reprisal of an active doing. But on the other hand, if analysands say, for example, that they find a certain something nauseating – a purely internal sensation – analysts may point out that the nauseating feeling is not properly theirs, but, for example, their father's. Analysts run with the hares of subjectivation and hunt with the hounds of alienation. Whether they condemn the presence of the Other in the interior life of the analysands or make them recognize subjective fantasies as transplants from the outside world, analysts always operate in a twilight zone between internal and external, between oneself and the other.

The most eloquent aspect of this uncertainty is the Freudian theory of melancholia (Freud 1915). Freud turns melancholia into a special, malign form of mourning; mourning is the psychic work that follows the loss of something or someone of great value to the subject. What specifies melancholic mourning is the fact that, on the one hand, subjects feel an ambivalence towards the lost object and, on the other, that this object was *already* narcissistic (i.e., what subjects loved about the lost other is what it reflected themselves as subjects). They loved what they were as subjects or what they would like to be as subjects. The lost object, the disappointing object, in other words, wasn't *other* enough; it was *another me*: it is thanks to this lack of alterity that I can introject it. It is introjected because it had never been entirely "outside": it's as if it shifted from an outside-half-inside to an inside-half-outside. Introjection is made possible (or in any case made easier) by the fact that the object is already *intro-*, so that it may be *-jected*. In melancholia, therefore, subjects seem to torture themselves severely: Freud calls this torturing *I Über-ich*. I call it the Beyond-the-ego rather than Superego because *Über* (above, beyond) has a negative sense; it is a non-ego. It is something that crushes the ego into guilt, shame and even death. The paradox is that this Beyond-the-ego or non-ego is still in any case subjectivity, i.e., it is still in any case *I*. For Freud, the Beyond-the-ego hounds not the other but the reflection of the other in the subject. In other words, the subject replaces the other without becoming it. We should therefore ask the subject: "*against who* are you depressed?" But also: "Is that person (or thing) you have lost not ultimately you?" Insofar as depressed subjects rack themselves as if they were the other, their subjectivity is particularly alienated: they treat themselves as if they were *another self*. Freud writes that it is not the object that enters the ego, but the ego that attacks the shadow the object makes.[17]

In a certain sense, the concept of narcissism allows Freud to correct the archicorismy thesis: this original separation in narcissism is partially flawed. The paradox of narcissists is that on the one hand, the others matter not as *truly other* but as reflexes or continuations of their selves, and on the other that this self is irremediably *dependent on "others,"* on the *vox populi*, on what others think or say or feel about them. Narcissistic frailty consists precisely in its dependence on others' admiration.

As we can see, the process of ego alienation and of subjective identification with the other does not have a beginning and an end: we cannot say there is a true ego entirely our own on the one hand and a pure alterity on the other. There is always some alienation in ipseity, and every alterity is infiltrated with ipseity. Consequently, any object narcissists lose can be seen as an image of themselves and everything they consider "ego, myself" is actually the introjection of the other. We can say that the other is always, to an extent, the shadow (or mirror image) of the ego and that the ego is always the shadow of the other. Narcissistic relations are always a sort of *mise en abyme*. A *mise en abyme* is when a detail of an image contains a copy of itself so that the copy, in turn, contains itself and so on in an infinitely recurring sequence. Narcissism and depression are the *mise en abyme* of subjectivity.

What Is Ego?

Before continuing, it would be useful not to clarify but to simply point out the obscurity of the concept of *ego*, another term Freud seems to deliberately use to lead to misinterpretation. In fact, he uses the term *Ich*, I, to designate subjectivity in general, or the psyche, as it was then referred to; but with the paper *The Ego and the Id* (Freud 1923) he set forth a topic (i.e., a spatialized model of subjectivity in which he deals with three instances or psychic "persons"): the *It* (*es*), the Superego or Beyond-the-ego or Meta-ego (*Über-Ich*) and the Ego (*das ich*). We can say that "*I*" in the primary sense is the *I* as the pronoun indicating the subject that expresses itself through words; I will write *ego* in the second sense – as an organized whole of a psyche – as "the Ego." Freud's heirs and his commentators have sometimes felt uncomfortable because it is often hard to understand whether by using *ich* Freud is referring to subjectivity as a whole or to the specific psychic instance, which is "the Ego," written as we've decided to write it here. For this reason, in languages other than German, the Freudian *ich* was eventually split into two. In English, a distinction was made between *the ego* and the *self,* giving the latter the topical sense of "ego" and the former the generic sense of "I" or "self." The French clearly distinguishes between *le moi* ("the ego") and *je,* the subject. Following the Anglo-American example, many analysts today consider the self a psychic organism and the Ego that governs this organism, in the same way our nervous system controls our entire organism.

A detailed analysis of Freud's texts, however, would show that only apparently in Freud does *ich* mean sometimes the whole and at other times a part of the whole. Freud does not see the difference between "I" and "the Ego" as a difference between the whole and a part of it. This is because the other topical components – *It* and *Beyond-the-ego* – are, on the one hand, *a part* of subjectivity and on the other, its *other*. *It* (id) – the drives, the libido – is, on the one hand, authentic subjectivity, the source of human activity in general; but on the other *It* also appears as something alien to the "ego," even a threat to its cohesion. The same applies to the Beyond-the-ego: on the one hand, it is the voice of the Other, as parent, educator and so on, of whoever represents a model or censor for the subject; on the other, it is the "interiorized" other, i.e., the Other that I am in relation to myself when I assess and judge myself. Beyond-the-ego is the subject *insofar as* it sees and judges itself from the outside, and hence thinks and feels in the same way as those who were external to it: parents, educators, mentors. The project of psychoanalysis seems to be that of letting us subjectivize as much as possible what presents itself as alien to ourselves, like the blind passions that may invade us or the moral norms that dominate us. The ambiguity between I and "the Ego" in Freud is not, therefore, a theoretical indecision (or at least it is not exclusively that) but the theme of the dialectics through which he considers subjectivity: that the latter always confronts and affirms itself in relation to its "other," to what looms over subjectivity as its alienation and coercion.

Is then Freud, a confused thinker? Or is he so complex to the point that he seems confused? To what extent is dialectics – i.e., a mode of thinking that accepts self-contradiction – a dignified word to refer to logical inconsistency?

If today the Freudian text, despite all the attempts to organize it into a respectable doctrine, still requires elaborate readings and exegeses, which tend to be divergent, it's precisely because Freud is a serious thinker: he is not satisfied with simple, clear formulae, with all-embracing solutions, with easy schemas all can use without (apparently) contradicting themselves. Freud tries to think out something contradictory *en abyme* of subjectivity. To what extent, then, can the theory afford the luxury of being linear and clear in order to account for human contradictions? And is this contradictory nature immanent to subjectivity, or is it Freud's contradictory theory that makes it seem so?

Reality-Tasting

Freud does seem to propose here an evolutionary model (from the primacy of pleasure to the primacy of critical realism) that corresponds to the most obvious clichés of contemporary anthropology. But we shall immediately see that this is not the case.

Here Freud describes a development from attributive judgment (good/bad) to judgment of existence (real/imaginary) that allows human beings to seize hold (*bemächtigen*) of the external thing to satisfy their needs. But for Freud, the ability to distinguish the real from the imaginary, to move from the desire-enjoyment principle to the reality principle, does not represent in any way a radical change. In fact, the reality principle is an adaptive progression from the desire-enjoyment principle – it's a way of doing without an egg today to have a hen tomorrow. Utilitarian philosophers like Hume had already said something similar: that reason ought only to be the slave of passion, not the other way around. The ultimate sense of the reality principle remains hedonistic in Freud. For him, the self-preservation instinct is a way of keeping for the ego the ability to enjoy again, above all, to enjoy life. We have, in other words, another *Aufhebung*: the primacy of desire-enjoyment is lifted but also preserved (raised up) in the relationship with reality. Enjoyment-desire affirms and perpetuates itself, denying itself in realism.

Says Freud: this progression from the desire/enjoyment-ego to the real-ego marks a passage from a frankly hallucinatory form of life to a new non-hallucinatory one. In fact, he affirms, "all presentations originate from perceptions and are repetitions of them."[18] This is the premise, already expressed in the *Project for a Scientific Psychology* (Freud 1895) he has always remained faithful to: that the human psychic apparatus is a representational repetition of perceptions. However, the original human consciousness senses as reality not only external perceptions but internal ones too: "[t]hus originally the mere existence of a presentation was a guarantee of the reality of what was presented." In short, there is still no separation between objective and subjective, reality and (re)presentation "originally" coincide. Note that Freud does not affirm this on the basis of thorough research on newborns (child observation was a later development) but on the basis of a fundamental metaphysical decision: that the discrimination between subjective and objective is the effect of a genealogical history, that the original subject is an ego-world. Reality and representation not only separate but become in antithesis [*Gegensatz*] only when "thinking possesses the capacity to bring before the mind [*gegenwärtig*] once more something that had once been perceived, by reproducing it as a presentation without the external object having still to be there" (Freud 1925, p. 237).[19] Every fantastic (re)presentation is, therefore, the repetition of the perception of something external; but the point is that "at an early stage" the ego does not discriminate between (re)presentation as the repetition of perception and a perception that repeats itself. Until reality-testing, or reality – tasting, appears.

The English translation fails to play on the double occurrence of *gegen*, "versus," in *Gegensatz* (antithesis) and *gegenwärtig* (before the mind): the repetition that makes something actual again is the very condition of the antithesis – not mere difference – between subjective and objective. *Gegenwärtig* is made up of *gegen*, against, in front of, and an adjectivization of *Wart*, caretaker, someone who watches over and safeguards something: thinking "brings before the mind," ultimately *against* the mind, what is facing us and we watch over. The presence – being before the mind – is what in the world, being awake and vigilant, is in contrast to us. We could therefore translate in a more enlightening way what Freud says:

> At first the subject and object are not one against the other (facing each other). This *being-one-in-contrast-to-the-other* only establishes itself once thinking succeeds in making us care again about something we perceived in the past as-like-the-one-in-contrast-to-us, insofar as it is reproduced in re-presentation.

Reality-tasting has a "primary and more immediate aim," i.e., there is an original primal mode of reality-tasting. This aim,

> is not to *find* an object in real perception which corresponds to the one presented, but to *refind* such an object, to convince oneself that it is still there [*vorhanden*] [*Freud's italics*].
>
> (Freud 1925, p. 237)[20]

An enigmatic and crucial statement. Here the English translation of *vorhanden* is "still there," but *vorhanden* refers back to *Vorhand, first hand*. It is still there in the sense of being ready to be handled. Further up, to say "before the mind," Freud used *gegenwärtig*: something that is in front of us, and we become caretakers of this thing. But it is a presence that can even be merely imaginary, a mere representation. Thanks to reality-tasting, the thing is not only *gegenwärtig*, fronting or facing up, but also *vorhanden*, i.e., ready to let itself be used, concretely seizable. We could say that the passage from *Lust-ich* to *Real-ich* is the passage from presence as *gegenwärtig* to presence as *vorhanden*, from facing up to availability. That is, from a presence as an astounded confrontation with the things of representation, we move on to a pragmatic presence to being able to use what is in front of us. Here we can only briefly mention the elaboration Heidegger (1927) would develop a few years later in *Being and Time* precisely on *Vorhandenheit* as "mere presence" and *Gegenwärtigung* as "presentation."

In fact, reality-tasting makes sense because the mind doesn't distinguish spontaneously, at first glance, the perception of the thing from the representation of the thing, the subjective from the objective. But we would be wrong in thinking that this testing or tasting aims at finding, in reality, something that coincides with the object represented in the subject. It's a case, Freud says, of finding the object itself again. That is, finding something that had already been present in our presence, and that was the origin of the re-presentation itself. Reality-testing or reality-tasting does not, therefore, amount to – as some tend to think – being able to say, "these are mere fantasies of mine; reality is different!" it means instead saying to ourselves, "what I thought was a mere fantasy of mine, I've now found right here, in the world within which I can operate."

Some think that the recovered object is the maternal breast as the original object of pleasure. Reality-testing has, therefore, nothing to do with a realistic discerning between fantasy and reality: it is a realization that the thing we are interested in is never found, but re-found. Reality-tasting makes possible what in classical theater was known as *anagnorisis*: when at the end of a play, the main characters recognize in strangers, loved or loathed, close relatives of whom they had lost trace, and so on.

Let's take someone we are sexually attracted to: for Freud, a delusion would be to think that – in the case of a woman – we have finally found the woman who corresponds to our mental representation of the partner we were looking for. Instead, we taste reality when we realize that the handsome woman we fancy is a woman who has been re-found – *in primis*, our mother. For Freud, to love is to find again: being realists is not finding something new that will fulfill our dreams but re-finding in reality what had once been there and was lost in re-presentation.

To this original function of reality-tasting, Freud adds another. He points out that "the reproduction of a perception as a presentation is not always a faithful one; it may be modified by omissions, or changed by the merging of various elements." So a second function (second both chronologically and hierarchically, it would seem) of reality-tasting is, therefore, the control of these deformations. And he ends by saying:

> But it is evident that a precondition for the setting up of reality-testing is that objects shall have been lost which once brought real satisfaction [*reale Befriedigung*].[21]

(Freud 1925, p. 238)

Here Freud seems to be saying that a primary condition or circumstance of this testing or tasting exists: the fact that the (re)presentation will always be inadequate compared to the thing itself. For many, this is the conviction they will never be as happy – i.e., *existent* – as when they were children ("to be happy is to be"). Precisely because there is a gap between the thing and its (re)presentation, re-finding the former is problematic, and always partial. But according to Freud, it is precisely this gap that *alienates* the objective from the subjective: the fact that the world essentially presents itself as an area where the reappearance of highly satisfactory but lost primary objects is possible. The archi-chorismy had thrown the baby (objectivity) out with the bathwater (the bad). As for Freud, the essential truth of humans is *die Lust*, desire or enjoyment, this famous objectivity or objectiveness, "realism," consists in acknowledging a dissatisfaction: that there is an irredeemable hiatus between original pleasure and the meager satisfactions that life later affords us. Cognitive objectivity is a surrender, and even cultivating science is a consolation for our weakness. Science is a way of controlling the world as best we can once we have entirely lost our delightful friendship with the world. In fact, Melanie Klein would talk of a depressive position: the depressing foregoing of primitive objects, i.e., of the full actual enjoyment of a golden age when pleasure could be *found*, not palely *re-found*.

A famous Italian song says, "*[t]he first love is so beautiful, but the second so much more!*" Perhaps for many of us, our first love may have been bland, yet there is an unrepeatable *first love*, one that, though repeated, remains a model that will never be re-actualized. It is our honeymoon with life that no conjugal happiness with our later life will ever be able to repeat. Reality-tasting means understanding that the objective will never live up to the subjective.

The Source of the Drives

In the third paragraph from last, Freud faces the relation between intellectual judgment (which for him is a judgment of existence) and action: "judging is intellectual action."

Here he talks about *Denkaufschub*, "this postponement due to thought."[22] Long before pragmatist philosophy, Freud already believed that thinking is not the mirror of nature,[23] but *to think is ultimately to act*. Thinking amounts to trying out, testing the waters, and saving motor energy by "acting" through thought.

Ethologists have given certain apes problems to solve, like picking a banana from a tree: some apes (the more stupid ones) make confused gestures and try to grab the banana, thus wasting muscular energy; other apes (usually the ones that find the solution) don't act immediately, but visibly think. Videos show them concentrating, motionless. And only when they have found a precise solution, so they act. Thinking is an imaginary experimentation without needless squandering of muscular energy.

But this ability – an adult and mature one – to deduce through thinking instead of acting immediately originates, for a change, in primal subjectivity. In fact, from the very beginning, perception through our sensory organs is not a purely passive process; it is not merely the retina being impressed with visual stimuli, it is not the ears registering sounds etc. Instead, with perception, the subject:

> periodically sends out small amounts of cathexis into the perceptual system, by means of which it samples [*verkostet*] the external stimuli, and then after every such tentative advance it draws back again.
>
> (Freud 1925, p. 238)[24]

The concept of tasting returns here, albeit in a different modulation – the English edition says, "*it samples.*" *Verkosten* is a rarely used term that we could render as "re-taste."

Freud stresses that after each advance, the subject draws back: *subjectivity is fearful*. The image of human beings Freud conjures here is different from Nietzsche's, who sees us as "thinking beasts of prey." More than a predator, the Freudian subject is like a turtle who retires into its armored home at the first hurdle; realism is cowardly cautiousness. This constant drawing back is the elementary form of *regression*: when the progressive movement of life backtracks, then we have neurosis and psychosis. At the first hurdles in life or in thinking, all of us are ready to regress – to run back into our mother's arms or whoever has taken her place. Our relationship with the world – the *extra moenia* world outside our homes, on the other side of the walls – is usually a punctual discontinuous one: tastings, quick advances, forays. We may even be great adventurers like Hemingway, but what counts is that after each blitz, we can return to our body/shell. And Hemingway killed himself; he went back to his mum when it was no longer possible for him to frenetically taste the world.

Freud is a pragmatist and activist vision of perception, one central to the debate today in cognitive psychology and neurosciences. Today neuroscientists who see perceptions not as passive reception but as a result of a series of actions and pre-visions agree with Freud. In his neural Darwinism, G. Edelman (1987) hypothesized a brain structure "with re-entry," which in several ways gives substance to Freud's idea of *Nachträglichkeit*, known as *après coup* in French, and which could be rendered with *afterwardsness*:[25] to the idea, in simple words, that with time subjects give a new sense and new forms to memories from the past. The neural maps of the brain link body receptors (like the skin or the retina) to the corresponding areas of the layers of the brain: in other words, they determine the image of the world the brain builds for itself. The crucial point is that these maps are *re-entering*: as the maps are interconnected, a selection that takes place in one implies similar selections in other maps. Reentry implies that our experiences in a given sector have repercussions on several mental levels, thus changing our categorization of the world and the structure we give it. In other terms, our experience is also retroactive: what we experience in the present remodels our past. It reshapes our memory, which is therefore never entirely objective but always re-elaborated.

In Freud's case, however, this idea of perception as action and thought as deferred action descends from his fundamental project, which we will summarize further: revealing *die Lust* as the *arché*, the principle and primacy of human life. In fact, immediately afterwards, he writes:

[t]he study of judgment affords us . . . an insight into the origin of an intellectual function from the interplay of the primary instinctual impulses [*Triebregungen*].
(Freud 1925, pp. 238–239)[26]

I would have preferred to translate *Triebregungen* with "drive movements."

Intellectual judgment too – the scientific reality of which he felt a champion – derives from primary drive movements. Like *everything* for Freud: neuroses, psychoses, dreams, parapraxes, sexual desire, humor, religious rites. Everything. The selection of intellectual judgment is a replacement of a division regulated by *Lust*: to include within me or to expel from me. What complicates the picture, however, as we have seen, is that the ego does not precede these inclusions or expulsions: it is their product, always unstable. There is no such thing as an empty space, a *tabula rasa*, a blank slate – ego – which is *later* filled with content, such as representations, perceptions, fantasies, and so on: these inclusive and expulsive acts open the space of the ego. In short, inclusion and expulsion have a precedence that philosophers call *transcendental*: they are not acts by the ego, but acts forming the ego. They are not acts directed at the world, but active conditions or conditions of possibility for the constitution both of the world and of the subject, in which the ego appears at once an agent and a product of its own acting. Freud does not talk of a transcendental condition, but he says something analogous.

In fact, for Freud, all drives refer back to a double source that separates transcendentality from phenomenality: Eros and Thanatos. He points out that affirmation (*Bejahung*) is a substitute or surrogate (*Ersatz*) of unification – and five years earlier, he had written that this is the specific quality of Eros, desire and life. Negation is instead a consequence (*Nachfolge*) of expulsion – the specific quality of Thanatos, destructive desire. Note that affirmation and negation are not precisely in the same relation with their symmetricities, Eros and destruction. Affirmation is a *substitute* for unification; negation is a *consequence* or *surrogate* of expulsion. To affirm is to replace, and to deny is to add. A structuralist linguist would say that affirmation is paradigmatic and negation syntagmatic. Affirming means choosing metaphors, and denying means slipping into metonymies.[27] The *no* adds an erasure to something that had previously been a substitute; it erases a substitution. The *yes* replaces what is present, thus repeating its presence; it is a re-present; the *no* retroactively erases the presence, adding to it a mark that continues it.

But unification and expulsion, Eros and Thanatos, are not actions started by anyone or that imply anything: they are transcendental processes – like space and time with respect to phenomena were, for Kant, openings starting from which something can be established. Therefore, the products of these two original movements, – the subject and its world – will enter the scene only in the form of repetition and re-finding. The subject will tend to repeat what established it, i.e., an original affirmation, and the world – that which has been denied – will be there for this subject to find something again in it.

Therefore, the negation from which Freud began is also a surrogate of the death drive. Here Freud evokes the negativism of certain psychotics. Negativist psychotics do not by any means react to what the other solicits them to do or say; they absolutely do not cooperate; they entirely detach themselves from the other. In this sense, psychosis gives plenty of space to the death drive because the libidinal affirmation is excluded. Yet earlier, Freud had said that the symbol of negation was the condition of the intellectual function: how can we then think that this intellectual function, the establishment of the *Real-Ich*, is something mortal? How can intellectuality be akin to psychotic negativism? Is Freud not becoming entangled in his own extremely intricate strings here?

In fact, to what extent does the *Real-Ich*, in correcting and denying the *Lust-Ich*, express the death drive? And is *die Lust*, desire-enjoyment, not in turn something that slides toward death if left to its own devices? Does Freud think that "the Ego" (*das Ich*) is a morti-fication of myself (*ich*)? Freud (1923, p. 46) had actually written:

> [b]y thus getting hold of the libido from the object-cathexes, setting itself up as sole love object, and desexualizing or sublimating the libido of the Thing (*es*), the ego is working in opposition to the purposes of Eros and placing itself at the service of the opposing drive impulses [my own translation].

Here I would translate the Freudian *Id* or *Es* (third person neutral singular) with Thing. These drive impulses or drive trends that oppose Eros are simply Thanatos. Is "The Ego" also steeped in death? Is the same "Ego" that we thought performed a vital function – which makes it possible to survive without being swept away by the drives –in the end a deadly instance that opposes a deadly inaction? Is life a struggle between death and death? Here Freud is evidently repeating the paradox we saw at the beginning of genealogy: that on the one hand, the affective is an affirmation, an appropriation, but on the other; it is also destruction and negation. Every affirmation has a negative side, and every negation reaffirms.

Negation of Denial

Basically, a "no" is the denial of denial (but not in the sense of classical logic, according to which denying a negation is equivalent to affirming). The "no" sign essentially denies death, i.e., the inaction of the desire-enjoyment domain that culminates in death. A "no," taken on its own, always ultimately means "I shall not die."

And in fact, Freud immediately adds that the intellectual function depends on the creation of the symbol of negation, which

> has endowed thinking with a first measure of freedom from the consequences of repression and, with it, from the compulsion (*Zwang*) of the desire-enjoyment principle.
>
> (Freud 1925, p. 239)[28]

Another statement that leads to more problems than it solves. Here *Zwang* is translated with "compulsion," referring to *Wiederholungszwang*, "repetition compulsion." For Freud, repetition compulsion manifests the death drive. Freud repeats here that the compulsion of the desire-enjoyment domain is deadly: the *Lustprinzip* forces us to repeat our satisfactions first of all, so we couldn't care less about reality. The paradigm of this could be an addiction: addicts repeat unceasingly the assumption of a pleasurable substance without caring about their health or their relations with others. So, the symbol of negation – as the seal of every intellectual ability – frees us from the effects of repression. Which effects?

Repression itself is undoubtedly a form of negation. (Though I would have translated *Verdrangung* not as repression but *removal*. Like after the fall of communism, many statues of Lenin were removed: not destroyed, only removed, dislodged.) The repressed is not destructible; it is only removed, concealed to the eyes of the conscious "Ego." To repress or remove is an act, a negation-in-action, a neg-action. From this point of view, the symbol of negation – not only in analysis but in general – is a sort of a homeopathic act: a "no" as a sign revokes and at once maintains (*aufhebt*) the effect of the neg-action represented by repression, i.e., the oblivion of (re) presentation. Denial, once it is symbolized as a "no," acts in the opposite way: what had been expelled from the ego returns to it, albeit equipped with a sort of verbal seal, a "not." This is the fundamental challenge of psychoanalysis as a whole: that symbolization allows a liberation from repression and its effects. Psychoanalytical practice as a whole, whatever the current, is based on this assumption, even though each school expresses it with different concepts. Verbalizing is a form of denial, but one that tends to annul negation *in actu* of repression. Verbal negation emancipates us from neg-action. Hence the preference psychoanalysis gives to the word and its mistrust of every form of action, of acting out.

But in what sense does any negative statement, even in everyday life, perform this function of de-negativizing the repressed or the removed?

Let's take a random statement like "the Freud book is *not* on the table." What on earth has a factual negation of this type have to do with negation in the Freudian sense, with a process of evasion from the domination of the dominion of desire-enjoyment?

Freud could say that I would pronounce such a statement in a situation in which, for example, someone else said to me, "go fetch me the Freud book on the table." And they could have said it only because this other *desired* to have the Freud book or because I desired it. At the root of every word, there is always a desire, in this case, the coveted book. Negation, therefore, responds to a repression, in this case, a physical rather than a psychic one: this book cannot be found, it is missing from where it should have been, it has been removed from that place. The negative statement further up is, therefore, not the result of a neutral observation but of the fact that someone else said, "the Freud book is, it could be, on the table." The "no" has a logical form, but actually remains a rhetorical "not." Negation interjects in a sort of dialogue between an affirming desire and a refutation *Verneinung*. What I say or think always ties in with what another says or thinks: the thought is not in me, but elsewhere – which is equivalent to a removal from me. But by saying instead that the book is not there, I emancipate myself from the other's desire, or from mine, insofar as it is other from what it is: by negating, I am affirming that the desire has remained unsatisfied.

One of the most significant contributions to psychoanalysis after Freud was linking closely not only negation, but the unconscious in general, to the function of the other. The difference between the intersubjectivistic currents and the Lacanian ones consists in the fact that the former thematizes the others as "subjects in themselves" who interact with me, while the latter distinguishes between the others and the Other, who is not an existing person in flesh and bones, but a topological figure; like the "line of the horizon," which doesn't correspond to a particular place on Earth; anything can be on the line of my horizon, all I need to do is move. In the same way, Lacan's Other is no one in particular, even though many can occupy their place. We may find a person in flesh and bones quite underwhelming; they may be quite irrelevant to us, while someone far away or dead may occupy the place of the Other and be decisive in our life. So, when an analysand says, "you ask who this person in the dream can be. It's *not* my mother," supposing the analyst to be an Other who is wondering who the person in the dream may be and saying that it is their mother, they are placing him in the position of the other who wonders and gives an answer; but in reality, the analyst in flesh and bones probably never asked this question and would have been even less likely to reply that the person in the dream was the analysand's mother. So, when Freud talks about the unconscious, he is implying that I, the subject, ascribe to the Other that which I desire, want and think.

If it's true that Freud did not explicitly thematize the central function of the other and of the Other, he certainly suggested it in various ways. For example, in his monograph on masses, Freud (1921) articulates a dynamic between the ego of each individual, the Ego ideal of each individual and an external object (the leader): the Ego ideal is evidently the place Lacan would call the Other, a crucial one to the formation of any group or mass; a place that can be occupied by various "others," in the same way as, for example, Popes succeed each other in the years, but the function of the Pope remains more or less the same across the centuries. The same is true for the *Über-Ich*, which we have rendered as Beyond-the-ego, to mark its alterity with respect to the ego: when we criticize ourselves or regret something we've done, our conscience takes the place of the Other, not of a particular censor, but of a generic critical or censorious function. In self-reproach, I take the place of the Other who judges me severely. Several psychoanalytical schools after Freud placed this constitutional function of the Other at the heart of the so-called unconscious; in this way, Freudian denial began to appear more and more as a negation of desire for and enjoyment of the Other. But it is precisely because of this negation that desire and enjoyment remain *other from me*, not my own, estranged: by denying that what the Other desires or thinks belongs to me, I am also disavowing what I desire or think by saying they are desires and thoughts that belong to the other.

An obsessional patient I followed had begun a relationship with a woman he considered too old to give him children and far from his ideal wife for a variety of reasons, including the fact she was a conservative Catholic while he was an atheist who despised the Church. But after only a few months, he actually married her in Church, and they had a baby boy. Why did he do this? The repeated reply was: "because *she wanted* to marry, and I couldn't say no!" Why couldn't you say no? "To avoid conflicts." He later admitted that his partner had never insisted on marrying, even though it was something she certainly desired. But for years, this patient never ceased to complain in the same repetitive way: "how could I have been such an arsehole to let that woman frame me?" It was as if everything he did – often even with great industry and zeal – wasn't desired by him but by someone else. He perceived his marriage and becoming a father not as what he desired but as what the other desired. His partner certainly wanted to marry and have children too, but what counts here is that the analysand placed this (supposed) desire of the other in the position of *the law*: "if the Other desires this, *I must* obey!"

What should the analyst then say? "What you did believing you were satisfying your wife's desire was, in fact, *your* desire"? Saying so, however, would be of no use because obsessional subjects don't perceive this desire as their own but as an inspiration from the Other: "I *did not* wish to marry her; it was she (the Other) who wanted to marry." The negation of desire as one's own casts them back into the Other, who isn't the poor wife herself, but the position in which he has placed her, which is the place of the unconscious. Because this patient actually did want to marry in Church and have a child with a Catholic woman, *unconsciously*; but when we say "unconsciously," we are *ipso facto* saying "the other wants this." The negation of our own desire makes it unconscious but reveals it as the desire of the Other: "I desire nothing at all, the Other desires."

Numeric and Analogue

In the final paragraph, Freud reaffirms what he already stated several times: that in the unconscious, there is no "no" and that the recognition of something unconscious by the "Ego" expresses itself with a negative formula. Only the non-unconscious ego is capable of verbal negation. And he concludes by saying that when a patient reacts to a discovery or revelation by the analyst with the words "I didn't think that" or "I didn't (ever) think of that," it is proof that the unconscious has manifested itself. Given that for Freud, the unconscious is made up essentially of thoughts, the affirmation that one had never thought about the analyst's revelation seals the fact that one had thought about it, but it had been repressed or removed.

Why does Freud think of the unconscious as negation in action that requires not the symbol of negation? If the unconscious is a form of thought, why is negating not a part of this thinking?

Freud belonged to a positivist culture, which had in many ways already conceptualized what would later be called – in information theory – the difference between numeric and digital language on the one hand and analogue language on the other. As we know, digital language is specific to human beings and is based on an all-or-nothing modulus: in this discreet language, it is possible to deny and use the symbol of negation, and the relation between signifier and signified appears arbitrary. The arbitrary nature of the linguistic sign – articulated by Ferdinand de Saussure – simply means that there is no similarity between a sign and the thing it signals; the various languages name the same thing with completely different sounds. The word "no" itself is pronounced with very different sounds according to the language; therefore, the sign "no" is arbitrary with respect to what it signifies, i.e., negating. Instead, analogue language only includes positive quantities, it is incapable of expressing negation, and it is impossible, for example, to use it to lie. If I want to express the concept of "cat," I could use the term of the English language I've just used (digital language) or draw a recognizable cat (analogue language).

Now, as Freud, at least on the surface, thinks of the unconscious as the irrational, animal, side of human beings, he tends to give it an analogic character. Instead, negation belongs to the digital order (the symbolic order, a psychoanalyst would say today) and cannot, therefore, be part of the unconscious. For this reason, Freud reaffirms that the unconscious does not acknowledge negation. The idea that the unconscious has no temporality also descends from this positivist semiotics of Freud's: in fact, if to signify "cat" I draw a cat, I cannot signify whether it is a cat of the past, present, or future or a mere atemporal paradigm of a cat. The analogue cannot state time, only the present. It cannot say that something no longer exists or doesn't exist yet; only numeric language can express temporality, including absence.

According to this positivistic semiotics Freud draws on, the affective universe does not include an "intellectual" process such as negation.

Instead, what sets Freud apart from positivist semiotics is the fact that for him, the analogical code – the unconscious – is in itself negation. In the unconscious, there is no "no" to be found; nothing is negated because the unconscious is entirely negative. And the function of "no" is precisely to negate the negation that constitutes affectivity: it is a way of bringing subjectivity back into the world.

In other words, Freud, though he had begun from a positivistic vision – seeing everything as positive – and ended up developing a conception that would be read more and more in a "negativistic," Hegelian key.

Notes

1 I will refer as *Vn* to the German original of "Die Verneinung," followed by the number of the volume and the page number. *Vn* 14, S. 11.
2 Today some use "disavowal" to convey the Freudian *Verleugnung*. But in fact, as we shall see, Freud also gives *Verneinung* the sense of disavowal, i.e., of a denial of something that had been somehow accepted at another level (Freud 1927).
3 *Vn* 14, S. 11.
4 "Konstruktionen in der Analyse," *GW* 16, S.
5 *Vn* 14, S. 12.
6 Lacan 1999, p. 529.
7 *Vn* 14, S. 12.
8 Vn 12, S. 12.
9 Vn 14, S. 12–13. z
10 Various authors have stressed the ambiguity of this term, e.g., Jean Laplanche (in Laplanche 1970) and Derrida (1980, p. 293).
11 S. Freud 1905, p. 135n; *GW* 5, S. 33n.
12 I have chosen to use the term "enjoyment" instead of "pleasure" for reasons that would be too long to explain here. I embrace the term *jouissance* used by Lacan, who, however,

in the context of his system of thought, gives enjoyment a sense almost alternative to that of pleasure.

13 The whole panoply of "good objects" and "bad objects" M. Klein never ceased to talk about comes from this primary function of attributive judgment, insofar as it separates the good and the bad, i.e., what we can introject and what is projected outside.

14 *Vn* 14, S. 13. In *GW*, 10, p. 229.

15 Heidegger played with the homonymy between the Greek *epoché* and our *epochs*: every historical epoch puts in brackets certain aspects of being. In Freudian terms, we could say that the original *epoché* I called archeo-corismy unfolds across various epochs of the subjective process, thus assuming different structures according to the various ages of life.

16 *Vn* 14, S. 13.

17 Freud, *GW* 10, p. 435.

18 *Vn* 14, S. 14.

19 Ibid.

20 *Vn* 14, S. 14.

21 *Vn* 14, S. 14.

22 Ibid.

23 In *The Philosophy and the Mirror of Nature*, Rorty (1979) tied the American pragmatist tradition (James, Dewey) to the great Continental European currents, starting from Wittgenstein and Heidegger: the basic idea was that the great 20th-century tradition – which he categorizes under pragmatism – had condemned any objectivist idea according to which we can have a detached, neutral or contemplative knowledge of the world. Knowledge is a specific form of manipulative action upon the world. Freud too – like for other reasons Vico, Hegel, Marx, and Nietzsche – undoubtedly belong to this critical, broadly speaking pragmatist, outlook on objectivity.

24 *Vn* 14, S. 15.

25 On *après-coup*, see Laplanche 2017, Benvenuto 2018.

26 *Vn* 14, S. 15.

27 In the linguistics of Roman Jakobson the two figures of speech of metaphor and metonymy (i.e., signifying the whole while naming only a part of it) have a special value insofar as the former is a mode of signifying that reflects the paradigmatic axis of language and the latter one that reflects the syntagmatic axis of language.

28 Modified translation. *Vn* 14, S. 15.

References

Allouch, J. (1998). Les impromptus de Lacan. Les Mille et Une Nuits.

Benvenuto, S. (2018). The Après-Coup, après coup: Concerning Jean Laplanche Problématiques VI. L'Après-Coup. Language and Psychoanalysis 7(2), 72–87. www.language-and-psychoanalysis.com/article/view/2829

Derrida, J. (1980). La carte postale de Socrate à Freud et au-delà. Flammarion.

Edelman, G. (1987). Neural Darwinism: The Theory of Neuronal Group Selection. Basic Books.

Freud, S. (1895). The project for a scientific psychology. SE 1, 294–397.

Freud, S. (1905). Three essays on the theory of sexuality. SE 7.

Freud, S. (1915). Instincts and their vicissitudes. SE 14.

Freud, S. (1917). Mourning and melancholia. SE 14.

Freud, S. (1921). Group psychology and the analysis of the ego. SE 18.

Freud, S. (1923). The ego and the id. SE 19.

Freud, S. (1925). Die Verneinung. GW 11. "Negation." SE 19, 234–239.

Freud, S. (1927). Fetishism. SE, 21, 152–157.

Freud, S. (1937). Constructions in analysis. SE 23.

Heidegger, M. (1927). Being and Time. Blackwell.

Heidegger, M. (1971). Nietzsche II (Franc., Ed.). Gallimard.

Lacan, J. (1999). Ecrits 1. Seuil.

Laplanche, J. (1970). Vie et mort en psychanalyse. PUF.

Laplanche, J. (2017). Après-coup. The Unconscious in Translation.

Laplanche, J., & Pontalis, J.-B. (1967). The Language of Psychoanalysis. Routledge. (2018)

Rorty, R. (1979). The Philosophy and the Mirror of Nature. Princeton University Press.

Winnicott, D. (1971). Playing and Reality. Penguin.

Section 2

Drive and Desire

Chapter 3

Turning Opportunities into Crises

The Lacanian Antidote to Toxic Positivity

Colin Wright

Introduction

The title of economic historian Philip Mirowski's 2013 book captures a problem with the negative I want to approach psychoanalytically. He called it *Never Let a Serious Crisis Go to Waste*, thereby suggesting a recuperation, without remainder, of the disruptive effects of the negative (Mirowski, 2013). The crisis in question was the 2008 credit-crunch when the fact that governments had to bail out the banking sector prompted much talk of the end of neoliberalism. Mirowski shows that the exact opposite happened: a re-entrenchment of free-market fundamentalism thanks to its ability to present itself as the solution to the very problems it had caused (as if the best way to put out a fire is pouring petrol on it). For example, the politics of austerity with which several countries responded to the credit-crunch were a further attack on the welfare state in the name of an economic "health" demonstrably bad for actual health, especially of the poorest (Marmot, 2016). So, what looked like a crisis of neoliberal doctrine turned out to be an opportunity to increase its global hegemony. Negativity there certainly was, in the sense of significant socio-economic suffering, but what it produced was not a dialectical *aufhebung* à la Hegel or Marx but an intensification of the status quo, as if the "labour of the negative" had gone on strike.

A decade on and this hegemony seems just as secure in the face of the vastly more challenging climate crisis. Rather than an existential threat to life on the planet, this is framed as an exciting opportunity for new green technologies – or as both, providing the latter is the only viable solution to the former. Carbon offsetting illustrates this faith in the market's recuperation of negativity well: by turning carbon dioxide emissions into "credits," we hope to trade our way out of trouble, surely akin to digging one's way out of a hole? Like the financial meltdown then, the climate crisis is a crisis for capitalism, not *of* capitalism. As Joseph Schumpeter (2008) and more recently Naomi Klein (2014) have pointed out, anything can be at stake in capitalism's "creative destruction", other than its own transcendental permanence. Thus, rather than accepting limits on our overconsumption of a finite planet, we delude ourselves that billionaire entrepreneurs like Elon Musk will keep the party going by terraforming Mars and then helping us to relocate there. Slavoj

DOI: 10.4324/9781003375920-5

Žižek has long observed that it is easier to imagine the end of the world than of capitalism. Today, this is because the world is being reduced to *a* world among others: each of these worlds can end, but capitalism cannot. *That* end never begins because negativity – as lack or limit or entropic loss – is constantly positivised away as profit.

I call this evacuation of the dialectical power of the negative *toxic positivity*. From self-help and life-coaching to neo-utilitarian happynomics, toxic positivity proscribes the poison as if it were the cure. It is toxic for the planet, for critical thinking about our predicament, and for broaching what Freud called the discontents of civilisation. Nevertheless, my claim is that it is best approached psychoanalytically, since Freud was already isolating a remainder that *cannot* be recuperated by civilisation, a negativity beyond mere discontent. He called it the symptom, and Lacan went on to underline it as a singular response to the economic problem faced by any civilisation: the regulation of jouissance. Thus, psychoanalysis reveals what even critics like Mirowski struggle to grasp, namely, the dimension of the death drive operative within this fantasy of an enjoyment that could outlive organic life, somehow persisting in a beyond of the Earth-bound pleasure principle. Lacan's concept of "surplus-jouissance" explains how capitalism renders loss itself productive, but also how this puts it on a collision course with castration as lack.[1] The *Communist Manifesto* had already captured the ensuing limitlessness by referring to capitalism as "melting all that is solid into air". If we are now seeing the polar icecaps literally melting and the air we breathe becoming toxic, it is because the prodigious waste-products of our own jouissance can no longer be negativised. Behind toxic positivity's refusal of waste, psychoanalysis can show how waste itself has become a drive-object, but also how a "real" symptomatic remainder nevertheless persists.[2]

Positive Individuals, Negating Subjects

Before being a series of interlocking institutions of transnational governmentality, neoliberalism is an apparatus for producing certain kinds of *individuals*.[3] Consumers primed for consumption, one of their key characteristics is now a relentless accentuation of the positive that mirrors, at the level of psychic economy, what Mirowski observed about the financial economy: individual crises are also de-negativised by being interpreted as opportunities for "personal growth".

This is clearest in the discourses of positive psychology and happiness studies, whose policy influence has grown exponentially since the 1990s (Horowitz, 2017), and whose consonance with neoliberalism is well-known (Binkley, 2014). In the work of someone like Martin Seligman – who made his name opposing the alleged miserablism of traditional psychopathology – moments of individual distress are in fact chances to "flourish", to enhance one's "resilience", and to accrue additional "mental capital". His antipathy for psychoanalysis, which he calls "a rotten-to-the-core doctrine" (Seligman, 2003: p. xii) due to its un-American pessimism, led him to turn the Freudian concept of trauma on its head in the 1970s. Far from being an element of the human condition rooted in a formative experience of *Hilflosigkeit* (helplessness), Seligman frames trauma as an opportunity to learn a glass-half-full optimism that reveals helplessness to be mere cognitive bias (Seligman, 2003). In other words, he aims to reinstate the ego as master in its own house, untroubled by division, impotence, or indeed the unconscious. And thanks to his alignment with the zeitgeist, he has been very successful: the alchemical transformation of negativity into the gold of "personal growth" has proved appealing not only to academia and the corporate world, but also to neoliberal states.

For example, he has received millions of dollars of funding from the US Army for his "Comprehensive Soldier Fitness" programme. This promises to turn Post-Traumatic Stress Disorder – an all-too human response to the negativity of war – into Post-Traumatic *Growth*, and thus the adversity of conflict into an opportunity for enhancing coping-skills and self-confidence. Like most positive psychology projects, its statistical evidence-base literally turns minuses into pluses by replacing the signifier by the number, a preference for data over speech typical of toxic positivity. If neoliberal life is becoming a Malthusian "survival of the fittest" akin to war, these discourses suggest we should not respond to this with critique (which just brings everyone down) but by welcoming it as the crucible in which we can forge our individual "grit" and "bouncebackability". Instead of bemoaning precarity, we should actively choose to live on the edge of survivability where the greatest adaptive gains are to be made. From "no pain, no gain" we slide towards pain *as* gain, and thus a kind of masochistic jouissance veiled as "self-improvement". In their systematic elimination of the negative then, positive psychology and happiness studies muffle the pain of living behind a performative rictus grin. The ill-being of the speaking-being gets lost amidst the averages resulting from Likert-scale surveys about well-being.

However, psychoanalysis has always made a topological distinction between the socialised individual and the *subject*, between the ego and the unconscious. The latter speaks not through statistics but first and foremost through the symptom, stubbornly returning in the real from all attempts at foreclosing it, like a psychic version of whack-a-mole. Without this minimal distinction between the individual and the subject of the symptom, the idea that speech under transference could produce a previously unknown knowledge, or any related dialectical change, would be nonsensical. If we coincided completely with our ideological interpolation as individuals, we would always say exactly what we mean and mean exactly what we say. Speech would be mere information transmitted between points A and B. Paradoxically, this positivity-without-remainder would make our sense of individual autonomy an ideological *méconnaissance*, for our speech would always already be alienated in the social Other. By contrast, the experience of the gap between what we intend to say on the one hand, and what can be heard in what is said on the other, testifies to this ethically and politically crucial difference between the individual and the subject. From a psychoanalytic viewpoint, a world expunged of the possibility of the *lapsus* – experienced egoically as a useless negativity, an embarrassing mistake – is already a subjectless world, but thankfully we are never as flawlessly mechanic as we might wish.[4]

What relationship pertains between the individual and subject? In his *écrit* on "Science and Truth", Lacan (2007) presents the modern individual, shaped by the scientific positivism to which positive psychology certainly subscribes, as "suturing" the subject, meaning that it erases its role as material cause. An objective knowledge supposedly without a knower, science has a passion of ignorance regarding the desire by which it is animated, and this is replicated at the level of the individual ego, which likewise wants to know nothing about its unconscious cause. As ever though, we should follow Lacan's specific choice of signifier. For just as Freud's ambiguous term "unconscious" has often been mistaken for another consciousness at a "lower" psychic level, one might erroneously take the subject for an individual "behind" the inauthentic persona. Lacan parodied this misconception with reference to the old idea of the homunculus by which consciousness was once explained with the image of a little man inside our heads. Countering this infinite regress on the imaginary axis, Lacan chose the signifier "suture" precisely to indicate the subject's *structural* correlation with the gap. In surgery, a "suture" is a stitch that closes a wound: healing might render its intervention invisible, but what makes it necessary in the first place is the wound *of* subjectivity, so to speak, not a wound *in* subjectivity. The difference between the subject and the individual then is not between two differently located positivities: the subject *is* a primordial lacuna. At the time of "Science and Truth", Lacan still designated this with the neologism *manque-à-être*, combining a want-to-be with a want-*of*-being to highlight the metonymy of desire as lack. Later, he would shift the accent away from symbolic lack and Oedipal castration towards the more complex topology of the hole, for example through the figure of the torus. In his Borromean clinic, subjectivity becomes a question of an inaugural void or hollow in a jouissance that can never be fully resorbed by the signifier – giving the lie to any idea of a recuperation without remainder, without waste. Nevertheless, this move from lack to hole, from desire to jouissance, and from the *manque-à-être* to the *parlêtre*, maintains a connection between subjectivity and negation, albeit one no longer limited to the minus phi of symbolic castration dominant in the Freudian era, but opening onto the various permutations of a knotting of the three register around a void. This supple connection between negation and subjectivity is one of the reasons we badly need Lacan in the context of today's toxic positivity. The relentlessly self-optimising neoliberal individual is "suturing" the subject and its symptoms behind a supposedly productive positivity, exposing itself, thereby, to a limitless jouissance indistinguishable from the death drive.

Analytic Crises and the Lesson of Loss

From this perspective, the Lacanian antidote to toxic positivity involves a reversal of the formula by which the "growth mindset" of capitalism turns all crises into opportunities. Undertaking an analysis can involve turning supposed opportunities – which is to say, received models of success or happiness – into crises, questioning them so that their relation to the singular desire of the subject (rather than to the conscious wishes of the egoic individual) can be interrogated. Indeed, the request for an analysis sometimes comes precisely at moments of disappointing "success", like the stereotypical Lottery winner whose newfound millions prompt a depressive *why-isn't-this-it*? Rather than opportunities for personal growth which follow the logic of accumulation, analytic crises can produce something truly novel. In other words, psychoanalysis can return to the category of crisis, if not the dialectical optimism we find in Marx, then its dimension of irrecuperable real, bringing out a stake beyond the mere repetition and accumulation of the same.

Etymology is helpful here. In ancient Greece *krisis* was precisely a clinical term referring to the turning point of a disease when the patient might live or die. Its root in *krinein* implied the need "to separate, discriminate, judge," meaning that it was a matter not of mere nosological confirmation but of decision-making in the absence of established guidelines. As such, it was also connected to *kritikē*, meaning "criticism" or "critique." The positivity of negativity was retained in thought's inventiveness when knowledge in the Other is lacking (which it always is, ultimately). Regarding temporality, *krisis* was not of the order of *Chronos*, meaning predictable metronomic regularity, but of *Kairos* and thus a fleeting urgency that calls for an act. In Lacanian terms, Guy Briole (2015: p. 25) has described crisis as "a breach in time that arises when the tradition that had framed the real disappears and when the new symbolic coordinates of the future are not yet known." The future is never really known of course, only imagined. But by risking uncertainty about its coordinates, a future other than the one we had destined ourselves for, even unconsciously, can open up. Such is the fecundity of the negative at stake in true crises.

Unlike toxic positivity's view of them as mere bumps in the road towards success, psychoanalysis views crises as potential crossroads at which the subject can choose the path of desire, rather than of the demand by which their ego remains permanently alienated. In a sense, psychoanalysis has its own version of Hegel's "labour of the negative" which puts crisis to dialectical work, though without ever promising redemption in Absolute Knowledge, or, indeed, in neoliberal happiness. Psychoanalysis is *not* a therapy (though it is not without therapeutic effects) because it does not aim to get rid of the symptom as if it were a malfunction. Indeed, it *constructs* the symptom, extracting its singularity from the discontents for which civilisation has a universal diagnostics and, in the era of Big-Pharma, a profitable one-size-fits-all pharmacological treatment. Thus, whereas Martin Seligman (2003: p. 235) recommended "viral optimism" as the cure for the financial crisis of 2008, reducing it to a crisis of consumer confidence easily rectified by positive thinking, Jacques-Alain Miller (2008) responded to that same global tumult by declaring, simply, that "the psychoanalyst is a friend of crisis." What the psychoanalyst welcomes in crisis is that fecund moment from which the singularity of the subject has the potential to emerge as a response not to a market opportunity for "growth," but to an eruption of the real.

However, it does not follow that psychoanalysis stands serenely outside crises as an ahistorical know-how with them. On the contrary, as its history of schisms shows, and as Miller (2022) has indicated many times – for reasons I would connect to his insistence on the Pass as a possible end to analysis that contrasts with the endlessness of capitalism – the analytic discourse is merely the other side of whatever version of the master's discourse reigns in a particular epoch. I add this in closing because one of the previously solid things which has "melted into air" is the Oedipal civilisation which in Freud's era treated jouissance via the Name of the Father, and thus a symbolic version of castration. There is absolutely no room in Lacanian psychoanalysis for conservative nostalgia, as if we could somehow "teach" today's analysands how to be more like Freudian neurotics from the good old days. One consequence of the subject's ontological emptiness is that it is only ever a discursive product of an Other that is itself in flux. Indeed, Freud's discovery of the unconscious arguably emerged precisely from the crisis of the prohibitive father already well underway in his epoch (as reflected in many of his case studies where we encounter weak fathers). Nevertheless, in the same way that a certain relation to negation remains across Lacan's conceptualisations of the subject, so the problematic of castration persists in the contemporary clinic but in a way that calls for invention. The cut for example, and thus the variable length session, can be seen as a carefully administered mini-crisis that brings out the time of *Kairos* rather than of *Chronos*. For the analysand, it can be an experience of castration regarding the push to say everything, yet it creates a gap that enables the well-saying of *something*, knotting the signifier and jouissance in new and unexpected ways. Empty speech, comprehensible as a social currency perhaps, becomes a kind of worthless *blah blah*, a form of waste, in fact, that one consents to losing once the value of the cut is felt. Today's consumers are often consumed by jouissance-phenomena they do not treat with desire or the signifier per se, but for precisely this reason they often experience the limits introduced by the analytic discourse, whether that be the cut, the fee, or the commitment to a particular time and place, as a profound relief.

In many ways, psychoanalysis is a lesson in the value of loss – from the loss of common-sense with the fundamental rule to the loss of the (want of) being that defined the individual ego, all the way to the loss of the analyst as a subject-supposed-to-know destined to be dropped as a piece of waste. As such, it is surely not an experience wasted on those who undertake it.

Notes

1 He indicated this in his matheme for the discourse of the capitalist by removing the disjunctive impossibility that marks the other four discourses. See Contri, Giacomo B. (ed.), *Lacan en Italie/Lacan en Italia 1953–1978*, Milan: La Salamandra, 1978, p. 40.
2 For the outlines of a Lacanian ecology, see Geert Hoornaert's chapter, pp. 267–310, in Litten, Roger, and Wright, Colin (eds.), *Returning to Lacan's Seminar XVII*, New York: Lacanian Compass, 2023.
3 See Chapter 9, "Manufacturing Neo-Liberal Subjects", in Dardot, Pierre, and Laval, Christian, *The New Way of the World: On Neoliberal Society*, London: Verso, 2013. This argues for the centrality of subject-formation in neoliberalism, but for reasons I am about to explain, I prefer to retain the term "subject" for a more restricted psychoanalytic usage.
4 It would also be what Badiou has called an "atonal world" without possibility of novelty or invention. See Badiou, Alain, *Logics of Worlds*, trans. Alberto Toscano. London: Continuum.

References

Binkley, Sam. (2014) *Happiness as Enterprise: An Essay on Neoliberal Life*, New York: SUNY Press.

Briole, Guy. (2015) 'Moments of Crisis', *Hurly Burly*, No. 12, January.

Horowitz, Daniel. (2017) *Happier? The History of a Cultural Movement that Aspired to Transform America*, New York: Oxford University Press.

Klein, Naomi. (2014) *Shock Doctrine: The Rise of Disaster Capitalism*, London: Verso.

Lacan, Jacques. (2007) 'Science and Truth', in *Écrits* (trans. Bruce Fink), London: W.W. Norton.

Marmot, Michael. (2016) *The Health Gap: The Challenge of an Unequal World*, London: Bloomsbury.

Miller, Jacques-Alain. (2008) "La crise financière vue par Jacques-Alain Miller", 10th October, 2008, available at: https://ampblog2006.blogspot.com/2008/10/ecf-messager-la-crise-financire-vue-par.html.

Miller, Jacques-Alain. (2022) *Comment finissent les Analyses: Paradoxes de la passe*, Paris: Navarin Editeur.

Mirowski, Philip. (2013) *Never Let a Serious Crisis Go to Waste: How Neoliberalism Survived the Financial Meltdown*, London: Verso.

Schumpeter, Joseph. (2008) *Capitalism, Socialism, and Democracy: Third Edition*, New York: Harper Perennial Modern Classics.

Seligman, Martin. (2003) *Authentic Happiness: Using the New Positive Psychology to Realise Your Potential for Lasting Fulfilment*, London: Nicholas Brealey Publishing.

Chapter 4

The Ethics of the Death Drive

Todd McGowan

Shoot the Hostage

When he conceives of the death drive, Freud sees it as a principle that undermines the therapeutic and ethical pretensions of subjectivity. It deals a blow not only to humanity's self-conception but also to Freud's own thinking about the prospects of psychoanalytic treatment. Rather than wanting to act on behalf of our own good or the good of the society, we are driven toward what is not good for us. We are driven to undermine our own good and the good as such. With this discovery, Freud comes to see that satisfaction derives not from achieving our aims but from undermining them.[1] This is why Freud becomes doleful about the prospects for human liberation after the discovery of the death drive in 1920. An inherently self-destructive being, he wagers, can have no hope of ethical coexistence with other such beings and no illusions about the possibility of creating a utopian future. His former dream of improving society by lifting its repressiveness melts away under the intense heat generated by the drive to destroy oneself, which is a drive that unconsciously seeks loss and failure rather than acquisition and success.[2]

This leads to the melancholy conclusion that wraps up Freud's speculation about the individual's relation to the social order in *Civilization and Its Discontents*. There, Freud concedes that, as a thinker, he has nothing in the way of hope for the future to offer humanity, due to his discovery of the destructive implications of the death drive. This separates him from many of his former fellow travelers, such as Otto Gross, Alfred Adler, and even Carl Jung, whose dualism offers the image a salutary complementarity. With an air of political defeatism, Freud states,

> I have not the courage to rise up before my fellow-men as a prophet, and I bow to their reproach that I can offer them no consolation: for at bottom that is what they are all demanding – the wildest revolutionaries no less passionately than the most virtuous believers.
>
> (Freud, 1961a, p. 145)

This is his refutation of Marxism but also of his own plans for psychoanalysis as a method. Freud envisions no possible consolation, no hope for a better future, because he recognizes the psychic primacy of the death drive.

DOI: 10.4324/9781003375920-6

But just as the death drive makes a utopian future unimaginable, it simultane-ously renders moral acts doable. Freud doesn't himself grasp this when he theo-rizes the death drive, but the connection between the death drive and the emergence of ethical action is implicit in his theorization. This is the ultimate paradox of the death drive as a conception and the reason for its political significance. As Kant was the first to show, morality requires that we have the ability to act against the constraints of our situation, that we be able to do what violates all the empirical incentives that determine what we are. This is the precise point at which the death drive intervenes. It is against the determinations of our situation that the death drive pushes us. Rather than driving us to pleasure or an oceanic feeling of oneness with the world, the death drive leads in the direction of alienation from the world.[3] We act against what our particular world tells us is for our own good or for its good. Under the compulsion of the death drive, the rule of self-interest takes a backseat to the dominance of self-destruction.

It is only the being driven to destroy itself and its own interests that can act ethi-cally, at least in the sense that Kant conceives ethical action. This is because ethical acts require a being capable of doing what directly violates its self-interest and puts this self-interest completely at risk. A purely self-interested being is a being incapable of ever acting ethically. For instance, when I decide to respond truthfully to the store-owner who asks if I've stolen a candy bar, my self-interest compels me in the opposite direction – toward the lie that would preserve my symbolic status in the store-owner's eyes and the candy bar's presence in my pocket. Honesty cuts into my symbolic identity and takes something away from it, which is what gives it a moral value for Kant. The acts that one can do as effortlessly as breathing – obey-ing traffic signals, greeting others politely, or not punching one's neighbor in the face – don't have a real ethical value in Kant's eyes. Because they don't require the subject to give up anything, they lack the sublimity of an authentic moral act, such as telling the truth when accused of stealing or even when it might put one's life in danger. Genuine moral acts require that one puts one's good to the side in favor of another principle – the moral imperative. We are able to sacrifice our good only because of the drive that animates subjectivity to act against itself, the drive that generates satisfaction through this sacrifice.

The death drive, despite the unethical implications that the term conjures up, is the basis for our ability to follow the moral law. Under the impetus of the death drive, the subject generates trouble for itself, erects obstacles, and thwarts its own good. It generates the loss that animates it as a desiring subject. By doing so, exhib-its an ability to act contrary to the demands of the situation, which always compels the subject to pursue some social good, no matter how perverse that that good might be.

The strangeness of the pairing between the death drive and morality derives from the radical singularity of the former. The death drive undermines the subject's good not by taking the Other into account but by subverting the subject's standing with the Other. Even though it involves subjectivity acting against its own good, this act always occurs in a way that distinguishes the subject from others occupying the same situation. The death drive puts one at odds with the Other and thus with most others. It is what allows the subject to stand out from other subjects. The death drive is the force that guards against ubiquitous conformity. And yet, the singularity of the subject's drive is at once the source of its connection to the universality of the moral law because of the radical break from the particular situation that it inaugurates. The ability to universalize an act depends on an ability to have one's particular situation count for nothing. The universality of the moral law requires that subjects evince disdain for the demands of their particular situation. This only occurs through the force of the death drive.

We do not act ethically when we accommodate ourselves to the ruling situation but when we act with allegiance to the universality that our particular situation obfuscates. Conformity is anathema to our moral being. Universality, in contrast, is the key to the moral act because it links this act to the fundamental solidarity that makes ethical activity possible in the first place. In *The Ethics of the Real*, Alenka Zupančič makes just this point. She contends,

> [t]hat which can in no way be reduced without abolishing ethics as such is not the multi-coloured variability of every situation, but the gesture by which every subject, by means of his action, posits the universal, performs a certain operation of universalization.
>
> (Zupančič, 2000, p. 61)

There is no such thing as an ethics of difference because accommodating particular differences is the basis for unethical behavior, not ethics.[4] The genocidal tyrant always insists on the particular difference that separates the conquering people from those being wiped out. Even if the condition is not as grave as this, the impulse of particularism always works against a moral comportment. When we act morally, we always do so with at least an implicit reference to the universal.

As long as we are acting for our own or the society's good, we will never find our way out of the particular demands of the situation. By lifting us out of the compulsions of our particular situation, the singularity of the death drive opens us to the universality of the moral law. While not every act of self-destruction has the status of a moral act, it is this self-destruction that provides the existential basis for our morality. As a result, moral questions are first and foremost questions of the unconscious, not of consciousness. Recognizing the formative role that the death drive plays in our moral capacity should transform how we think about morality itself and its link to the unconscious. This is clearest in the case of Kantian morality.

Kant's Missing Relative

Far from linking Kantian morality to the death drive, Freud sees it as a manifestation of superegoic pressure. Like the superego, Freud claims, Kant's moral law represents not a fact of reason but the internalization of a figure of social authority. In this sense, it has exactly the status of the superego for the subject. Both mark the subject's internal capitulation to an external authority that has been introjected. In Freud's telling, obeying the moral law becomes nothing more than obeying the internalized father.[5] It is not so moral at all.

But Freud is much too quick to reduce Kant's moral law to demands of the superego. His conventional interpretation of Kantian morality as a form of social capitulation rather than political emancipation leaves him unable to recognize that the moral law has an intimate relation with the death drive and not the superego. When we obey the moral law, Kant insists, we act in defiance of not only our own good but also that promulgated by social authorities. The moral law cannot be akin to the superego because it drives us away from what the authorities command.[6]

It is not coincidental that Kant develops his moral philosophy just prior to the outbreak of the French Revolution. While the French Revolution introduces the revolutionary potential of universality into politics, Kant does so in theorizing about morality. The partisans of the French Revolution attempt to introduce universal values – *liberté, égalité, franternité* – into a political arena completely dominated by the particular interests of the king, the nobility, and the clergy. In the same way, Kant rejects morality based on particular sentiments or traditions in favor of the universal fact of reason. After the onset of the Revolution, he considers it in relation to our moral being. The Revolution's universal appeal becomes for Kant an indication of the inherent moral leaning within everyone.[7] Although he never develops this linkage any further after mentioning it, there is a sense in Kant's philosophy that both the French Revolution and his moral philosophy participate in a radical break that constitutes a new universe for the subject. What neither Kant nor the revolutionaries in France grasp is that this break emerges out of the disruptiveness of the death drive. When Freud theorizes the death drive over a hundred years later, he has no intimation of this connection.

The fundamental weakness in Kant's theory of morality lies in his inability to identify what makes a subject capable of heeding the imperative that the moral law lays down. In the *Critique of Practical Reason*, Kant proves that freedom is actual on the basis of the representation of the moral imperative: beings without freedom simply follow their instincts without posing a law that requires them to act against these instincts. What Kant calls the fact of reason – the existence of a moral commandment within the field of representation – indicates that one can always do otherwise than follow one's immediate compulsions.

But Kant never attempts to theorize what enables the subject to act against its own good. For him, proving that the subject has the ability to do so – and must do so – is already the great breakthrough, a breakthrough that distinguishes his first articulation of the moral law in the *Groundwork of the Metaphysics of Morals* in 1785 from its mature version in the *Critique of Practical Reason* in 1788. In the earlier text, just like in the *Critique of Pure Reason* of 1781, Kant contends the concerns of morality constrain us to presuppose that freedom exists. The absence of the presupposition of freedom would imperil us as moral actors because it would throw our potential autonomy for moral decisions into question. But then, when he writes the Second Critique, Kant silently alters the situation, contending that the bare existence of the moral imperative telling us what we must do implies that we can do it. Even though Kant lays out the different versions of the categorical imperative in the *Groundwork*, the Second Critique constitutes the great leap forward because it eliminates the presupposition that renders the argument of the earlier work tenuous.

Kant proceeds from an earlier necessary assumption that we are free – what most moral thinkers throughout history have assumed – to a proof that we are. This is a move that none before Kant had dared. From Étienne de la Boétie to Adam Smith, the exponents of moral philosophy began with the presupposition of human freedom without even conceiving the possibility that it might be provable. Kant himself goes to great lengths in the First Critique to show precisely that we cannot prove it. This is the entire point of the Third Antinomy. But this all changes, without Kant himself mentioning the radical transformation, with the publication of the *Critique of Practical Reason*.

The imperative of the moral law becomes the evidence that we are free, but it leaves unexplained the source of that freedom. This remains a lacuna in Kantian morality even after the advance of the Second Critique. Kant never uncovers – or even attempts to uncover – the source of our capacity for heeding the moral law, even though he convincingly proves that we can do so, despite the determinants of our biology or our situation. What Kant could not yet conceive as the condition of possibility for adherence to the moral law is the death drive, the drive of the subject to find satisfaction in acting against its own interests rather than for its own good or the good of the community. Only a subject that can act directly against the good can obey the moral law, which enjoins one to act for the sake of duty regardless of the good that will result from one's action. Kant is the first to see that the good is a moral lure, a temptation, to be rejected for the sake of moral duty, and only a subject of the drive is capable of rejecting this lure and acting out of duty. One who is not a subject of the death drive has no ability to act against its own good. Such a subject would be a prisoner of the good.

In order to act morally, the subject must be able to put its good to the side for the sake of its duty. Kant has his doubts about the possibility of accomplishing a genuine moral act because, he fears, some conception of our own good will always sneak back into the calculus. Although the existence of the moral law is a fact of reason that no one can doubt, this doesn't imply that there are instances where we can clearly identify someone obeying it. In the *Critique of Practical Reason*, he writes,

> the moral law is given, as it were, as a fact of pure reason of which we are a priori conscious and which is apodictically certain, though it be granted that no example of exact observance of it can be found in experience.
>
> (Kant, 1996a, p. 177)

Kant rejects the notion of an identifiable moral act because he believes that the subject always smuggles considerations of the good back into its acts, even when it attempts to act morally. He takes up this skepticism about moral acts because he doesn't theorize the moral law in terms of the death drive.

Once we see the death drive as the foundation for our moral being, we can inte-grate the unconscious into morality, which is what Kant was unable to do, thanks to being born too early. Unlike Kant's vision of our moral activity, the unconscious death drive doesn't always come up short in experience. We are really able to sabo-tage ourselves and act without reference to our own good, even if we consciously have a good in mind. A moral law rooted in the death drive is a moral law that we have the capacity to enact, not despite the injury that it does to our own good but precisely because of this self-damage.

Mad About You

Perhaps the best example of the intimate relationship between the death drive and an ethical act occurs in the first season of the television series *Mad Men*. Despite chronicling the activities surrounding a Madison Avenue advertising agency and focusing primarily on two characters tasked to create advertisements that will manipulate people into purchasing commodities that they don't need, the show is not primarily a critique of capitalist society, much to the chagrin of the Marxists who tuned in waiting for this. It does advance a critique of capitalism, but it does so obliquely rather than straightforwardly. This critique emerges through the depic-tion of how capitalism is able to take advantage of the priority of the death drive within the psyche, which is actually the primary concern of the series.

Interestingly, *Mad Men* begins with an explicit mention of Freud's conception of the death drive. It is as if the show articulates its controlling idea for the audience only to hide itself behind its explicit rejection in this first episode. At its beginning, the focus of the series is the Sterling Cooper advertising agency, where Don Draper (Jon Hamm) and Peggy Olson (Elisabeth Moss), the primary figures of the show, work. The initial problem that confronts Draper, the agency's artistic director, is how to sell cigarettes at the moment when their dangers have become thrust into public consciousness. An expert in psychology working at the agency, Dr. Greta Guttman (Gordana Rashovich), draws on her experience in Europe working with Alfred Adler in order to come up with a creative solution.

Guttman floats the idea of appealing directly to Freud's conception of the death drive to sell cigarettes. They could even go so far as to put a skull and crossbones on the package in order to highlight the self-destructiveness inherent in smoking. She tells Draper, "Before the war, when I studied with Adler in Vienna, we postulated that what Freud called the 'death wish' is as powerful a drive as those for sexual reproduc-tion and physical sustenance." For Guttman, who disappears from the series after this episode, a straightforward appeal to the death drive makes sense, since this is what actually impels people to continue to smoke when they know that it's killing them.

Don Draper rejects the direct appeal to the death drive in favor of a fantasy sce-nario that will speak to what consumers imagine they want rather than what drives them. He recognizes, albeit implicitly, that the death drive has to function uncon-sciously and that open appeals to it will always miss their mark, which is why auto racing doesn't advertise the number of deadly crashes that occur, despite the role that such crashes have in attracting additional spectators. Don Draper opts out of the death drive campaign on behalf of cigarettes, but *Mad Men* nonetheless begins with the idea that the death drive is the source of all our activity.

Although the idea of explicitly appealing to the death drive disappears from *Mad Men* after the first episode and the concept is never mentioned again throughout the seven seasons of the series, the death drive in action becomes the primary focus of the show, especially as it manifests itself in the characters of Don Draper and Peggy Olson. They exist in a world of mendacious and rapacious capitalism, and yet both manage to comport themselves ethically at times in ways that none of their colleagues are able to do. Their ethical behavior is in each case linked to the role that the death drive plays in their subjectivity, as the series is at pains to point out. Don and Peggy's willingness to destroy themselves, to abandon all self-interest for no foreseeable profit at all, elevates them above the other characters on the show. The other characters are almost entirely the products of their situation, while Don and Peggy act constantly at odds with their situation. One of their ethical high points comes in the penultimate episode of the first season, entitled "Nixon vs. Kennedy." During this episode (which takes place during the 1960 US presidential election), Account Executive Pete Campbell (Vincent Kartheiser) attempts to blackmail Don into giving him a promotion.

Through prying into a delivery meant for Don, Pete learns that Don Draper is really someone named Dick Whitman and that his false identity undoubtedly covers up an unsavory (and likely criminal) past. Faced with Pete's blackmail that threatens to torpedo not only his advertising career but also the middle class life that he enjoys with his wife Betty (January Jones), Don appears to be in a position where resistance is futile. Pete simply forces his hand and pushes Don to give him the promotion rather than allow Pete to decimate Don's entire life. And in the midst of this blackmail campaign, Peggy, unaware of the blackmail, comes into Don's office and points out the rampant injustice in the world, as her attempt to do the right thing results in the firing of two completely innocent workers in the building.

Peggy is in Don's office crying. She laments the horrible injustice that rules in their office and in the world. Peggy tells Don, "[i]nnocent people get hurt, and other people, people who are not good, get to walk around doing whatever they want. It's not fair." Peggy clearly has Pete in mind as one of those "not good" that can act with impunity. Don looks concerned but doesn't respond with anything more than a prompt for Peggy to finish the drink that he poured for her. But clearly Peggy's frustration with the injustice of the office had an effect on Don. After their meeting, the show cuts to outside Don's office. An unusual tracking shot follows Don from close behind as he walks to Pete's office and enters without knocking. This shot, as the tracking shot often does formally, shows the character's separation from the milieu – Don's alienation from the rest of the office – which is barely visible because of the proximity of the camera to Don's back. Don is separate from his situation in the form of the show. In this shot, we see Don intent on acting ethically at the same time as he embraces his own imminent self-destruction. In this scene, doing the right thing requires Don to simultaneously accept the destruction of his symbolic status.

After telling Pete that he is refusing the blackmail and not giving him the promotion he wants, Don leaves Pete's office to see Bert Cooper (Robert Morse), one of heads of the Sterling Cooper Agency. As Don strides toward Bert's office, we see Pete run him down in the middle of the agency, in front of numerous coworkers. When Pete catches Don, their conversation makes clear Don's acceptance of his own symbolic destruction:

Pete: What are you doing? Where are you going?
Don: I'm going to take care of this right now.
Pete: Is this some sort of thing like in the movies where I have a gun and you don't think I'm going to shoot you. I will shoot you.
Don: I won't let you hold this over my head.
Pete: So you'd rather blow yourself up than make me head of accounts?

Don answers Pete not with a verbal assent but by striding again toward Bert's office, outside of which Pete once again confronts him. Rather than allowing Pete to convince him to do what's in his own interest, Don insists on acting morally, on refusing to cave into Pete's blackmail. But this refusal entails the path of the self-destructive death drive. In this scene, self-destruction and the moral act come together and reveal their interconnectivity. Don can act morally because he enacts an annihilation of his own symbolic status. He follows his duty by acting against his own good and that of Pete.

The refusal to give in to blackmail is the basis for all moral activity. Kant thinks, for reasons linked to his conception of what holds the social order together, that truthfulness is the fundamental moral stand, that all other moral acts have their basis in the subject's refusal to lie, no matter what the personal or social cost. But he fails to recognize how immorality makes its inroads. One does not start down the road to perdition with a lie but with a first capitulation to the blackmail that the situation poses against one's morality.

For most, their situation blackmails them straightforwardly with money. This is capitalism's standard operating procedure. A corporation offers me a raise for trimming the pay of others; a government offers me a bonus for overseeing a crackdown on protesters; or a boss offers me a higher salaried position for being willing to speed up production at a factory, despite the harm that it will cause those workers there. A moral blackmail occurs: more money in exchange for compromising my moral position.[8] Often, the blackmail doesn't involve money but social standing: by ceding my moral principles for the sake of the particular situation, I allow myself to rise within the situation. Almost every social advance comes with this blackmail at least implicitly contained within it. As a result, those who rise to the top in organization end up being almost inevitably the most morally compromised. Those who refuse this moral blackmail end up in the mailroom.

Because the death drive functions through the destruction of one's symbolic status, it provides the moral backbone for resisting blackmail of this sort. When one is ready to destroy oneself symbolically, one can resist those who offer to build up one's symbolic identity for the sake of a moral transgression. The damage that one does to oneself is the source of one's resistance to the inducements that the social order makes. One can disdain social advancement only on the basis of a destructiveness that itself evinces disdain for any such advancement.

Shooting Oneself in the Foot

As long as one assumes that aggression is a fundamental impulse of subjectivity, it is only possible to envision ethical action through the curtailing of this impulse. One sets up incentives, such as social approbation or an eternal reward, in order to direct people's actions away from this fundamental aggressiveness. But in the end, such incentives can only function as stop-gap measures, as attempts to put a finger in the dike to hold off the onslaught of aggression and the violence that it portends. The problem is that stemming acts of aggression would not alter the impulse and would surely have the effect of heightening it. Restrictions always make transgression more enjoyable. But when aggression is no longer the basis for subjectivity, the moral equation changes. This is why Freud's discovery of the death drive marks such a revolutionary moment in the moral history of humanity, even if the twentieth century itself stands as something of a moral catastrophe.

The introduction of the death drive entails a complete reversal of the relationship between sadism and masochism in Freud's thought. Whereas the early Freud recognizes the primacy of sadism, the later Freud inverts their relationship and comes to see masochism as psychically more primordial. If sadism has psychic primacy, Thomas Hobbes is correct and the project of universal emancipation has no chance. All that we can do is, as Hobbes suggests in *Leviathan*, find ways to minimize the damage and put up ramparts against the outpouring of this sadism. If masochism has primacy over sadism, however, then the greatest danger for humanity is not murder but suicide. Murder will always be a variation on suicide, not the converse. The project of emancipation must wrestle not with the primacy of aggression but with the tendency to self-destruction and the damage that this tendency unleashes. But it is precisely this tendency to self-destruction that makes us moral beings in the first place, which is a fact that neither Kant nor Freud are able to articulate.

Kant of course never has the opportunity to think about the relationship between the death drive and his theory of morality. Freud, for his part, did not immediately comprehend the ramifications of his own discovery. He did not see that, after conceptualizing the death drive, masochism must be psychically prior to sadism. Writing in the same work in which he announces the discovery of the death drive, Freud continues to assert that masochism is inverted sadism rather than the contrary, which is what the death drive would imply. We can only conclude that Freud himself is confused by the consequences of what he uncovers. In *Beyond the Pleasure Principle*, Freud claims, "masochism [. . .] must be regarded as sadism that has been turned round upon the subject's own ego" (Freud, 1955, p. 54).[9] This statement that assumes the primacy of sadism is one that belongs in Freud's earlier work, the work that occurs prior to 1920. And yet, here it appears just after the introduction of the death drive into his theoretical edifice. This reveals that Freud himself does not see the radicality of his own intervention, even though he does hint throughout *Beyond the Pleasure Principle* at the threat that the death drive poses to his earlier thinking.

Once one integrates the death drive into one's thinking, it is clear that masochism must have psychic primacy over sadism. It takes Freud a few years after the discovery of the death drive to make this step, but eventually he does. Freud finally affirms this primacy late in his intellectual trajectory. He does so explicitly, for instance, when he writes the *New Introductory Lectures on Psycho-Analysis*, where he provides a final overview of some of the most important insights derived from psychoanalytic thinking.

Near the end of his life, Freud becomes convinced that the role of the death drive in the psyche gives masochism not just a logical but also a chronological primacy relative to sadism. In a clear reversal of his earlier view, Freud states, "we are led to the view that masochism is older than sadism, and that sadism is the destructive drive directed outwards, thus acquiring the characteristic of aggressiveness" (Freud, 1964, p. 105). Here, the moral implications of the death drive begin to make themselves felt. If masochism is prior to sadism and self-destruction precedes and shapes aggression, then the problem of morality takes on a completely different shape. To act morally is not to find a brake on the subject's fundamental drive but to unleash it. Our moral being resides not in constraining our darkest impulses but rather in giving free rein to them.[10] Subjectivity's self-destructiveness that arises through the subjection to the signifier is the foundation of our moral being.

Situating the death drive as psychically prior to aggression changes the moral equation. The problem is how to resist the compromises to one's drive, how to follow one's impulses without forcing others to pay the price for one's self-destructiveness. The death drive isn't inherently moral. It provides a structure that leads to moral action when we don't retreat from the damage that it promises to visit on the subject's own ego.

Clearly, there is still plenty of aggression that exists after 1920. Given the horrific events that took place in the decades following the publication of *Beyond the Pleasure Principle*, no one would try to claim that aggression doesn't remain a stumbling block to moral action and political change. But given Freud's discovery, we have to change the way that we regard this stumbling block. If the death drive has psychic primacy, then aggression is always a secondary phenomenon that arises as a result of the death drive becoming derailed.[11] To act according to the moral law requires putting the death drive back on the tracks and aligning it with its primary target. When we act according to the primary structure of the death drive, we are engaging in what Kant calls a moral act.

The problem that trips up the emancipatory project is not so much people on top who sadistically want to hold onto their authority. It is rather the universal impulse to self-destruction that finds an outlet in repressive regimes that enable people to discover satisfaction in how badly things are going. But it is precisely what hobbles the emancipatory project that also fuels it. The death drive hinders emancipation while at the same time making possible the ethical activity that underlies it. Thanks to the primacy of the death drive, people have the ability to destroy a regime constructed around the promulgation of self-interest in order to construct a more egalitarian system. This possibility only exists through the self-destructiveness that also gets in the way of its emergence.

The introduction of the death drive into thought demands that thinking about ethical activity becomes more dialectical than Kant would have it be, even though Kant marks the great breakthrough in moral philosophy. What he doesn't see is that, while the moral law itself may be a fact of reason, our capacity for heeding its imperative belongs to the self-destructiveness that Freud finds in the death drive. Our ethical being struggles against the drive that animates it. There is not a moral agency that confronts immoral impulses but rather a death drive that constantly confronts another manifestation of itself. To be ethical is not to vanquish one's impulses, as Kant would have it, or to accede to them, as the early Freud and the Herbert Marcuse of *Eros and Civilization* would have it. Instead, it is to opt for one form of self-destruction over another, to choose the form of self-destruction that comes without the illusion of abundant recompense. When we can recognize that loss itself provides the basis for our satisfaction, we are ready to act ethically.

Notes

1 In *Imagine There's No Woman*, Joan Copjec provides a description of the death drive that captures nicely its structure. She states, "the death drive achieves its satisfaction by *not* achieving its aim. Moreover, the *inhibition* that prevents the drive from achieving its aim is not understood within Freudian theory to be due to an extrinsic or exterior *obstacle*, but rather as part of the very *activity* of the drive itself" (Copjec, 2002, p. 30). As Copjec makes clear, the death drive doesn't run into an obstacle. It generates an obstacle in order to create a form through which the subject satisfies itself.

2 Freud was sanguine about the possibilities for psychoanalysis improving the human condition by lifting repression and curing neurosis until at least 1910. In this year in "The Future Prospects of Psycho-Analytic Therapy," he writes, "all the energies which are to-day consumed in the production of neurotic symptoms serving the purposes of a world of phantasy isolated from reality, will, even if they cannot at once be put to uses in life, help to strengthen the clamour for the changes in our civilization through which alone we can look for the well-being of future generations" (Freud, 1957, pp. 150–151). At this advanced point in his career, Freud still dreams of changing civilization through the process of freeing the psychic energy trapped through repression. This dream would die with the discovery of the death drive.

3 Possibly the worst misreading of the concept of the death drive, promoted incidentally by Freud's discussion of the oceanic feeling at the beginning of *Civilization and Its Discontents*, interprets it as the nirvana principle, a return to a sense of oneness with all creation. This interpretation actually mistakes the death drive for the pleasure principle, which is indeed the elimination of all excess excitation.

4 Alain Badiou rejects the recent association of difference with ethics. In his work on ethics, he notes, "we can never go back on universalism. There is no earlier territoriality calling for protection or recovery. The whole point is that differences be traversed, conserved and deposed simultaneously, somewhere other than in the frozen waters of selfish calculation" (Badiou, 2001, p. 113). Badiou stands out in the theoretical universe by always insisting on universality.

5 In his essay "The Economic Problem of Masochism," Freud lays out the link between the Kantian moral law and the superego. This connection stems from the development of the Oedipus complex and the unconscious role that this complex plays in Kantian morality, according to Freud. He states, "The super-ego – the conscience at work in the ego – may then become harsh, cruel and inexorable against the ego which is in its charge. Kant's Categorical Imperative is thus the direct heir of the Oedipus complex" (Freud, 1961b, p. 167).

6 Mladen Dolar corrects Freud on this point. In *A Voice and Nothing More*, he states, "The superego is not the moral law, despite Freud's declarations to the contrary, but a way of eluding it" Dolar, 2006, p. 99). Once we see the connection between the death drive and the moral law, Dolar's claim comes to appear almost self-evident.

7 Kant discusses the impact of the French Revolution on the rest of the world in "this revolution, I say, nonetheless finds in the hearts of all spectators (who are not engaged in this game themselves) a wishful *participation* that borders closely on enthusiasm the very expression of which is fraught with danger; this sympathy, therefore, can have no other cause than a moral predisposition in the human race" (Kant, 1996, p. 302). Our inability to remain impartial observers of the events in France suggests to Kant that the politics of this Revolution have moral implications. In both cases, universality has a primary importance.

8 In season three of *Mad Men*, Don falls for precisely this form of moral blackmail. When his personal charm prompts Conrad Hilton to become a client of Sterling Cooper, Don must do what he has hitherto resisted doing – sign a contract that commits him to the agency for three years. At the same time, he turns against his colleague Salvatore Romano (Bryan Blatt), a closeted gay man who refused a major client's advances and thus threatens the account for the agency. Earlier, Don displays acceptance when he accidentally sees Salvatore with another man, but this acceptance disappears when an immense sum of money is at stake.

9 In *Death and Desire*, Richard Boothby clarifies the position that Freud comes to after 1920 relative to masochism and sadism. He writes, "It became clear that although masochism and sadism are intimately bound up with one another, masochism is the more primary impulse. Sadism is to be conceived as a turning outward of a more primitive masochistic tendency. This view led Freud to the revolutionary thesis that all aggression and destructiveness in human beings is, according to its original nature, self-destructiveness" (Boothby, 1991, p. 5).

10 Even though *Civilization and Its Discontents* seems to read like an extended lament about the dangers of aggression for the survival of human society, Freud is nonetheless clear in this work that aggression represents a redirecting of the death drive outward, a turn away from its primary target, which is the self.

11 Ironically, conceiving of masochism as more primary than sadism makes it more difficult for Freud himself to theorize human emancipation, even though it shouldn't. Early on in his thinking, he equates emancipation simply with the lifting of repression. Later, he gives up on the possibility altogether. Psychoanalytic practice, in his thought after 1920, becomes a matter of easing the suffering of individuals rather than changing the nature of the social order. That dream is over, reserved for Marxists whom he sees as driven by resentment and in desperate need of an enemy to destroy.

References

Badiou, A. (2001). *Ethics: An Essay on the Understanding of Evil* (Peter Hallward, Trans.). Verso.

Boothy, R. (1991). *Death and Desire: Psychoanalytic Theory in Lacan's Return to Freud.* Routledge.

Copjec, J. (2002). *Imagine There's No Woman*. MIT Press.

Dolar, M. (2006). *A Voice and Nothing More*. MIT Press.

Freud, S. (1955). Beyond the Pleasure Principle (J. Strachey, Ed. and Trans.). *The Standard Edition of the Complete Psychological Works of Sigmund Freud*. Hogarth Press.

Freud, S. (1957). The Future Prospects of Psycho-Analytic Therapy (J. Strachey, Ed. and J. Riviere, Trans.). *The Standard Edition of the Complete Psychological Works of Sigmund Freud*. Hogarth Press.

Freud, S. (1961a). Civilization and Its Discontents (J. Strachey, Ed. and Trans.). *The Standard Edition of the Complete Psychological Works of Sigmund Freud*. Hogarth Press.

Freud, S. (1961b). The Economic Problem of Masochism (J. Strachey, Ed. and J. Riviere, Trans.). *The Standard Edition of the Complete Psychological Works of Sigmund Freud*. Hogarth Press.

Freud, S. (1964). New Introductory Lectures on Psycho-Analysis (J. Strachey, Ed. and Trans.). *The Standard Edition of the Complete Psychological Works of Sigmund Freud*. Hogarth Press.

Kant, I. (1996a). Critique of Practical Reason (M. J. Gregor, Ed. and Trans.). *Practical Philosophy*. Cambridge University Press.

Kant, I. (1996b). The Conflict of the Faculties (M. J. Gregor and R. Anchor, Trans.). *Religion within the Boundaries of Mere Reason and Other Writings* (A. Wood and G. di Giovanni). Cambridge University Press.

Zupančič, A. (2000). *Ethics of the Real: Kant, Lacan*. Verso.

Chapter 5

Humility and Humiliation of the Drive

Comedy and Tragedy in Philosophy and Psychoanalysis

Simone A. Medina Polo

Three Interventions

In *Why Psychoanalysis?*, Alenka Zupančič has highlighted three interventions that Freudo-Lacanian psychoanalysis had in philosophy at the levels of ontology, practical philosophy, and aesthetics through the drive as a fundamental concept of psychoanalysis. Zupančič describes the drive as the inherent fissure in being itself where reality experiences itself as parallaxes through the assumption of different strategies for coping with this fundamental split as what is called sexuation. For ethics, Zupančič addresses the notions of freedom and cause, as their separation is unwarranted since the split in reality itself is also a tie whereby objectivity and subjectivity are entangled in one another as a generative short-circuit occurring between nature and culture as well as ontology and epistemology. Lastly, she discusses the realism of desire and the realism of the drive as two ways of navigating different nothingnesses. Whereas the former concerns the uncanny and the logic of constitutive lack as transcendental nothing, the latter focuses on the logic of constitutive dislocation as immanent nothing in comedy.

At each intervention, Zupančič attests to the reconfiguration of philosophical concepts through the insights of psychoanalysis – in an interview with Agon Hamza and Frank Ruda, she notes:

> At the moment when philosophy was just about ready to abandon some of its key central notions as belonging to its own metaphysical past, from which it was eager to escape, along came Lacan, and taught us an invaluable lesson: it is not these notions themselves that are problematic; what can be problematic in some ways of doing philosophy is the disavowal or effacement of the inherent contradiction, even antagonism, that these notions imply, and are part of. That is why, by simply abandoning these notions (like subject, truth, the real . . .), we are abandoning the battlefield, rather than winning any significant battles.
>
> (Zupančič et al., 2019: 435)

Through these inherent conceptual contradictions, Lacan developed a productive intervention for philosophy and psychoanalysis: theories can have effects outside

DOI: 10.4324/9781003375920-7

theory and clinical practices can have profound philosophical implications. Antag-onisms between philosophy and the clinic miss this point through unwarranted claims that psychoanalysis should stay in its demarcated field of practice or that philosophy is too theoretical.

This essay expands on Zupančič's interventions. Ultimately, we will question that the end of analysis takes place when the analysand traverses their fantasy to assume their drive and jouissance through subjective destitution. Instead, we pro-pose the dual end of analysis in the humility and humiliation of the drive as the impossibility of harmony in the constitution of the subject. This dual edge is best characterized through comedy and tragedy as a solidarity of suffering between eve-rything alive. Furthermore, the end of analysis gives way to the experience of love as sharing lack in non-relation.

The Artwork as Borderspace

The drive articulates the locus of an ontological torsion where reality experiences itself as "missed encounters" (Zupančič, 2008: 6–11, 2017: 24). Thus, drives do not have a clear set object that they aim at to arrive at their satisfaction; instead, the very form of satisfaction of the drives is substitutional.

Sexuality and the drive are central to psychoanalysis because of the way that we position ourselves in sexuation, whereby any prospects of an original, unprob-lematized satisfaction are problematized in the clinic. Psychoanalysis navigates the idiosyncratic strategies of a person's way of being as well as their insights into themselves and others in what we call the unconscious. The unconscious is sex-ual since it is partial to the sexuated position assumed around the lapsed moment. Therefore, not only do we have meaningful and fleshed out psychological lives, but these lives are situated around fundamental conflicts that implicate the very nature of psychic lives and how these lives tell a story about themselves.

Furthermore, Bracha L. Ettinger's matrixial borderspace shows us that the missed encounter for individual life is articulated at the limits of personalized sub-jectivity. The borderspace facilitates this encounter to allow subtle transmissions and acts of witnessing between everyone interweaved therein (Rousselle, 2021: 81–82). For Ettinger, the artwork is one such place. The painter draws the viewer's eye through visual allures and situates the spectator's gaze as coinciding with the picture's stain of the almost-impossible encounter (Ettinger, 2006: 42, 72–73).

In a lecture, Ettinger shows the ambivalence of the screen through the difference between the artwork and the digital screen – while we are plagued by individual dramas in perpetual "doomscrolling" through social media, the artwork facilitates matrixial transgressions of subjectivity which the self-composed gaze of digital screens resists in order to preserve itself. The digital screen flattens experience to a point where time and space as the coordinates that orient our psychic lives are at risk. The stupor of digitality flattens psychic life to immediate enjoyment without the mediations and reflections of desire – and desire takes time and space to cultivate because we find a significant collapse of the dimensions of the human experience by succumbing to reactivity and positive feedback without timespace for desire to form (Ettinger, 2020).

Digital screens intensify the experience of obsessive living dead self-preservation and the homogenization of otherness; whereas the artwork drags us into the trouble of being alive. The regime of positivity disintegrates the profundity of desire by reifying it into a pure demand and supply as its erosive compulsion – if psychoanalysis entertains this positive orientation, then its inability to sustain the negativity required for desire's development would amount to a crisis of psychoanalysis since its very motor collapses. Ettinger provides a way to weave the shared lack expressed through the medium of visual art. Thus, museums can be rethought as the spaces for facilitating affective borderspaces and the transmission between co-emerging subjects, as she notes in the lecture:

> What is the role of a museum? It enables borderlinking and borderspacing in webs of severality that are affected, that is embodied being – we are embodied-being even in a world of hyperconnectivity in the web of webs.
>
> (Ettinger, 2006: 24, 44–48)

The Death Drive in Comedy and Tragedy

Hegel's *Phenomenology of Spirit* is the process of becoming enchanted with the wisdom that one may suppose in Hegel or another figure, and then deciding to pursue wisdom as a philosopher. This is harder than it seems because one bumps into contradictions in all claims to wisdom one makes. Thus, Hegel's *Phenomenology* is an exhaustion of all possible avenues of wisdom through their failures and contradictions.

Whereas in the *Phenomenology* we traverse all the fantasies of wisdom that the loving pursuit of wisdom constructs, the end reveals that the only wisdom is the philosophical drive that frustrates and mobilizes this pursuit repeatedly – as Slavoj Žižek notes, we move from an impasse to the pass.[1] By patiently learning to fail better, we let go of being a mere philosopher. In the end, spirit is nothing more than the living, reflective gallery of failures and contradictions of its own making as the wisdom that one grasps is that of fundamental contradiction, which is not just generative and structuring of thought, but also of being itself (McGowan, 2019: 21). Thus, spirit is the collective development and actualization of reasons, where the process of philosophy takes time, space, labor, social failures, ethical impurities, historical mishaps, and crucifixions of the divine for it to take place properly at all.

Comedy and tragedy are exemplar dramatizations of these contradictions. In the *Phenomenology*, religion traverses the representational fantasies of philosophy when it is self-aware of itself. Through artworks, Hegel introduces the epic as the elementary narrative where a protagonist is an active universality as opposed to the abstract universality of forces in ancient poetic songs. Ironically, Hegel introduces comedy when gods and heroes are shown to be in "a comical self-forgetfulness of their eternal nature" (1977: 442).

Heroisms deflate to repetitious bickerings of the divine insisting on an irrational void of necessity as their unconscious – we will refer to this as the Hegelian death drive (Hegel, 1977: 442).[2] Whereas in comedy, the artist disavows the gods' sorrows, tragedy cannot allow that distance. In tragedy, the death drive loses the ease of comedies to show its humiliating side as the tragic hero's fate.

Even then, the hero is split between an actor and a mask that mark a distance from the death drive. Thus, Hegel returns to comedy since nothing remains to be seen at this point where nakedness and ordinariness is not distinct from the genuine self, the actor, and the spectator. The truth of living comedy is the actual actor coinciding with what they impersonate in the death drive. As Žižek notes through a Marx Brothers' joke: "Don't let him fool you. He may look like an idiot, talk like an idiot, but he really is an idiot."

Death Drive All the Way Down

Hegel's approach to tragedy and comedy stays within the representations of spirit which solely belong to individuals who are not yet part of a community of believers. These dramas remain privatized whereby only one's own struggle can be considered a tragedy and only certain individuals can be comedic.

After the communion of believers, this community is pushed to get over representational idolatry when it realizes that it is spirit itself in its activity. Then, to see these dramas to the end, we must place them in the context of Absolute Knowing. In the realm of spirits, we are concerned with actual tragedy and comedy, not solely their representations. Though there may be an immediate loving recognition of the death drive in these actualities of the living spirit, we caution against their romanticization by an outlook of pure love. Loving recognition goes beyond to a love that does not purify the negative away from these dramas; as in witnessing the actual tragedies and comedies in the community of spirit, we witness just how humbling and humiliating history can be. Therefore, tragedy and comedy connect us with the concrete universal as they deal with the death drive rather than their privatization and romanticization to an untouchable sublimity.

Like Ettinger's museum, the gallery of spirits remains a place for the living community grasping its own aliveness. Hegel's philosophy shows how psychoanalysis can bridge the outlooks of individualized tragedy and comedy over to their universalistic implications for our humanity and spiritual community (Mills, 2002: 165). The crux is how this connectedness to others is necessary for us – we know that we are connected because it hurts: we care because we feel the lack and through this lack as this social bond and a zone of paradoxical union (Rousselle, 2021: 34, 132–134). What brings us together is anxious, and feeling compassion for others is not happiness – happiness might be secondary here. Love is sharing a lack: not as possessing someone or as the possession of something that will fill the void of who we are; but as a sharing of a void as that which we don't have.[3]

"Love Is Watching Someone Die, So Who's Gonna Watch You Die?"

Our question is simply: who are we? As Zupančič (2019: 438) notes in an interview:

> no, my point is that philosophy *can* assimilate psychoanalysis, and if it doesn't, this constitutes a genuine philosophical, conceptual decision and necessitates a philosophical invention; the distance/gap is produced in this case from within philosophy itself [. . .] *to think differently* in philosophy.

Our capacity to witness our humanity and that of others is on the table. When we take psychoanalysis into the philosophical questioning of what we are to ourselves, we are deciding something about the very concept of what we are. This is the encounter that is missing, as we fail to witness humanity for some sanitized idea that obscures its fundamental impurities – we are not trying to witness an innocent pure humanity, but when we uphold the pretext of pure innocence, we fail to witness how implicated humanity is in its own impurity. We embrace this as the condition of human existence as humbling and humiliating as it is.

The missed encounter of our originary experience is not as easy to retrieve as getting over its repression and making do with substitutes. In fact, we have to consider that such an originary experience is not integrally our own, at times felt in the solipsistic experience of feeling guilty for one's own life – compassion and love can only be done as an interweaving and not a singular strand of a person (Ettinger, 2007: 115). We are not protagonists, nor is there such a thing. The original experience is not integrally our own since it is the experience of transsubjective transmissions akin to birthing, where a mother intimates the perfect strangeness of her own child as a non-I. Here, lack is a sharing space as the matrixial borderspace.

Lack can insist as a death drive that permeates living individuals and communities, which are interwoven through aesthetic means. Hegel's depictions of tragedy and comedy shows how they retain the outlook of the individual and the articulation of universal humanity in the actual dramas of the community. Despite the privatization of these dramas, tragedy and comedy attempt to articulate a concrete universality rather than abstract universality and concrete particularities. These dramas captivate humanity in contradiction with itself rather than a rivalry of differences one-upping each other. Encountering radical humility and humiliation intimates us with the death drive and the death driven in ourselves, among others, and in the very fabric of reality in the end.

Since we can think differently in philosophy, such a difference can be introduced in psychoanalysis too. While traditionally the end of the clinic moves from desire to drive so that the drive as jouissance can be enjoyed, this positive solution can give way to the humility and humiliation of the drive as the true end of analysis. Rather than enjoying the drive, we maintain the restlessness that we are left with as a contention of just how humbling and humiliating the drive can be every step of the way. Psychoanalysis is not about desire getting in the way of the drive, but

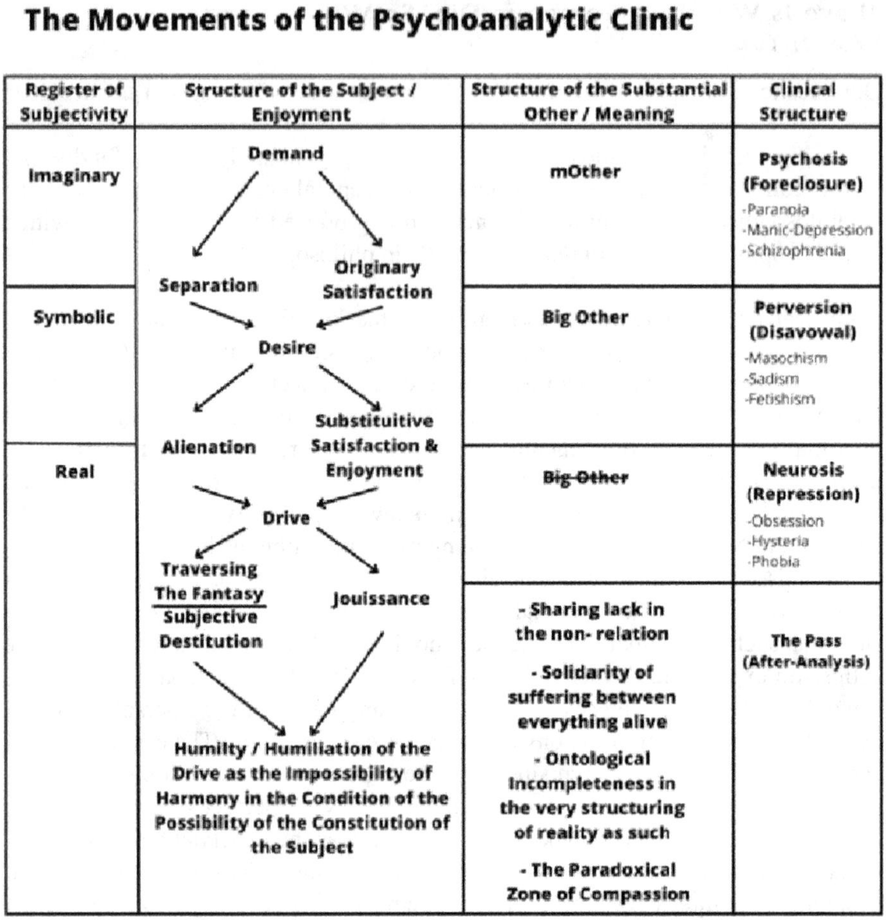

The Movements of the Psychoanalytic Clinic

Register of Subjectivity	Structure of the Subject / Enjoyment	Structure of the Substantial Other / Meaning	Clinical Structure
Imaginary	Demand / Separation / Originary Satisfaction	mOther	Psychosis (Foreclosure) -Paranoia -Manic-Depression -Schizophrenia
Symbolic	Desire / Alienation / Substituitive Satisfaction & Enjoyment	Big Other	Perversion (Disavowal) -Masochism -Sadism -Fetishism
Real	Drive / Traversing The Fantasy / Jouissance / Subjective Destitution / Humilty / Humiliation of the Drive as the Impossibility of Harmony in the Condition of the Possibility of the Constitution of the Subject	~~Big Other~~	Neurosis (Repression) -Obsession -Hysteria -Phobia
		- Sharing lack in the non- relation - Solidarity of suffering between everything alive - Ontological Incompleteness in the very structuring of reality as such - The Paradoxical Zone of Compassion	The Pass (After-Analysis)

Figure 5.1 Charting the clinic's trajectory via the imaginary, symbolic, and real.

about the drive itself in the constitutive lack of the subject. When we assume jouissance and the drive, we measure the drive in the terms of desire and enjoyment; but by accounting for the drive's full restlessness, the drive is measured in its own way. This psychoanalytic approach is outlined in Figure 5.1.

When we are witnessing this trouble of being alive, we are plagued by the band-aid solutions that overlook how fundamental our troubles are. Love and compassion are not simple and easy positive solutions, rather they are a complex invitation into the infinite abyss in ourselves and others as a shared void – love is what makes up for the missed encounter and what finds something fundamentally real in that abyss; compassion is what attests that, as much as we witness this utterly humbling and humiliating predicament in ourselves, we are witnessing this in others and with others.

Notes

1 "The pass is what had initially seemed to be the impasse" (see Žižek, p. 2, pp. 24–25).
2 "Absolute negativity, the 'nothing' that pushes the dialectical movement forward, is precisely the intervention of the 'death instinct' as the radical ahistoric 'zero hour' of history" (Žižek, 2014: 185).
3 "The infinitude of the concept is nothing but the concept's own self-limitation. The enjoyment that the death drive produces also achieves its infinitude through self-limitation. . . . A society centered around the death drive would allow us to recognize that we enjoy the lost object only insofar as it remains lost" (McGowan, 2013: 284–286).

References

Ettinger, Bracha L. "The Matrixial Gaze" in *The Matrixial Borderspace*, Ed. Brian Massumi. Minneapolis: The University of Minnesota Press, 2006.

Ettinger, Bracha L. "From Proto-Ethical Compassion to Responsibility: Besidesness and the Three Primal Mother-Phantasies of Not-Enoughness, Devouring and Abandonment" in *Athena: Philosophical Studies*, issue: 3, 2007, pp. 100–145.

Ettinger, Bracha L. "Digital PTSD. The Practice of Art and Its Impact on Digital Trauma." *YouTube Video*, Castello di Rivoli Museo d'Arte Contemporanea, 18 December 2020. www.youtube.com/watch?v=5nzgimnrFhE

Hegel, G.W.F. *The Phenomenology of Spirit*. Trans. A.V. Miller. Oxford: Oxford University Press, 1977.

McGowan, Todd. *Enjoying What We Don't Have: The Political Project of Psychoanalysis*. Lincoln: University of Nebraska Press, 2013.

McGowan, Todd. *Emancipation after Hegel: Achieving a Contradictory Revolution*. New York: Columbia University Press, 2019.

Mills, Jon. *The Unconscious Abyss: Hegel's Anticipation of Psychoanalysis*. New York: State University of New York Press, 2002.

Rousselle, Duane. *Real Love: Essays on Psychoanalysis, Religion, Society*. New York: Atropos Press, 2021.

Žižek, Slavoj. *The Most Sublime Hysteric: Hegel with Lacan*. Trans. Thomas Scott-Railton. Great Britain: Polity, 2014.

Zupančič, Alenka. *Why Psychoanalysis? Three Interventions*. Uppsala: NSU Press, 2008.

Zupančič, Alenka. *What Is Sex?* Cambridge, MA: The MIT Press, 2017.

Zupančič, Alenka, Agon Hamza and Frank Ruda. "Interview with Alenka Zupančič: Philosophy or Psychoanalysis? Yes, Please!" in *Crisis & Critique*, volume 6, issue: 1, April 2019.

Chapter 6

Apophatic Psychoanalysis
The Plenitude of the Negative

Mark Gerard Murphy

The Era of the Positive

In his new work *Surplus Jouissance: A Guide for the Non-perplexed*, Žižek states the spiritual plight of our situation:

> [We are saturated in] extreme right-wing conspiracy theories about the COVID-19 pandemic [and how they] get combined with New Age spirituality. Melissa Rein Lively's focus on wellness, natural health, organic food, yoga, ayurvedic healing, meditation, etc., led her into a violent rejection of vaccines as a source of dangerous contamination.
>
> (Žižek, 2022: 10)

What we call spirituality today plays an important ideological supplement in modern political discourse in online spaces and much more. We see the rise of a spiritual-therapeutic-moralist discourse that replaces old forms of morality while creating new anxieties (Waldman, 2021). We also see it being utilised to re-instantiate the reign of a lost paternalism. Thus, we see it in Jordan Peterson's self-help and QAnon's reactionary mythology building (Bowles, 2018; Dickson, 2020; Peterson, 2018). We can term this therapy-spiritual discourse Toxic Positivity (Wright, 2014: 791–813).

It is part of what we can call the attention economy (Seymour, 2019: 23–24). The attention economy is what Marika Rose's work *On Machines of Loving Grace* highlights in the transition from the old analogous worldview of participation to our disembodied techno-spiritual world that works on exotic algorithms and formulas operating to create a fused form of cyborg subjectivity optimised so these systems can extract and circulate labour value (Rose, 2017: 240–258).

In more detail, Richard Seymour's new work, *The Twittering Machine*, suggests that our new digitally mediated experientialist paradigm functions through an economy of addiction and attention (Seymour, 2019: 19–21). He argues that this addiction should be framed as a type of malformed devotion we are commanded to engage in at an unconscious level through the hidden injunction of the screen. Reflecting this, Lembke argues that since the turn of

DOI: 10.4324/9781003375920-8

the millennium, behavioral – as opposed to substance – addictions have soared. Her new book stresses that we are now all addicts to a degree due to the attention and experience economy bolstering our attachment to the Smart Phone (Lembke, 2021).

Seymour's work is an expanded critique and analysis of the attention economy's movements and the effects on subjectivity and politics. In his view, the use of spirituality, self-help, and other technologies of the self, in this paradigm, are merely other methods through which our attention is captured. By capturing our attention, we are monetised through the promise of experiential wholeness and bliss. In short, the promise of happiness.

Jacques-Alain Miller detected the outlines of this problem in 2002 when he explained the following:

> Robert Reich's idea is that there is an economy of attention and an offer of attention, therefore a market for artificial attention. [. . .] He, thus, delineates the development of a whole sector of specialized activities in the service of attention. This allows him to create a category where we also find personal gym teachers, those who do shopping . . . and the entire set of psychological, spiritual advisors. [. . .] The functioning of this machine . . . exacerbates nostalgia for the master signifiers, and this appeal to the master signifier is all the more exacerbated as it appears detached from the rest, and all the more insistent that it clearly appears as supplementary.
>
> (J.-A. Miller, 2019: 116–117, 123)

For Miller, this new era of addiction – what he calls the machine of the *not-all* – is the era of jouissance-as-such, an era of regimes of spiritual and psychological enjoyment and nostalgia for master signifiers. All are defined by a truncated return for positivity and wholeness.

The Negativity of Psychoanalysis?

But this raises the question, what is the place of the negative in our world today as a solution? How does it insert itself into and disrupt the 'libidinal economies' of healing, spirituality and commodified moralism that saturate our discourses today? What is the place of the negative in Lacanian psychoanalysis, and how does it operate in a world that has fundamentally changed in the last decade? Further still, how, in a world saturated with a toxic positive jouissance that isolates, how do we situate the last Lacan with his turn to the positive?

This work explores the negative in both psychoanalytic practice and what we can call the logics of darkness spirituality as the antithesis of our attention economy. It traces a shift in our modern predicament where what we call the libidinal economy has become defined not by negativity but an overbearing positivity.

The apophatic is a term from mystical theology that means negation. It stems from the early days of Christianity and neo-platonic thinkers like Pseudo-Dionysius, who argue that we cannot say what God is but only what he is not. The apophatic is a necessary negation at the centre of the Christian tradition. However, we can also suggest that negation is at the heart of the psychoanalytic tradition, and we see this in Freud's central text, *On Negation*.

The problem today, however, is that the negative is either related to discourses of pure negativity and emptiness or to extraordinary religious experience and healing discourses that focus on wholeness at the imaginary level.

I also believe that certain psychological healing discourses fall into these categories also. But, unfortunately, some also can fall into a cynical end of analysis – which is presenting in modern culture as doomerism – focusing on pure emptiness, or they veer into a cloying optimism defined by shallow sentimental positivism (Coaston, 2022; Millman, 2022).

In opposition to this, I state that the concept of the apophatic in mystical theology leads to a plenitude, a clo(u)d of unknowing, an ineffable encounter with the divine. I argue that 'negative abundance' should not be judged at the level of 'sublime pre-discursive experience.' Instead, it relates directly to an ancient practice of apophasis that relates to a wider structure and its excessive element.

My argument here is if we wish to preserve the potency of psychoanalysis that resists logics of psychologistic utility, then, ostensibly, it should borrow from the structural discourse of mystical theology.

But a problem arises: how can we talk about Lacan's overall teaching being apophatic when the very late Lacan is distinctly positive in its operation, focusing on Jouissance, the One and the body? Surely this would be the opposite of Lacan's earlier apophatic phase being cataphatic in operation?

I attempt to answer this herein. I argue that traditional apophasis is not merely structurally negative (it is not merely mysticism),[1] as the negative always desires to be filled; nature abhors a void. The true mystical is always – in the end – radically opaque and full to the extent that it elides all epistemic, psychological, experiential and linguistic frameworks. And it is this understanding of the mystical as disruptive fullness that coheres with Lacan's later teaching and the concept of the School. To do this, I show how questions of the Sinthome and the body connect with ideas stemming from Bauerschmidt's radical interpretation of Julian of Norwich.

The apophatic and cataphatic are terms related to mystical theology. Apophatic means 'without words,' and cataphatic means 'with images and representation.' This form of theology is rooted in Pseudo Dionysius's work in the 6th century (Dionysius, 1987). In short, his work, *The Mystical Theology*, argues that we must learn to unsay the divine in approaching the divine. It is a theology of unsaying God (McIntosh, 1998: 125–126). To know anything of the divine involves a process of unknowing: it is divine ignorance; as Nicholas of Cusa would later say, 'all we know of the truth is that the absolute truth, such as it is, is beyond our reach' (Cusanus, 2007: 11–12).

Over time though, the mystical concept has taken on a different resonance. In the past, it was more associated with a past textual, structural and communal practice

(McIntosh, 1998: 44–56). The apophatic mystical was thus about entering more deeply into a community that cannot be fully said, defined or captured. It was less about a given extraordinary 'experience' and more about how a measured operative negativity sustains itself in a communal-structural framework. It was thus inherently catechetical, *mystagogical* and liturgical. The latter term comes from the Greek *leitourgia*, which means work of the people. It was about a structure we participated in, which organises itself around a central mystery that constantly causes the structure to revise itself through a 'work' we can never fully understand (McIntosh, 1998: 44–56).

But unfortunately, the mystical is now associated precisely with religious experience as a passive vitalist mysticism: the idea that we give up words to focus on an internal, emotional experience that words fail to grasp (Tyler, 2011: 3–25). And this now goes hand in hand with modern individualism and the commodification associated with a saturated self-help culture.[2] We see plenty of work co-opting this experientialist understanding of the mystical into self-help and mindfulness schemas. As Carrette and King argue, the mystical is no longer merely a 'private experience' of the sublime Good but a privatised experience (2004: 26–27).

Like Pseudo Dionysius, negation is at the heart of Freud's theory, as seen in his first publication of 1925 of the same name:

Only one consequence of the process of negation is undone – the fact, namely, of the ideational content of what is repressed not reaching consciousness. The outcome of this is a kind of intellectual acceptance of the repressed, while at the same time what is essential to the repression persists.

(Akhtar & O'Neil, 2018: 55)

However, the radical negativity of Freud's discovery of the unconscious has arguably given way to treating the negative as a kind of transitionary point toward from which we can find emotional healing, affective wholeness and the like. The negation of repression in its various guises – neurosis, hysteria – gives way to knowledge and healing, the positive.[3]

And although we can talk about radical negativity in Freud, the tendency toward a *joui-sense* – meaning – is always there. This is due to the Freudian articulation of the symptom and the unconscious. Indeed, the Symptom for Freud is something that 'wants to say' (Stevens, 2007: 211–221). And the work of an analysis aims to connect, interpret and uncover the meaning of the symptom. Hence any apophasis that exists ends up becoming positive. So, maybe the transition to psychological positivism – as described earlier – was due to its inherent attachment to sense?

The Negative in Lacan

Lacan was aware of this radical negativity and its absolute centrality in psychoanalysis. The negative starts in Lacan's writings in the imaginary with misrecognition, which he borrows from Hegel's master-slave dialectic (Eyers, 2012: 15n). We then see the symbolic order's inherent negativity as Lacan places precedence on the signifier and how it cuts into the body to create metonymy and metaphor. Later, we see how Lacan focuses on the Real as the final instance of the negative.

The latter concept came to the fore in 1953 in a lecture called *Le symbolique, l'imaginaire et le reel*. Lacan introduced the Real in this lecture as connected with the imaginary and the symbolic. However, its negative operation really starts to come to the fore in Seminar VII (Kesel, 2009). Here he relates the concept of *Das Ding* with the figure of Antigone in seminar VII as one who refuses to give up on her desire in the face of the law.[4] As Paul Allen Miller states:

> Antigone's choice, her desire, is pure precisely to the degree that it rejects the claims of the Other to dictate its objects or form. For Lacan, it is the beauty of Antigone's choice of a Good beyond all recognised goods, beyond the pleasure principle, that gives her character its monumental status and makes her a model for an ethics of creation as opposed to conformity.
>
> (Miller, 2007: 1–14)

The logic of Antigone is a logic toward the negative. She gives up false positivity and aims with a Kantian-like duty toward negation as the full expression of desire at the expense of any utilitarian expression (J.-A. Miller, 2019). This is a pure apophasis with the void as the goal. Seminar VII represents a turning point in Lacan's seminars, where we see the intersection of apophatic negativity associated with the logic of desire toward the apophasis associated with the fullness of Jouissance as a transgression of a barrier (J.-A. Miller, 2019).

The Positive in the Last Lacan?

However, a theoretical problem arises here. The general view is that the early Lacan focused on the negative and, later on, the positive. How, then, can we say that the products of the later Lacan (the Sinthome, The One-All-Alone, The Not-All and the Analytic Act) are still apophatic? How can this be the case when Lacan speaks of Jouissance-as-such without any opposition? What are we to make of Lacan's insistence that the subject is happy? Surely this negativity should apply only to the middle and early Lacan? This is all the more the case when we focus on desire and negative theological proponents.

But this is not entirely accurate. Indeed, it is the case that radical negativity as practice first took the role of explication on desire, the subject and later *object a and the drive*. It was explained as the gap between the signifier and signified regarding the bedrock of castration. However, the negativity of the early Lacan ran into issues precisely because the signifier's trajectory always relates to absence calling out to be filled in some way. So, there is a temptation there to fill negativity.

The later Lacan starts with the radical positive of jouissance but insofar that its negative operation plays out not in an absence but in its senseless opacity. He states in seminar 24:

> What does it mean to deny? What can one deny? This plunges us into the *Verneinung* of which Freud has put forward the essentials. What he enunciates is that negation presupposes a *Bejahung [affirmation]*. It is starting from something that is enunciated as positive, that one writes negation.
>
> (Lacan, 1977: 117–118)

In this specific passage, Lacan addresses the nature of speech as being predicated on the positive. But writing – rather than speech – becomes associated with failure and negation. Speech, for Lacan, becomes less related to the work of the signifier and more to do with what he calls *lalangue*. Moreover, the opacity of such speech beyond the signifier is even more negative than absence because density resists meaning in a way an analysis predicated on the chain of signifiers of the early Lacan could not (Dupont, 2020: 15–37).

Interestingly enough, this radical fullness reflects modern scholarship in mystical theology. Lacan's later work follows modern theological ideas about how we should reject the tendency to oppose non-experiential structural contemplative practice to a supposed cataphatic imaginary. For instance, Julian of Norwich is usually seen as the archetype of an experientialist cataphatic mysticism, focusing wholly on apparitions and sensations in opposition to the desirative emptiness of contemplative prayer. In contrast, mystics like John of the Cross and Meister Eckhart are seen as the pinnacle of a negative theology that hollows out the self entirely.

However, as Frederick Christian Bauerschmidt argues, this is not quite correct. He argues that Julian's mystical encounter with the speaking body of Christ that we see in Julian's work goes beyond cataphatic and apophatic distinctions as a radical confrontation with the negative fullness of Christ's mangled body as the letter. Moreover, the encounter leads to a disruptive effect and the creation of a new social bond – born from Love – over her lifetime as a confrontation with her mother tongue (*lalangue*), as Christ – the word – is perceived as a mother. Raul Moncayo speaks of the relationship between *lalangue* and Sinthome as the inverse relation between signifier and symptom. Lalangue is the mother-tongue, the singular use of the word without meaning. In this field, the symptom becomes Sinthome as the style of writing that allows the imaginary, symbolic and real to hold together (Moncayo, 2019, p. 30).

I argue that this encounter with the body is a type of positivised void that allows for space of radical invention that typifies Lacan's approach to Jouissance-as-such. In other words, Julian's encounter with *lalangue* represents the creation of the Joycean Sinthome, but also a leaving behind of that name toward the invention of the Other.

The Not-All?

Seminar XX is famously known as the mystical seminar (Lacan, 1999). In the seminar, we begin to see the full transition from an understanding of the mystical apophatic from a practice of constitutive lack and desire to a disruptive mute opacity that becomes connected to disruption, silence and the body. As Miller states succinctly: '[t]he not-all is not a whole that contains a lack. On the contrary, it is a series in development without limit' (J.-A. Miller, 2019, p. 120).

Miller explains that if the clinic operated by the classifications of the 'All' with clear demarcations and categories in the past, societal transitions have now resulted in 'globalisation' (J.-A. Miller, 2019). This new economic and political order has removed paternal ordered limits and resulted in many symptoms beyond the previous nosological categories of past analysis. In short, our current political and economic paradigm is the machine of the not-all, as it is saturated with a totalising positivity precisely because all external limits or means to categorise are removed. Other Jouissance, then, can be understood as the space that is opened up by analysis that disrupts this totalising tendency. Lacan located this other Jouissance with what can be called the mystical. But it should not be understood solely as an extraordinary individual experience. Indeed, in the globalised machine of the not-all and how it consistently captures attention and experience, psychoanalysis cannot be just another psy-spiritual experience among many.

Other Jouissance, to be sure, is *not without affective experience*, but to focus on extraordinary experience as the arbiter of content is to miss the point.[5] Moreover, this idea of a pre-discursive experientialist substance as being the experientialist 'presence' of mystical Other Jouissance in seminar XX is taken directly to task by Miller in his *The One Is the Letter*, where he states:

> The dividing line passes through this term I have used of prediscursive being. [The Real] arises from language working on language, it presupposes the logical apparatus seizing what is said [. . .] in order to make [it] emerge. This real at the level of existence is a signifier – nothing to do with the presence that palpitates.
>
> (Miller, 2021: 13–44)

The real is not a direct confrontation with some pre-discursive mystical substance: the transgression of the early Antigone and her massive Jouissance. No, Other Jouissance is the failure of the totalising tendency to fully capture us. It thus gives us access to what is at stake in the failure of the non-rapport: the one of the letter – the nonsensical letter all alone *is* our confrontation with the Real.[6]

In this sense, Other Jouissance can be understood far less bombastic than what is otherwise made out. It relates – Brousse argues – to the unsaying of speech in the various contexts we engage in daily. It means becoming disruptive mute points in a field of saturated signifiers. It is to disidentify with semblants – moment to moment – by relating directly to the antagonism inherent in the social bond that is otherwise excluded in repression.

For Brousse, this apophatic operation comes in several categories: hiding, disappearing, disobedi-sense, silence, anonymity. In each category, what is at stake is a mode of subtle resistance to ascribed identity by saying what I am not or, more accurately, it is a way of not being fully present by not being wholly there by being something that does not belong to the set itself. As Zupančič says, what takes place is that an external point is brought into the field of totality (2017: 10). It presents as a 'negative surplus' – a clod of unknowing – in the symbolic field. To reduce it to an imaginary affect, albeit in negative language, is to miss the point.

The Sinthome: Beyond Apophatic and Cataphatic

What comes into view in the later Lacan is the Sinthome as an expression of the Real. The latter is unrelated to the signifier but rather that radical un-meaning of *lalangue* as opposed to the binary of the signifier. In this sense, it is 'One.'

In seminar 23, Lacan shows that the desirative logic that we attribute to those of neurotic structure with their reliance on the Name-of-the-Father is not a special signifier but just another signifier amongst others that works to bind together the triadic structure of the subject. His point in this seminar is that Joyce – being the psychotic that he was – did not have the paternal signifier and so – through the use of artifice – fashioned a Sinthome himself to stabilise his subjectivity.

A sinthomatic analysis – much like negative theology – moves through the structure of an analysis until there is a stripping away of ephemera, and one hits an opaque point. This is the symptom in all its opacity. It is at this point that Voruz argues that there is a choice between two kinds of negativity: two kinds of apophasis (2022: 118–119). The first is to approach it as something to believe in – a space which can be filled with meaning. The symptom is something that can be answered by the Other. It can be interpreted. This is the traditional approach to psychoanalysis, the Freudian endeavour, and the deadlock where negativity always wishes to be filled (Voruz, 2022: 118–119). Moreover, this is the way of desire and the dark night of the soul as emptiness.

The second is much more radical and tries to start from the symptom's radical fullness. It is radically without meaning, but it constantly returns in iteration – this term is differentiated from repetition, as repetition has to do with sense and meaning. And meaning is linked to the call of the symptom, not the Sinthome (Stevens, 2007).

The Sinthome encounter repeats our first encounter with language itself, the first bite of the linguistic that carves a hole in the body for sense to appear. The first encounter subtracts the one and leaves the 0. And from this point of *ex nihilo*, the signifier appears as S1. But – as Dupont explains – beneath the signifier, a trace exists 'as an inarticulable defence against the real' (Dupont, 2020: 15–37). And it is this trace as speech that functions as the substance of what Lacan calls *lalangue*. It emanates from the Real itself through 'use' as a defence against the Real. And as Lacan points out, there is a Real of the Symbolic, The Imaginary and the Body.

In Žižek's *Surplus Jouissance*, he takes to task the supposed monism and positivity of Meister Eckhart and his supposed predilection toward the One:

> The unique role of Christ is something that escapes mysticism even at its best, which means, of course, Meister Eckhart. Eckhart was on the right track when he said that he'd rather go to Hell with God than to heaven without – but his ultimate horizon of the mystical unity of man and God as the abyssal Oneness in which man and God as separate entities disappear prevents him from drawing all the consequences from his insight.
>
> (Žižek, 2022: 315)

Žižek is correct in positing the problem of 'mysticism,' but mysticism is – as I have argued – not the mystical. Hence, my contention here is that Žižek is wrestling with the value of Eckhart's apophatic tendency in a world saturated with a toxic positivity that reduces all to the One. Indeed, toxic positive healing discourse is a discursive practice that reduces all to a false wholeness that acts as an ideological supplement to our hellscape. Hence, he needs to create a fundamental difference in the sophisticated theology of Eckhart by showing that it is not-one. However, his mistake is found in moving forward from a position of constitutive negativity. He must show Christ as the negative point that stops an all-encompassing positivity. Consequently, he alters the mystical apophasis of Eckhart by literally introducing the body of Christ to disrupt the oneness; he says:

> It is my contention that one should replace here 'God' with 'Christ' one cannot be without God in Heaven because God IS Heaven, and the only way God can be in Hell is in the figure of Christ. The reason we have to replace 'God' with 'Christ' is thus simply that this is the only way to make Eckhart's proposition meaningful in a Christian sense.
>
> (Žižek, 2022: 317)

However, in contrast to this, Julian of Norwich directly shows the limitations of an empty contemplative mysticism and directly introduces the body of Christ from the position of radical positivity. With Julian, there is a radical aloneness that is disrupted not with negation but with a further encounter with the positive.

Even in her visions of the bleeding hellish crucified body of Christ on the Cross, she tries to lift her eyes toward heaven to see God (the constitutive exception), but her eyes are pulled directly to the speaking body: the full antagonistic point within the symbolic field. Further still, it is from this bleeding body of Christ that we see her accused literally emptying out Hell:

> Behold and see the virtue of this precious plenty of his dearworthy blood! It descended down into Hell and burst their bonds and delivered them, all who were there who belong to the court of heaven. The precious plenty of his dearworthy blood overflows all the earth and is ready to wash all creatures of sinne

who are of good will, have been, and shall be. The precious plenty of his dear-worthy blood ascends up into heaven in the blessed body of our lord Jesus Christ, and there is in him, bleeding, praying for us to the Father, and is and shall be as long as we need.

(Julian of Norwich, 2015: 21)

Moreover, Julian shows directly how it is possible to escape from the 'one-blunder' – a term I shall expand on later – through an encounter with the speaking body and through into a Love in the Real, which is synonymous with the field of invention.

For Bauerschmidt, we can suggest that Julian is a mystic who, in their encounter with their own Sinthome, goes beyond affectivity and negative contemplation. She is a mystic who exists beyond the apophatic and cataphatic by focusing on the negative fullness of Christ's body.[7] And how her own encounter with this opaque body leads to the creation of her own *Sinthome*[8] of 'all shall be well,' an injunction that was basically impossible and incomprehensible in her own context:

[For Julian] Jesus crucified body is the concrete reality to which she clings for solace and the mysterious hieroglyph that she insistently probes and questions. It is a body whose mysteries seem beyond articulation, not because it is beyond words (for it is precisely as the Word of God that Jesus is crucified), but because in the image of the crucified Julian is presented with what Paul calls the *logos tou staurou* (1 Cor.1:18), which may be read as both 'the word of the cross' and 'the crucified word,' God's disarticulated eloquence.

(Bauerschmidt, 1999: 51)

Julian's encounter with the body operates as a kind of opaque point that constantly invites endless inventive interpretation:

For Julian, what she sees-Christ's body is like an inexhaustible detailed land-scape that requires more than a lifetime to comprehend, and her subsequent interpretation of what she saw is always more seeing, by which the revelation is shown again and again 'with more fullness in light of his precious love.'

(Bauerschmidt, 1999: 49)

For Bauerschmidt, Julian's encounter with the Body of Christ becomes a nodal point by which one becomes part of a wider community through an interpretative encounter that creates a social bond:

It is Jesus's crucified body that Julian 'reads' as her revelatory text; what is primary is not the subjective response aroused by meditation on Christ's body, but the message of Love that is revealed there. In this [. . .] understanding of Christ's body, Julian moves away from the experiential emphasis of affective piety, yet we shall see that she does not succumb to the 'contemplative' [apophatic] temptation to consign all that is sensual to merely a preparatory stage of prayer. . . . [Moreover] we see this Love displayed not simply as an individual's consolation amidst the brute forces of a heartless world, *but* as the social bond that grounds 'the lyfe of alle mankind that shalle be savyd.'

(Bauerschmidt, 1999: 36)

Proceeding with a sinthomatic analysis must be seen as a clinical response to the forms of subjectivity that come from this globalised totality without limit. Miller argued that the previous era of the paternal metaphor means that it had the security of discontinuity – categories and segmentation of concepts – but in this era, the nosology of psychosis, neurosis and perversion are defunct manifestations of the All. Thus, what takes precedence in a sinthomatic analysis is a response to the saturating effect of the 'machine of the not-all.' It, therefore, proceeds not through categorisations but via the concept of knotting. The Sinthome is what radically does not work, but it will knot together the body as imaginary, symbolic and real in a way that is specific to that person. Interesting, the knot as a conceptual point was important for Julian of Norwich also:

The soul is preciously knitted to Him in its making by a knot so subtle and so mighty that it is oned into God. In this oneing, it is made endlessly holy.

(Julian of Norwich, 2015: 80)

However, Lacan believed that the encounter with the Sinthome needs to go beyond pure inward contemplation – a problem he encountered with Joyce. He criticised this in his Seminar 24, which can be interpreted as 'Love is the failure of the one-blunder.' In short, his argument centres on the importance of the creative act and encounter with the Sinthome, moving from this point outward to create a social structure.

Another interpretation of this seminar is 'Love is the failure of the One-conscious.' Meaning that our confrontation with the Sinthome and the Oneness of its encounter entails an ethical encounter outward. For Lacan – and like the mystic Julian – this can only happen through an act of Love.

However, this Love should not be understood as pure sentimentalism; it is based on the importance of creating a symbolic structure in which it can take place. For Julian, it is, therefore, political, but for Lacan, it relates to the concept of the School – the necessary place where analysts learn to handle transference and the place for invention.

Conclusion: A Revised Letourgia – The Work of the School and Negativity

When looking at the work of Pseudo-Dionysius and Nicholas of Cusa, the combinations of negation and affirmation are always set within a structure: a hierarchy. This is a necessary structure that must be transmitted. (Hierarchy is a term not invented by some dry scholastic theologian but by the Father of Mystical Theology himself.)

And can we not see this traditional apophatic element at work in Lacanian practice today where the One-All-Alone of the analytic act takes place in the Body of the School, thus negating any tendency toward the idiotic (the privatised)? The Millerian concept of the School is one of the distinguishing aspects of its current focus in the analytic community. As Papada states:

> The School is 'the organism in which there is work to be accomplished. It is inseparable from the training to be dispensed.' The contribution Lacan makes to the formation of analysts is to assert that analysts are not taught and trained by other analysts. There is nothing universal about the analytic discourse. The analytic discourse cannot be taught. Instead, analysts are formed by their own analysis, as Lacan made clear in the proposition of October 9 1967, on the Psychoanalyst of the School.' One becomes a psychoanalyst through the experience of encountering the real through one's symptom.
>
> (Papada, 2020: 6)

The idea of psychoanalysis as a profession cannot be communicated positively in university pedagogy as a build-up of positive experience that makes one an analyst. No, knowledge of psychoanalysis is different from becoming an analyst. On the contrary, it is much more negative than this. The transmission of psychoanalysis is equal to the analysis itself. One becomes an analyst on the completion of their own singular analysis.[9]

Just as an analyst is singular and becomes an analyst through their own analysis, so the operation of the School operates not like a normal community but through a singularity. As Miller explains,

> there is no exception, but rather an ensemble, or rather a series of exceptions, of solitudes incomparable to each other [. . .] the school is Not-All in the sense that it is logically inconsistent and presents itself in the form of a series in which a law of formation is missing.
>
> (Papada, 2021)

Reflecting on this, Tassara states:

> [The School reflects] the productive *docta ignorantia* Lacan took from took from Nicholas of Cusa, a thirteenth-century German philosopher and theologian. In opposition to crass ignorance, docta refers to a wise ignorance, which is situated in the juncture between knowing and not-knowing.
>
> (Tassara, 2020: 63)

The question of non-knowledge and ignorance is central to the experience of the School. The analyst is defined by his passion for ignorance. This non-knowledge – something intricately linked to the mystical tradition – should be distinguished from the Bataillian notion of non-knowledge, which Lacan has always tried to distinguish. For

Lacan, this is not to be confused with the experience of ineffable affective alterity. Instead, it is primarily structural and defined with a craft; work – a use of cultivated ignorance put to work in the structure of the analytic setting to create the field of invention.[10]

And what is this analytic identity that comes from the School's not-all? It is a non-identity. It is an attestation of a desire that is – ultimately – negative by saying what has been stripped away. As Brousse states:

> Passing from analysand to analyst is to mobilise the logic of the not-all, a plunge into the unknown. Homophonic in French, you may read this as you will: 'un' or 'One.' In fact, it is a matter of agreeing to occupy that place which J.-A Miller, in his 2007–2008 course, characterised as the *place de plus personne* – the place of no-one anymore. The void, the null . . . Noting here that truth is related to Jouissance he proposed, 'the truth says of itself *je me demens, je demens, je me defile, je me defends* – I'm ducking, I'm dodging, I'm flitting, I'm fending off.'
> (Brousse, 2022: 66)

And as these candidates are speaking, the analysts of the Jury listen to a change in speech. They listen to rhythms and repetitions that show a transformation: a negative shift that says all that is left is a body and a 'mark. It is to identify as waste, surplus, outside phallic systems of value' (J.-A. Miller, 1989). Ultimately, an analysis aims at a form of subjectivity that has become a positivised void. They are left with the bare essentials for inventing fictions – new ways of situating themselves in the social bond.

In the final instance, the 'full apophasis' of the psychoanalytic, like traditional negative theology, is about the possibility of creating a structure, not a singular positive experience, in a world that horrifically saturates us with false positives.

Notes

1 'Mysticism' is a modern term that appeared after the term 'mystical.' It has connotations of changed inward states and religious experience, while the earlier term – related to mystical theology – did not have this experientialist focus.

2 This transition to the 'affective' has its roots in the Western Christian tradition as 'affective Dionysianism,' as we can see in the work of Thomas Gallus, which had an influence on the Victorines with their emotional understanding of divine receptivity as opposed to a divine form of epistemic unknowing. This 'affective' strand is eventually passed down through the west until finally, we come to the psychologisation of the mystical with the work of William James. He argued that religion's root is a private, affective, emotional experience of the divine on which institutional, linguistic and intellectual elements are bolted as secondary phenomena.

   Much work has been undoing this misapprehension of the apophatic as synonymous with the affective. We see this in the work of Andrew Louth, Peter Tyler and Denys Turner. They argue that the mystical concept – in short – is not being given the negative weight that it is due because of this psychologisation.

3 This idea is something that Wilfried Ver Eecke follows in his work *Denial, Negation, and the Forces of the Negative*, which makes a comparison and reading of the role of

the negative in the work of Freud and Hegel. For Hegel, negation plays a crucial role in the unfolding of his philosophy, but for Freud, dissolution is central in the mechanisms of denial and repression. However, Ver Eecke argues that negation mediates toward the absolute spirit in Hegel and individuation in Freud.

Moreover, we also see this in the work of Mari Ruti with her focus on the need to recover the sense of healing in structural psychoanalytic perspectives. She believes that the heuristic of constitutive lack – although crucially important – can leave one cold to existential agony. Of course, negativity is central in articulating contradictions in power systems and the formation of subjection/subjectivity, but psychoanalysis – in its original Freudian conception – is a practice of healing; it aims toward making sense of the negative, of sublimating it.

4   But also – I think – the more interesting negation regarding Lacan is his negation as a clinician. Indeed, if you look at the anglophone reception of Lacan, it's almost as if his radical negativity can only exist in critical theory and a kind of dispersal amongst the humanities. Yet, when it comes to pure analysis – clinical analysis, the training of analysts – his presence exists beyond intellectual curiosity in France and Brazil, and to a lesser extent, Ireland. Why? It is no coincidence that these countries are also Catholic; Catholicism being home to western mystical tradition; a symbolic that was pre-determined for Lacan's radical work of unsaying and negation as therapy.

5   In his work *The Psychoanalytic Mystic*, Michael Eigen is a primary example. He argues that pleasure and desire as positive manifestations protect us from Jouissance. Jouissance – for Eigen – becomes a kind of arch-affectivism, a sea of wordless feeling. Apart from creating a common conflation that many scholars do when it comes to overusing the term for Eigen, it almost becomes an affective meta-language, a pleasure greater than pleasure itself that involves a leaving behind of things for a sublime wordless *private* experience. However, as soon as we present Jouissance as an 'affective grounding' of any kind – it does not matter how dark and radical it is – we are operating in the positive realm of what Lacan called phallic jouissance.

Another example of this affective approach to a positivised absence is found in the work of Amy Hollywood in her mystical theological work *Sensible Ecstasy*. She argues that the distinction between the poles of phallic Jouissance and other Jouissance are to do with experiences of unitive religious experience and experiences of fragmentation. The latter, for Hollywood, is synonymous with the feminine mystic. Again, this framing within an affective framework locks it in a logic of phallic jouissance, even if framed in negative language.

6   The letter is the first mark on the body that instantiates language. The analytic act involves confronting this letter.

7   A neologism that means speakingbeing invented by Lacan.

8   Indeed, the idea of a signifier cut off from context directly applies to Julian for Bauerschmidt argues that the audience for who she was writing her work is strangely absent. She says that her work has yet to be performed.

9   The process of identification means identifying oneself as an analyst to an inverted jury – inverted in that it is not made up only of the qualified but of unqualified analysands, who vouch for the candidate's transformation. The candidate's identity will be ascertained by listening to an account of what they deem a successful analysis.

10 Miller expands on this form of non-knowledge and shows how its apophatic operation needs to be distinguished from the common usage we usually attribute to it today in terms of the affective. Reflecting on this subtle operation of Jouissance so as not to lock it within a primary affective interpretation, Lacan said in seminar 23 that the 'real sets fire to everything, but the real is cold. The fire that burns hot is really a mask of the real. The real must be sought elsewhere on the side of absolute 0.' This zero is mentioned to separate it from the Freudian conception of libido linked to the positivism of the era.

There is a warning here for analysts not to get caught up in the realm of the affect when interpreting jouissance. The 'hot fire' is a mask of the real means that to get caught up in the affect is to misrecognise its operation. Miller, in his seminar in the Analysts Banquet explains that to navigate the 'confusion of the zero' to access the function of non-knowledge, which is necessary for an analysis, then 'it is necessary to, first of all, emphasise the non, not to remain ignorant about the non, and without going so far as to say that negation does not exist, to be attentive to the modalities of negation.' He then explains that to explain this modality of negation, it is crucial that one does not get caught up in its pathological presentation, what is known as the horror of the real as we confront it in the singularity of an analytic case. Hence, he sets out a way of transcribing it in a transmissible and propaedeutic structure.

References

Akhtar, Salman, & Mary Kay O'Neil. (2018) *On Freud's Negation*. Routledge.

Bauerschmidt, Frederick Christian. (1999) *Julian of Norwich and the Mystical Body Politic of Christ*. University of Notre Dame Press.

Bowles, Nellie. (2018, May 18) "Jordan Peterson, Custodian of the Patriarchy." *The New York Times*. As retrieved on August 10, 2022, <www.nytimes.com/2018/05/18/style/jordan-peterson-12-rules-for-life.html>

Brousse, Marie-Hélène. (2022) *The Feminine: A Mode of Jouissance*. Lacanian Press.

Carrette, Jeremy, & Richard King. (2004) *Selling Spirituality: The Silent Takeover of Religion* (1st ed.). Routledge.

Coaston, Jane. (2022, July 23) "Try to Resist the Call of the Doomers." *The New York Times*. As retrieved on September 10, 2022, <www.nytimes.com/2022/07/23/opinion/climate-doomers-possibility.html>

Cusanus, Nicholas. (2007) *Of Learned Ignorance*. Wipf and Stock Publishers.

Dickson, E. J. (2020, September 15) "Wellness Influencers Are Calling Out Qanon Conspiracy Theorists for Spreading Lies." *Rolling Stone*. As retrieved on August 1, 2022, <www.rollingstone.com/culture/culture-news/qanon-wellness-influencers-seane-corn-yoga-1059856/>

Dionysius, Pseudo. (1987) *Pseudo-Dionysius: The Complete Works*. Paulist Press.

Dupont, Laurent. (2020) "Formation of the Analyst, the End of Analysis." *Psychoanalytical Notebooks*, *36*, 15–37.

Eyers, Tom. (2012) *Lacan and the Concept of the Real* (1st ed.). Palgrave Macmillan.

Julian of Norwich. (2015) *Revelations of Divine Love*. Oxford University Press.

Kesel, Marc De. (2009) *Eros and Ethics: Reading Jacques Lacan's Seminar VII* (1st ed.). State University of New York Press.

Lacan, Jacques. (1977) *Seminar XXIV Final-Sessions 1976–1977* (C. Gallagher, Trans.; 1st ed.). Lacan in Ireland. As retrieved on August 8, 2022, <www.lacaninireland.com/web/translations/seminars/>

Lacan, Jacques. (1999) *The Seminars of Jacques Lacan Book XX: On Feminine Sexuality the Limits of Love and Knowledge 1972–1973* (Jacques-Alain Miller, Ed.; 2nd ed.). W.W Norton & Company.

Lembke, Anna. (2021, August 13) "Digital Addictions Are Drowning Us in Dopamine." *Wall Street Journal*. As retrieved on July 4, 2022, <www.wsj.com/articles/digital-addictions-are-drowning-us-in-dopamine-11628861572>

McIntosh, Mark A. (1998). *Mystical Theology: The Integrity of Spirituality and Theology (Challenges in Contemporary Theology)* (Lewis A. Jones & Gareth, Eds.; 3rd ed.). Wiley-Blackwell.

Miller, Jacques-Alain. (1989) *The Analysts Banquet* (A. Duncan, Trans.). NLS.

Miller, Jacques-Alain. (2019) *Paradigms of Jouissance*. London Society NLS.

Miller, Jacques-Alain. (2021) "The One Is the Letter." *Psychoanalytical Notebooks*, autumn/winter (37/38), 13–44.

Miller, Paul Allen. (2007) "Lacan's Antigone: The Sublime Object and the Ethics of Interpretation." *Phoenix*, *61*(1/2), 1–14.

Millman, Oliver. (2022, May 19) "Suicides Indicate a Wave of 'Doomerism' Over the Escalating Climate Crisis." *The Guardian*. As retrieved on October 1, 2022, <www.theguardian.com/environment/2022/may/19/climate-suicides-despair-global-heating>

Moncayo, Raul. (2019) *Lalangue, Sinthome, Jouissance, and Nomination: A Reading Companion and Commentary on Lacan's Seminar XXIII on the Sinthome*. Taylor & Francis Group.

Papada, Peggy. (2020) "Editorial." *Psychoanalytical Notebooks*, *36*, 5–8.

Papada, Peggy. (2021, March 3) "Formation of the Analyst." *The Lacanian Review*. As retrieved on October 1, 2022, <www.thelacanianreviews.com/2988-2/>

Peterson, Jordan. (2018) *12 Rules for Life: An Antidote to Chaos*. Penguin UK.

Rose, Marika. (2017) "Machines of Loving Grace." *The Journal of Cultural and Religious Theory*, *16*(2), 240–258.

Seymour, Richard. (2019) *The Twittering Machine*. The Indigo Press.

Stevens, Alexandre. (2007) "Love and Sex Beyond Identification." In Veronique Voruz (Ed.), *The Later Lacan: An Introduction* (1st ed., pp. 211–221). State University of New York Press.

Tassara, Patricia. (2020) "Supervision." *Psychoanalytical Notebooks*, *36*, 57–63.

Tyler, Peter. (2011) *The Return to the Mystical: Ludwig Wittgenstein, Teresa of Avila, and the Christian Mystical Tradition* (1st ed.). Continuum.

Voruz, Veronique. (2022) "Acephalic Litter as a Phallic Letter." In Luke Thurston (Ed.), *Reinventing the Symptom* (pp. 111–140). Other Press, LLC.

Waldman, Katy. (2021, March 26) "The Rise of Therapy-Speak." *The New Yorker*. As retrieved on August 2, 2022, <www.newyorker.com/culture/cultural-comment/the-rise-of-therapy-speak>

Wright, Colin. (2014) "Happiness Studies and Wellbeing: A Lacanian Critique of Contemporary Conceptualisations of the Cure." *Culture Unbound*, *6*(4), 791–813. As retrieved on September 20, 2022, <https://doi.org/10.3384/cu.2000.1525.146791>

Žižek, Slavoj. (2022) *Surplus-Enjoyment: A Guide for the Non-Perplexed*. Bloomsbury Academic.

Zupančič, Alenka. (2017) "The Apocalypse Is (Still) Disappointing." *Journal of the Circle for Lacanian Ideology Critique*, 10 & 12.

Section 3

Clinical Implications

Chapter 7

Negation beyond Neurosis

Leon S. Brenner

Between 1885 and 1899, Sigmund Freud attempted to substantiate his meta-psychological model of a group of disorders which he termed "neuro-psychoses." This group included hysteria, obsession, phobias, hallucinatory psychosis, and paranoia. Developing a psychoanalytic etiology, in his papers, "The Neuro-Psychoses of Defense" (1894) and "Further Remarks on the Neuro-Psychoses of Defense" (1896), Freud posited that all of these disorders originate in an *active effort* on behalf of the subject, rather than an exterior, deterministic, or hereditary factor. Freud (1894) specifically described the origin of these disorders as a moment when the subject is:

> faced with an experience, an idea or a feeling which aroused such a distressing affect that the subject decided to forget about it because he had no confidence in his power to resolve the contradiction between that incompatible idea and his ego by means of thought-activity.
>
> (p. 47)

At the time Freud called this type of *active forgetting* "repression" and argued that it operates by detaching a sum of excitation or affect from a disturbing idea with the aim of turning a strongly conflictual ideal into a weak one.

As Freud developed his metapsychology, he arrived at the conclusion that a single repression does not operate at the origin of every neuro-psychosis. He (1896) argued that in the case of psychosis, "a special method or mechanism of repression which is peculiar to it" is at play (p. 175). Freud (1894) described the workings of this mechanism by positing that, unlike neurotic repression, in psychosis, the subject "rejects [*Verwift*] the incompatible idea together with its affect and behaves as if the idea had never occurred to the ego at all" (p. 58). On the same note, in his later papers "Fetishism" (1927) and "Splitting of the Ego in the Process of Defense" (1938), Freud develops the concept of "disavowal" (*Verleugnung*) to connote a denial of a perception of an unacceptable piece of reality situated at the origin of perversion.

Freud (1914) asserted that "the theory of repression is the corner-stone on which the whole structure of psychoanalysis rests" (p. 15). He further elaborated on three

DOI: 10.4324/9781003375920-10

different modes of "repression" that are involved in the constitution of the subject in its three structural modalities that are commonly referred to in psychoanalysis as neurosis, perversion, and psychosis. It is worth noting that, building on Freud and Jacques Lacan's teaching in another publication, I have developed a concept of "autistic foreclosure" as the underlying cause of autism (Brenner, 2020).

Freud's investigation of the different modes of "repression" provided him insight into the unique facets of the neuro-psychoses. He accomplishes this by analyzing the subject "at the level of its language" (Foucault, 2006, p. 339) to distinguish the different "repressions" underlying its different formations. Correspondingly, in the psychoanalytic clinic, Freud (1915) asserted that the psychoanalyst must listen to the analysand's speech and outline the intricacies of their discourse. By analyzing the unique alterations in their discourse, the psychoanalyst can determine the nature of the "repression" that shapes psychic reality, allowing them to effectively guide the analysand through the course of analysis (p. 150).

The present chapter centers on a specific form of discursive alteration that Freud labels as negation (*Verneinung*). The chapter begins by demonstrating how Freud addresses negation as a unique discursive structure that is the hallmark of repression (*Verdrängung*); proceeding to demonstrate how negation also functions as the hallmark of the structure of the neurotic subject. Following a discussion of the varied discursive implementations of negation in psychotic and perverse discourse, negation is posed, not only as the hallmark of neurosis, but as expressing a distinctive feature of each and every subjective structure. Finally, the chapter presents a distinction between the archetypal use of negation in neurosis and autism through a comparison between the "fort da" game and "on/off conducts," offering a more nuanced reading of the discursive manifestations of negation in psychoanalytic practice.

Negation and Repression

In his paper "Negation" (1925), Freud attempts to explain the nature of the relationship between a linguistic negation (*Verneinung*) and the mechanism of repression (*Verdrängung*). Freud begins his paper by providing the reader with several examples of some peculiar uses analysands make of negative judgments in their speech. For instance, Freud gives a classic example of a repudiation of an idea that comes to the analysand's mind through its projection: "[n]ow you'll think I mean to say something insulting, but really I've *no* such intention" (p. 235). These kinds of negations appear many times in the course of analysis, rightfully drawing the analyst's attention to them. In the same vein, an analysand might begin recounting a dream by saying "the dream began like this, but it is *not* very interesting, so I'll go straight to what is important." This type of articulation might compel some analysts to quickly ask the analysand to concentrate on that "*not* interesting" part and recount it in great detail. In one of the examples provided by Freud in the paper, an analysand spontaneously formulates the following negative judgment: "you ask who this person in the dream can be. It's *not* my mother" (p. 235). Freud states that in these examples, the analysands voluntarily articulate their response in the form of a negation: they introduce an explicit opposition to something that was not addressed by the psychoanalyst and could well have been disregarded. As a result, Freud insists that such negations cannot be simply disregarded; on the contrary, they should be scrutinized by the analyst.

Freud (1925) comments that it might be tempting to interpret these negations in an inverted form, thinking to oneself: "so *it is* his mother!" However, Freud hints that such rash interpretations should be reserved for party tricks, where one might ask their interlocutor: "what do you think was furthest from your mind at that time?," proceeding to interject that it is that thing exactly that was at stake (p. 235). Accordingly, Freud emphasizes that the clinical value of negation is not confined to the notion that a negated predicate such as "it is *not* my mother" can yield the affirmation of the same predicate, namely, "it *is* your mother." We see that it is through his account of negation that Freud attempts to convey something of the nature of repression itself. This is rendered explicit when Freud emphasizes that what is at stake in the patient's voluntary use of a negative judgment is not strictly related to the negated predicate but rather his opposition to the affirmation of something unconscious. In other words, it concerns the work of a defensive censoring mechanism that Freud calls repression (p. 236).

Repression as a form of defense (*Abwer*) is one of the most salient concepts in Freud's work. Freud describes repression as a dual mechanism entailing: (1) a specific form of defensive censorship that diverts distressing content from consciousness into the unconscious; as well as (2) the persistence of repressed content in consciousness through symptomatic behavior. Freud (1915) explains that repression functions in relation to two elements that are generally linked together in the psyche: ideas and affects. According to Freud, in repression, a conflictual idea that exceeds a certain threshold of affective strength is detached from its corresponding "quota of affect" and diverted from consciousness into the unconscious (p. 152). Both the ideas and the detached affects that come under the sway of repression are termed by Freud the "derivatives of the repressed" (p. 154). They are the by-product of repression and shape the reality and the behavior of the subject. These derivatives take part in the formation of new meanings between ideas in the unconscious and are also portrayed through the insistence of isolated affects in consciousness. When doing so, they are considered to be the indications of a "return of the repressed" (p. 154) and manifest themselves in what Freud calls neurotic symptoms such as conversion disorders or obsessive thoughts, dreams, slips of the tongue, jokes, and, in our case, *negative judgments* (p. 177). Freud argued that the psychoanalysis of neurosis revolves around these derivatives. He claimed that in psychoanalysis these derivatives are produced by the analysand in an attempt to pass the censorship of repression (p. 177). By removing the resistance to repression, Freud argues that one can experience a decrease in the magnitude of the suffering produced by his or her symptoms.

Freud's interest in negation basically stems from the assumption that subjective reality cannot be solely identified with what a person consciously says or thinks but is also determined by what he or she denies, refuses, or represses from consciousness (Ronen, 2014, pp. 21–22). Many times an obsessive analysand would confess to "not wanting to leave his partner" but "constantly fantasize about breaking it off and being with others." In other cases, a hysteric analysand will describe the painstaking process of studying to a final exam yet remain baffled as to the cause of the disabling bodily pains that again and again prevent them from actually going to the university and taking the test. It is this split between what one says and the contradictory way one acts that is exemplified in Freud's development of the concept of negation. Negation, therefore, is considered in psychoanalysis as a passage from one register to another: from the unconscious to consciousness (Lacan, 1997, p. 155). As Freud (1925) puts it: "to negate something in a judgment is, at bottom to say: 'this is something which I should prefer to repress'" (p. 236). It is its quality of being one of the most evident manifestations of the return of the repressed in the subject's speech that brings Freud (1925) to argue that negation is the "hallmark of repression" (p. 236).

Already in Freud's (1894) early work, repression is defined not only as a mechanism of defense but, more specifically, as an affirmation and demarcation of the division between consciousness and the unconscious (p. 162). Basing himself on Freud's (1938) notion of the *Spaltung*, Lacan (1992) argues that this division is an essential quality of the neurotic subject (p. 102). When addressed as the "split subject" (Lacan, 2001, pp. 70–185), that is, when not reduced to either of the domains or agencies presented above, the neurotic subject is identified by Lacan as nothing but the psychic construct embodying this very division (Fink, 1997, p. 45). Now, if repression is defined as the psychic mechanism constituting the division between consciousness and the unconscious, and the neurotic subject is defined as this very division, we can then describe repression as the most fundamental mechanism in neurosis: in other words, as its cause. Further, because negation is the "hallmark of repression," we can now say that it is in fact the hallmark of neurosis as well. Therefore, Freud suggests that psychoanalysts pay attention to such linguistic formulations and use them to lend weight to a diagnosis of neurosis based on the evidence of repression. Following this diagnosis, the analyst can better situate themselves in the transference in order to direct the treatment.

Negation beyond Neurosis

Negation is a multifaceted type of linguistic operator. Accordingly, in the field of logic, negation takes on itself many forms such as: modal negation, intuitionistic negation, paraconsistent negation, and many-valued negation as well as contraposition negation, de Morgan's negation, double negation, and more. Therefore, going back to Freud's paper "Negation" (1925), we might say that in his paradigmatic example he particularly refers to a modal negation of an existential type in which the analysand negates the existence of at least one instance of a property ("it is *not* my mother"). And indeed, Lacan (1997) emphasizes that there is a whole range of negations in different languages, each with different characteristics (p. 155). Therefore, I suggest that the investigation of the variance in their discursive structure might provide hints to the diagnosis of the subject in its varied manifestations.

Recall that the negation in Freud's paper is a linguistic utterance that testifies to the work of repression. Be that as it may, even Freud himself studied the use of negations in his investigation of other psychic structures. A good example can be found in his work on the concept of disavowal (*Verleugnung*). In his paper on the case of Little Hans, Freud (1909) describes the former testifying that his sister has a penis, even when experiencing contrary evidence. Hans' disavowal of his sister's lack of a penis is then said to be expressed on a conscious intellectual level "she does *not not* have a penis" ("her widdler's still quite small") which contradicts him knowing that she doesn't (p. 11). Freud takes this unique "both/and logic" expressed in Hans' negation as a hallmark for the working of disavowal and the perverse subjective structure (Swales, 2012, p. 80).

In his seminar on the psychoses, Lacan (1997) argues that, in the same way negation is an emblem of the return of the repressed in the neurotic's conscious speech, it can also attest to the relationship between what has been rejected by the psychotic and reappears in the real (p. 13). Lacan directs us to Freud's "Psycho-Analytic Notes on an Autobiographical Account of a Case of Paranoia" (1911), where he discusses how Schreber's delusional erotomania materializes in relation to four different types of contradictory statements that include a negative judgment: "it's not I who love him, it's she," "it's not him that I love, it's her," "I do not love him, I hate him," and finally, "I do not love him at all – I do not love anyone" (pp. 63–65). Lacan (1997) argues that in each of these statements and "the not, the negation" demonstrates a different type of alienation in psychotic phenomena such as jealousy, depersonalization, and the deterioration of the other (p. 42), all of which culminate in Schreber's "divine erotomania" (p. 311). In doing so, Lacan demonstrates that negation can also function as a hallmark for psychotic phenomena and the progression of the psychotic process.

Negation in Autism

The final section of this chapter will draw the reader's attention to a particular type of negation that seems to be a hallmark of autism. It presents itself in what Jean-Claude Maleval (2009, 2015, 2021) calls "on/off conducts." Its singular nature will be emphasized by contrasting it with another brand of neurotic negation that Freud identified in the "Fort-da" game.

"Fort-da" is a term coined by Freud (1920) to describe a game he observed his young grandson playing. The game involved the child throwing away a wooden spool (a simple cylindrical toy) with a string attached, and then pulling the string to retrieve it. Freud observed that the child seemed to be using the game as a way of dealing with the anxiety rendered by the absence of his mother (pp. 14–17). It enables the child to deal with this unbearable absence by becoming an active factor in the object's loss rather than merely a passive victim. The child does so by selecting an object that is detached from the mother but retains some of her dynamic qualities and inserting it into a symbolic dialectic where its absence is rendered present through its negation. Freud identifies in the child's game the use of a symbolic opposition between two arbitrary terms that he refers to as "Fort" ("gone" in German) and "da" ("there" in German). In the "Fort-da," the negated object is not directly stated but signified in the opposition between these two terms. In this sense, the opposition between the "gone" and the "there" does not refer to the mother itself but to a loss associated with a primal type of repression (Freud, 1925, pp. 237–238).

Laplanche and Leclaire (1972) add that it is through the Fort-da game that the child's whole symbolic universe is established (p. 153). Their argument corresponds to Lacan's (2006) reformulation of the Fort-da game as the moment "at which the child is born into language" (p. 262). He adds that, in this moment, a "symbol" that eclipses the negation of the object is introduced in its place. Lacan describes this as an act that "gives birth to the symbol" (p. 262) – that which Jean Hyppolite terms the "symbol of negation" in one of Lacan's seminars (Lacan, 2006, pp. 752–753).

The negation implemented in the Fort-da game is homologous to the one presented in Freud's paper "Negation" (1925) where it is also a hallmark of the movement between unconscious and conscious discourse. Like the analysand's "it is *not* my mother," the Fort-da game is a reiteration of the derivatives of the repressed. In other words, it is a signifying structure that attests to the return of the repressed in a different guise. It entails a representation of something that is solely lacking through its negation. Just as the negative judgment concerning "mother" does not divulge the repressed content but only testifies to the working of repression, the "Fort-da" attests to the fact that something was lost without us knowing what that something is.

According to Maleval (2021), autistic subjects do not typically engage in the Fort-da game in its variations. However, many autistic subjects are attracted to a particular type of behavior that he calls "on/off conducts" (*conduites on/off*) (p. 246). These types of behavior commonly entail turning lights on and off, opening and closing doors, or breaking or throwing away objects without awaiting their return but they are also expressed through particular forms of linguistic utterances. Maleval refers to a detailed description of the latter in a case study of a six-year-old autistic child named Arnold (Guillas, 1999). Arnold's therapist reports how he uses an on/off conduct to temper his uncontrollable urge to swallow every object he sees, as though it was food – i.e., to treat his unregulated oral drive. Arnold bases this conduct on his acquaintance with a book of images that also includes images of food stuff. He skims these images, tapping each of the images, naming it, articulating sentences which affirm their presence and absence: "the strawberries"/"no more strawberries"; "the potatoes"/"no more potatoes"; "the plums"/"no more plums"; "the chocolate"/"no more chocolate, finished"; etc. In a later session, Arnold generalizes this conduct to include objects that do not refer to oral satisfaction but, according to his therapist, have to do with other issues that are important for him: "the snowman, goodbye, no more. The soup, not here, later, no more. The little boy, goodbye, not here, no more. Grapes, no more, goodbye," etc. All of these linguistic utterances implement negative judgments that are organized in the structure of "there is"/"there is no more" (cited in Maleval, 2021).

According to Maleval (2021), both on/off conducts and Fort-da games in their many variations come to deal with the negativity of language and the pain of the loss of an object of libidinal investment (p. 246). However, he emphasizes that they illustrate two distinct modes of relation to the object and attest to specific ways to treat it. I will expand on their distinction in the following section of this chapter.

In Arnold's on/off conduct, he attempts to engender the loss of an object that is experienced as being intrusive and excessively present in the child's world. He first designates its presence with a word tied to an image ("strawberries") and then opposes it with a negation that symbolizes its absence ("*no* more strawberries"). The child does so because no initial symbolic designation of loss is established in his world (Maleval, 2009, pp. 144–145). Conversely, in the Fort-da game the absence of the object precedes its presence in the oppositional couple Fort-da. In other words, in the Fort-da game, the child attempts to compensate for the real absence of the mother through the affirmative symbolic designation of a loss (Lacan, 1988, pp. 173, 178, 2001, p. 62).

On/off conducts and Fort-da games are also distinct in their designation of the object at stake. While in on/off conducts the object is clearly stated and only then negated, in the Fort-da game, neither the "Fort" nor the "da" designate the object at stake. They refer to an absence without explicitly naming what is absent. Therefore, we see that the Fort-da is a mode of symbolic play, where the negation of the presence of the mother is symbolized and mastered. In contrast, with the on/off conduct, there is no substitution, metaphor or symbolic play, there is a negation that is implemented for a sake of establishing a limit to jouissance and a sense of order and predictability in the world (Maleval, 2021, p. 246).

The Fort-da game is sometimes described as a coping strategy associated with the loss of the object. In contrast, on/off conducts are considered to be coping strategies that provide many autistic subjects with a way through which jouissance can be rendered tolerable. Starting from a very basic coupling between bodily sensations and objects associated with sounds, we see many autistic subjects progress in their on/off conducts to associations between words, developing more intricate coping abilities, strengthening their protective function and enriching their capacities (Maleval, 2015, p. 772).

Maleval (2009) proceeds to argue that the distinction between the Fort-da game and the on/off conduct is also rooted in the fact that the former is applied at the level of the signifier, while the latter is achieved at the level of the sign (p. 144). The distinction between the signifier and the sign in Lacan's teaching is thoroughly developed in another publication (Brenner, 2023). For the sake of our discussion, I will briefly mention that, for Lacan, a sign is a signifying unit that embodies a direct and rigid bi-univocal relationship between a sensory form and a referent (Lacan, 1997, p. 167). A signifier, on the other hand, is a phonological element that by itself does not signify anything and does not refer to any object or concept.

Therefore, there is no natural relationship between the signifier and the signified. It is only when several signifiers are opposed one against the other that the signified is produced. In the Fort-da game, two signifiers are brought in opposition in order to signify the dimension of loss. In the on/off conduct, an object invested with jouissance is linked with a sign that is then effaced by the use of a linguistic negation. In other words, through the on/off conduct, the subject gains mastery over a sum of jouissance by associating it with a sign that can be controlled by being linguistically negated (Brenner, 2020, p. 243).

In summary, we see that on/off conducts exemplify the use of a negation in singular discursive structures that are reserved to the autistic subjective structure. Through a negation of a sign, on/off conducts are able to treat the jouissance of the body by engendering a lack in a world that is characterized by an excess of presence. They do so by directly naming the object at stake, not through symbolic play, but through a conscious delimitation of the boundary of the body, establishing a regulation of what goes in and out. Because there is no repression in autism, the negation in the on/off conduct does not function as the hallmark of repression but as the hallmark of a different type of psychic mechanism which is the cause of autism: autistic foreclosure (Brenner, 2020).

Conclusion

A major heuristic in psychoanalysis states that, unlike an intake with a psychologist, the analyst must not be rash in making a diagnosis. Be that as it may, many times when analysts make a diagnosis they are led to make quick assumptions about the analysand's speech based on their biases, passions, difficulties, or inadequate information (Lacan, 2006, p. 225). Therefore, Lacan suggests that the analyst should *support the analysand's speech* by listening carefully rather than just thinking that they know what their speech has to say; that is, they should endeavor to *not understand too quickly* (p. 359). In this chapter I have applied this psychoanalytic dictum to the analysis of negation in the analysand's speech. After discussing its varied discursive implementations we come to the conclusion that negation might be the hallmark of repression, and in that sense neurosis, but *not* only of that. Beyond neurosis, I suggest negation might be considered a hallmark of the subject in general. It is the elaboration of the different discursive structures of negation and the function they fulfill for different subjective economies that is put forward as a stepping stone to the development of a differential psychoanalytic clinic. This in turn warrants a different direction in the treatment of neurosis, perversion, psychosis and autism based on the analysis of negation.

References

Brenner, L. S. (2020). *The Autistic Subject: On the Threshold of Language*. Springer Nature.
Brenner, L. S. (2023). The Autistic Pseudo-Signifier: Imaginary Dialectization of Signs in the Clinic of Autism. *Theory & Psychology*, 33(4), 535–554. https://doi.org/10.1177/09593543231176543

Fink, B. (1997). *The Lacanian Subject: Between Language and Jouissance*. Princeton University Press.

Foucault, M. (2006). *History of Madness in the Age of Reason*. Routledge.

Freud, S. (1894). The Neuro-Psychoses of Defence. In J. Strachey (Ed.), *The Standard Edition of the Complete Psychological Works of Sigmund Freud, Volume III (1893–1899): Early Psycho-Analytic Publications* (pp. 41–61). Hogarth/Institute of Psycho-analysis.

Freud, S. (1896). Further Remarks on the Neuro-Psychoses of Defense. In Strachey (Ed.), *The Standard Edition of the Complete Psychological Works of Sigmund Freud, Volume III (1893–1899): Early Psycho-Analytic Publications* (pp. 157–185). Hogarth Press/Institute of Psycho-analysis.

Freud, S. (1909). Analysis of a Phobia in a Five-Year-Old Boy. In J. Strachey (Ed.), *The Standard Edition of the Complete Psychological Works of Sigmund Freud, Volume X (1909): (1909): Two Case Histories ('Little Hans' and the 'Rat Man')* (pp. 1–150). Hogarth Press/Institute of Psycho-analysis.

Freud, S. (1911). Psycho-Analytic Notes on an Autobiographical Account of a Case of Paranoia (Dementia Paranoides). In J. Strachey (Ed.), *The Standard Edition of the Complete Psychological Works of Sigmund Freud, Volume XII (1911–1913): The Case of Schreber, Papers on Technique and Other Works* (pp. 1–82). Hogarth Press/Institute of Psycho-analysis.

Freud, S. (1914). On the History of the Psycho-Analytic Movement. In J. Strachey (Ed.), *The Standard Edition of the Complete Psychological Works of Sigmund Freud, Volume XIV (1914–1916): On the History of the Psycho-Analytic Movement, Papers on Metapsychology and Other Works* (pp. 1–66). Hogarth Press/Institute of Psycho-analysis.

Freud, S. (1915). Repression. In J. Strachey (Ed.), *The Standard Edition of the Complete Psychological Works of Sigmund Freud, Volume XIV (1914–1916): On the History of the Psycho-Analytic Movement, Papers on Metapsychology and Other Works* (pp. 141–158). Hogarth Press/Institute of Psycho-analysis.

Freud, S. (1920). Beyond the Pleasure Principle. In J. Strachey (Ed.), *The Standard Edition of the Complete Psychological Works of Sigmund Freud, Volume XVIII (1920–1922): Beyond the Pleasure Principle, Group Psychology and Other Works* (pp. 1–64). Hogarth Press/Institute of Psycho-analysis.

Freud, S. (1925). Negation. In J. Strachey (Ed.), *The Standard Edition of the Complete Psychological Works of Sigmund Freud, Volume XIX (1923–1925): The Ego and the Id and Other Works* (pp. 233–240). Hogarth Press/Institute of Psycho-analysis.

Freud, S. (1927). Fetishism. In J. Strachey (Ed.), *The Standard Edition of the Complete Psychological Works of Sigmund Freud, Volume XXI (1927–1931): The Future of an Illusion, Civilization and Its Discontents, and Other Works* (pp. 147–158). Hogarth Press/Institute of Psycho-analysis.

Freud, S. (1938). Splitting of the Ego in the Process of Defense. In J. Strachey (Ed.), *The Standard Edition of the Complete Psychological Works of Sigmund Freud, Volume XXIII: Moses and Monotheism, An Outline of Psycho-Analysis, and Other Works* (pp. 271–278). Hogarth Press/Institute of Psycho-analysis.

Guillas, G. (1999). Que l'Autre Soit. Du Changement Dans l'autisme? *Journée de l'ACF/VLB*, 197–199.

Lacan, J. (1988). *The Seminar of Jacques Lacan, Book I, Freud's Papers on Technique (1953–1954)*. Norton & Company.

Lacan, J. (1992). *The Seminar, Book VII, the Ethics of Psychoanalysis (1959–1960)*. Norton & Company.

Lacan, J. (1997). *The Seminar of Jacques Lacan, Book III, the Psychoses (1955–1956)*. Norton & Company.

Lacan, J. (2001). *The Seminar of Jacques Lacan, Book XI, the Four Fundamental Concepts of Psychoanalysis (1964)*. Norton & Company.

Lacan, J. (2006). *Écrits* (B. Fink, ed.). Norton & Company.

Laplanche, J., & Leclaire, S. (1972). The Unconscious: A Psychoanalytic Study. *Yale French Studies*, (48), 118–175.

Maleval, J.-C. (2009). *L'Autiste et sa Voix*. Seuil.

Maleval, J.-C. (2015). Extension du Spectre de l'Autisme. *L'évolution Psychiatrique*, 90, 764–781.

Maleval, L.-C. (2021). *La difference autistique*. Presses Universitaires de Vincennes.

Ronen, R. (2014). *Art Before the Law: Aesthetics and Ethics*. University of Toronto Press.

Swales, S. (2012). *Perversion: A Lacanian Psychoanalytic Approach to the Subject*. Routledge.

Chapter 8

Spiraling

Cyrus Saint Amand Poliakoff

Language of Our Time

Psychoanalysts listen to words. We listen to read the part of the symptom that addresses the Other, and to bring forward what exists between the lines – what cannot be said. We listen to meet at its horizon, the subjectivity of our time (Lacan, 1953/2006). Words and their gaps implicate a subject within discourses that organize social bonds; they speak the contemporary symptoms of civilization's discontents. These are language inventions that circulate, modalities of jouissance. Lacan often returned to his definition of the signifier that founded the structural clinic: the signifier represents a subject for another signifier, a new definition of subjectivity, the subject of the signifier. The language of the times constitutes a style that responds to what Lacan named the real. Style, the vibe of social symptoms, reflects the encounters with the impossible at stake in each era (Miller, 2022). One enduring name of the real for Lacan was *the impossible to bear*. In psychoanalysis we follow the signifying path of each patient noting what gets repeated and what remains unsayable. Figures of speech reside in the locus of the Other, the dimension of the said. We are subjects of the words of the times. With the digital residence of signifiers, social media, words travel long-distance fast. Turns of speech, witticisms, trends, and their use, cycle rapidly. The meme is the best example of contemporary signifying style.

I'm Spiraling

Since the year 2020, I began to hear a phrase repeated by patients across different sessions: *I am spiraling*. It appeared to be a way to announce and identify a state of subjective disarray. It joins the legacy of various expressions of *I am going crazy*. These expressions employ metaphors: *I'm falling apart, I'm losing my grip, I'm tripping, I'm going off, I'm on one*. They also identify someone with a particular action. They express a state of being, *I am* . . . I heard *I'm spiraling* enough that I began to wonder about the status of this spiral. Naturally, there are the associations that each analysand produces from the word "spiral." This is the nature of the signifying chain according to the definition of the subject of the signifier Lacan

DOI: 10.4324/9781003375920-11

established. A spiral represents a subject for another signifier, and another. Particular significations of "spiral" will not hold across different analysand's constellations of being. Resisting the temptation to generalize from meaning, we can instead investigate the spiral at the level of structure. How to approach structure without folding back into the imaginary of meaning? Lacan's proposal was topology.

Man Is a Torus Animal

As a form, the spiral illustrates a pathway around a central void – circular tracing through repetition that creates a volume. In Lacan's topology, we encounter the spiral within another form, a paradigmatic structure, the torus. From his 1953 Rome Report through his last teachings, the torus preoccupied Lacan. The use of the torus and its conceptualization continued to develop alongside Lacan's evolving response to the project of the Freudian unconscious. Jacques-Alain Miller has elucidated the paradigm shifts following the development from the unconscious to the speaking being to the speaking body (Miller, 2016). In 1953, the topology of the torus served to approach the structure of the subject. Later in *Seminar IX* from 1962, he employed the torus to model the dynamics of demand and desire to account for "the structure of the subject insofar as he speaks" (Lesson March 21). Finally in *Seminar XXIV* from 1976 by studying the manipulation of the torus through cuts, reversals, and knots, Lacan evoked the world and even the universe as toric (Lesson December 14).

In *Seminar IX* Lacan hails man as "a torus animal" (Lesson March 21). Later in *Seminar XXIV*: "[t]here is no progress. Man turns in circles if what I say about his structure is true, namely that the structure of man is toric" (Lesson December 14). Lacan reminds us on March 7th, 1962, that he had first introduced "the structure of the subject as that of a ring" in his Rome Report. Logic establishes the topological schema of the torus:

> [t]o say that this mortal meaning reveals in speech a center that is outside of language is more than a metaphor – it manifests a structure. This structure differs from the spatialization of the circumference or sphere which some people like to schematize the limits of the living being and its environment: it corresponds rather to the relational group that symbolic logic designates topologically as a ring.
>
> (Lacan, 1953/2006, p. 264)

On March 3rd 1962, Lacan presented the torus to his audience,

> [i]t is something that one plays with when it is made of rubber, it is handy, a torus can be deformed, it is round, it is full, for the geometer it is a figure of revolution engendered by revolving a circumference around an axis situated on its plan; the circumference turns; at the end you are surrounded by the torus.

What is generated is a closed surface that looks like an innertube, a holed structure. The structure is distinguished by consisting around two voids, internal and external, where the peripheral exteriority and the central exteriority are continuous. Leaning on topology, Lacan highlights "the surface in the function of the subject" (Lesson March 3).

Lacan challenged longstanding philosophical traditions of employing the sphere to describe organisms and beings. It was a departure from the binary of inside and outside founded by the spherical model. A sphere with a tube pulled through it is a torus. This is also a schema of the body: "[w]hy not note that what we see of the living body is organized like what I called the other day a stick, which is nothing other than a torus" (Lacan, Lesson December 14, 1976). In contrast to a bubble, there is an inside that is also the outside. The interior space, the digestive tract with two orifices, one at the top and one at the bottom, is continuous with exterior space, most notably when both holes are open. Because topology studies surfaces and volumes, it permits us to recognize a logic throughout different deformations and imaginary extrusions. The shape or image changes, but the structure can be apprehended beyond representations. This principle has lasting clinical implications. By the time we reach *Seminar XXIV*, Lacan had proposed that based on the status of the torus as a hole, "everything having to do with the Borromean knot can only be articulated as being toric" (Lesson January 18). This allows us to consider how psychoanalysis can produce holes, holes that give consistency and permit the three registers to hold together. Structure is then conceived of as the Borromean knot itself.

Jacques-Alain Miller clarifies the logic of the torus in Lacan's *Seminar IX* where the two holes of the torus are used to illustrate the spiraling circuit of demand and the object of desire,

> I invited you to consider that the spiral of the chained turns of the cylindrical circle, which encircles the body of the torus, when it loops itself, draws the central circle of the torus, the one that communicates, that makes one with the space where the torus is located. [. . .] [H]e immediately uses it to represent in it the turns of demand, turns of the cylindrical circle which, when they eventually come together draw the circle that encloses the central hole as the hole of the object of desire.
>
> (Miller, January 26, 2011)

Miller evokes the torus to show the structure of Lacan's discourse. Seminar after seminar, Lacan returned to address an audience of psychoanalysts. With Lacan's project, Miller notes that we see repeated turns of the demand to speak about psychoanalysis, going in circles around his own object cause, the real, through repetition.

The torus can also be thought of as a structure within the analytic experience. Sessions trace the turns of the demand. Over time patients return for each session to repeat this circuit of the demand known as the drive. The object *a* is gradually encircled as the central exterior hole of the torus. The void at the center becomes delimited and rendered through the accumulation of all the traces of the demand in an analysis. Desire is what cannot be spoken via the demand, what is impossible to

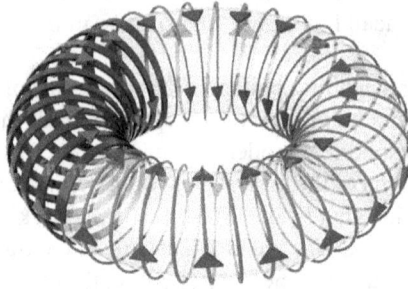

Figure 8.1 The Spiral of the Torus: A torus formed by the spiral of the turns of the demand that trace the central exterior hole of the object of desire.

say. Speaking implies the circular dynamics of the demand. Demand comes from the Other's speech (Lacan, 1958/2017, p. 336). To ask for what you want, it must pass through language, becoming encoded by signifiers. Because language is the locus of the Other, the demand, by virtue of being spoken, must pass through the detours of the Other. The speech projected from inside our bodies is made of the Other, a signifying material. In psychoanalysis, the symbolic produces a body with words. What we believe to be interior, proper to ourselves, comes from the outside. What you say you want is never your desire, which is necessarily unconscious. Something is missing, inarticulable. We have to speak again, to return and try to say it another time. With each failure in saying, a loop of the spiral is posited. In *Seminar XIX* Lacan examines supply and demand. Referring to the analyst, "but the demand that he satisfies is the recognition of the fundamental fact that what is being asked for, this isn't it" (Lacan, 1972/2018, p. 77). Lacan uses circular repetition to describe how the demand relates to the drive. Jacques-Alain Miller succinctly proposes that a drive is a demand, "[w]hen translating Lacan, 'demand' [*demande*] would really be valid only on the level of the drives. Lacan tells us that the drive is a signifying chain" (Miller, 2011, p. 13). The drive is at once a signifying articulation, an effect of speaking, and a bodily demand. It is the peculiar product of bodies plus language. The object *a* represented by the center hole of the torus in *Seminar IX* is later modeled after separated remainders of the body in *Seminar X, Anxiety*. There we learn the adage that anxiety is not without an object (Lacan, 1962/2014).

Metonymy and Anxiety

In clinical practice, the object *a* is closely related to anxiety. Accounts of spiraling, almost always described with the presence of anxiety, lead us to the following hypothesis. Spiraling has a metonymic action. *I am spiraling* is a metonymic episode. An analysand relayed, "a spiral is a spiral of thoughts." One thought, one signifier slides into another, not through metaphor but through a metonymic avalanche characterized by displacement and combination in the signifying chain. The sense of acceleration and exacerbation, the catastrophic slope of the spiral, lends to the effect of tailspin, a signifying process out of control. The action of metaphor, which depends on the function of the Name-of-the-Father, is a substitution that might offer a temporary halt, stabilizing the subjective drift of representation. This often fails to stop spiraling. The central void of the spiral, the object of loss, gains consistency through each of the turns, the demand as the speech of the Other experienced as unbearable thoughts.

Highlighting the dimension of loss essential to this object of metonymy, Lacan says in *Seminar IX* lesson of March 14th, 1962, "[i]f we push metonymy further, as you know, it is the loss of something essential in the image, in this metonymy, which is called the ego, at this point of the birth of desire." With each successive circuit of articulation, the lack in being is exposed. There is an erosion of the belief that we are how we imagine ourselves, the ego. The effect is a renewed demand to frantically fill the lack with more signification. Troubling because signification opened the gap in the first place. This in turn further gives shape to the loss at stake. The more we say, the further we are from saying it, and the closer to the appearance of the metonymical object, the central exterior hole of the toric spiral. Lacan proposes how we might use the torus clinically in this lesson of March 14th,

[t]his is how the schema of the torus is going to be of the greatest use to me – as you are going to see – by starting from the experience so highly valued by psychoanalysis and the observation that it gives rise to. The subject can attempt to speak [about] the object of his desire. He does nothing but that. It is more than an act of enunciating; it is an act of imagining.

A few words later,

the desire of the object as such in so far as it resonates to the very foundation of the subject, that it shakes him well beyond his constitution [. . .] as revealing his fundamental lack, and this in the form of the Other as bringing to light both metonymy and the loss it conditions.

Shaking the subject "well beyond his constitution," spiraling presents as a crash course. Where does the trajectory end? It doesn't. This is the nature of the torus, a closed surface that is a ring looping back on itself. One account of an analysand characterized the spiral as a succession of "I am not (x)" phrases eventually funneled down to the statement, "I am alone." The motion halted once reduced to this axiom of solitude. Thoughts related to death have also been observed as the conclusion of the spiral. It is not surprising that the affect of the spiral is anxiety. In *Seminar X*, Lacan indicates that anxiety is the only affect that doesn't lie (Lacan, 1962/2014). Anxiety is a subjective means of approaching the real, the closest we can get to something that can never be met. In this sense, anxiety is a reference to the real, a way to approach the space between subject and real. This space, the center exterior hole of the torus, known as the object *a*, is continuous with the exterior void that surrounds the torus and extends infinitely. Spiraling is a signifying approach to the real via anxiety. Spiraling is a shape of anxiety, a form, the torus.

Spiraling under Transference

During the toric interlude of *Seminar IX*, Lacan emphasizes the difference between thinking and speaking. By the time we arrive at Lacan's later seminars, thinking, speaking, and writing seem to be radically distinct modalities concerning the three registers, imaginary, symbolic, and real. This is critical to distinguishing between the private thought spirals of the subject and spiraling in analysis. Encountering the presence of the analyst together with the act of speaking insinuate the body. Psychoanalysis is a speaking spiral, a directed spiraling.

Free association in analysis passes through all sorts of circuitous detours. I recall the words of my analyst at the end of one session, "[y]ou beat around the bush, around and around the whole session, then boom, finally the object." Spiraling under transference can have an effect of delimiting jouissance by localizing the object, circumscribing the environs of a hole. There is necessarily anxiety and division in the encounter with the analyst that institutes the analytic discourse. Yet directed spiraling in analysis can also have organizing effects for speaking beings. It establishes vectors that conduct the circuits of the drive in our rather disorienting contemporary moment. The object *a* contours the drive in transference with the analyst occupying the position of the cause of desire, as a semblant of it, or an absence. We know from Freud that transference is a phenomenon of love that constitutes the motor force of the treatment and its fundamental obstacle. Referring to Lacan's formulation of the demand as fundamentally a demand for love, the turns of demand in analysis are spun with transference set in motion by the gravitational force of the lost object. Formed by bodies that speak, the torus establishes a structure that accounts for the effects of cuts, inversions, and knots that allow us to operate in psychoanalysis.

The homophonic masterpiece on the absence of the sexual rapport that Lacan wrote under the title, "L'etourdit," explores an aphorism, "[t]hat one might be saying remains forgotten behind what is said in what is heard" (Lacan, 1973/2001, p. 449). Here Lacan pries apart the signifier, statement, sense, and saying to expose the lack of sense in the sexual that founded psychoanalysis: "Freud puts us on the track of the fact that lack-of-sense (*ab-sens*) designates sex: it is by the inflation of this lack-of-sex-sense (*sens-absexe*), that a topology is unfolded where it is the word that decides" (p. 451). Lacan's title, "L'etourdit," plays with the comedy by Mollier, "L'Etourdi," translated in English as "The Blunderer" or "Bungler." The addition of the "t" at the end introduces *dit* (said). Within the title, we also hear *tour* (circuit or turn) and of course *torus*. Impossible to translate the neologism, we can approach it as an equivocation between the turns of the said and the subject who errs in a state of discombobulation, dizziness. Colloquial English has a few excellent spiral words: *turned up*, meaning high or wild, and *spun*, also connoting intoxicated to a point of madness.

I am spiraling. It contains a grammatical equivocation due to the gerundive form of the verb. Spiraling describes the action of the subject of the statement; taken as a gerund, it represents the subject of the enunciation itself: *I am this spiraling.* I am the spiraling condition of speaking beings. Lacan goes to great length over the course of three lessons in *Seminar IX* to demonstrate that the subject of the unconscious is a subject of the toric spiral. Contemporary subjectivity attests to the topological destiny of speaking beings. When someone says they are spiraling, so long as they are a speaking being, we can be sure that spiraling is not only a metaphor. Taken at the level of structure, it is topological. *Spiraling is real.*

References

Lacan, J. (1962). *L'identification Séminaire IX 1961–1962* (1st ed.). l'Association freud-ienne internationale.

Lacan, J. (1976). *Jacques Lacan, l'insu que sait de l'une-bévue s'aile à mourre (1976–1977)*. (P. Valas, Trans.). http://www.valas.fr/Jacques-Lacan-l-insu-que-sait-de-l-une-bevue-s-aile-a-mourre-1976-1977,262

Lacan, J. (1973/2001) "L'etourdit" in *Autres Écrits*. Éditions du Seuil.

Lacan, J. (1953/2006). "The Function and Field of Speech and Language in Psychoanalysis," in *Écrits*, trans. Bruce Fink. W.W. Norton & Company.

Lacan, J. (1962/2014). *Anxiety: The Seminar of Jacques Lacan, Book X*, ed. Jacques-Alain Miller, trans. A.R. Price. Polity.

Lacan, J. (1958/2017). *Formations of the Unconscious: The Seminar of Jacques Lacan, Book V*, ed. Jacques-Alain Miller, trans. Russell Grigg. Polity.

Lacan, J. (1972/2018). . . . *Or Worse: The Seminar of Jacques Lacan, Book V*, ed. Jacques-Alain Miller, trans. A.R. Price. Polity.

Miller, J-A. (2011). "The Economics of Jouissance," in *Lacanian Ink*, N° 38. Wooster Press.

Miller, J-A. (2016). "The Unconscious and the Speaking Body," in *Scilicet: The Speaking Body*. New Lacanian School.

Miller, J-A. (2022). "Lacan Clinician," in *The Lacanian Review*, N°. 12. New Lacanian School.

Chapter 9

What Is Non-Negativisable Jouissance?

From Negation to a Singular Norm

Aino-Marjatta Mäki

Introduction

The title of this book initially proposed a *conjunction* between the terms 'positivity' and 'negativity' for psychoanalytic thought. My contribution to this collective effort begins from this minor observation. I find myself asking if positivity always requires a conjunction with negativity?

Logically speaking, the semantic effect of any conjunction – that is to say, what is implied by the *and* joining two terms – is that there is not one without the other. One term, so a conjunction reads, is to be thought *not without* the other term. Conjunction in this way replicates the binary structure of language, which Lacan represented in the formula S1–S2. In both a conjunction and in this basic structural dyad, one signifier has meaning only in relation to another signifier. But, as Lacan teaches, this meaning is never stable nor in fact the same for all speaking beings, insofar as this binary structure does not produce a universal conjunction between the signifier and the signified. The signified for Lacan (1999) is only an effect of the signifier (p. 18).[1] Thought in this way, the structure of language does not guarantee that this effect is always the same *for all*.[2] Universal meaning, logically speaking, is therefore a (phallic) fantasy.[3] For this structural reason psychoanalysis is suspicious, to say the least, of 'common sense' meaning in the register 'for all'.[4] It then becomes necessary to distinguish logical conjunction from any articulated signification. With Lacan it is impossible to suppose or rely upon on general meaning. Conjunction as such does not imply preordained meaning. It only stipulates that one signifier is to be taken in relation to another said signifier. The question is, what would it mean, in logical terms, to dissolve a proposed conjunction?

In this chapter my task is precisely this. I propose to consider the positivity of jouissance, insofar as it is separated from the plasticity of the Freudian libido, and distinct from any relation to negativity.[5] But in order to introduce this task properly, it's important to lay out some parameters. First, jouissance concerns the actual living body, but cannot be thought of properly without a reference to a living body in relation to language. Secondly, once characterised with the term positivity, this jouissance escapes being fully conjoined with the symbolic and the operation of negation constitutive to it. It is, in other words, *non-negativisable* jouissance of

DOI: 10.4324/9781003375920-12

the living body. It by definition is removed from negativity. However, positivity of jouissance does not refer to some primordial pre-linguistic 'pure' enjoyment or pleasure of the body. Positivity of jouissance is not a vitalistic proposition. Rather, it is a consequence of a conjunction between the signifier, all-alone and outside of meaning, and the body (Stevens, 2021).[6] For this reason, jouissance cannot be thought of completely without the signifier.

Thirdly, the notion of the speaking body [*corps parlant*] to which, if it could be put like this, the idea of the positivity of jouissance contributes to, finds its actuality in the speaking beings [*parlêtres*] encountered in the psychoanalytic experience. That is to say, positivity of jouissance is not only a theoretical proposition. It is not merely theoretical, even if it relies on the fundamental change in the way Lacan, towards the end of his teaching, thinks of the effects of language on a living body. The idea of the positivity of jouissance has major clinical consequences, including on *how* an analyst listens, and *what* they listen to. Furthermore, it clarifies what can be read during the course of an analysis of the singular effects the signifier has for a particular speaking being. As Miller already demonstrated in 1998, this holds consequences for the idea of the end of an analysis (Miller, 2018). And finally, the idea of the positivity of jouissance leads towards a trans-structural orientation in psychoanalysis. That is because this particular positivity concerns all clinical structures. It allows contemporary psychoanalysis to orient its practice towards the incorporation by a speaking being of the utmost singular consistency. This possibility exists for each case.

For these reasons, it is necessary to trace several theoretical steps in order to grasp this conception of jouissance. These theoretical shifts ultimately concern the changing status of the signifier for Lacan – and with it, his approaches to the status of the body for a speaking being, the jouissance of this body, and finally his very understanding of language itself. The tracing of these theoretical movements is the life-long work and teaching of Jacques-Alain Miller, without which it is simply impossible to read Lacan in these terms, or to appreciate the consequences of his work for contemporary psychoanalysis. But in the English-speaking psychoanalytic context, we can only follow Miller's theoretical trajectory in a piecemeal fashion, given that very little of his teaching, interventions and contributions throughout the Freudian field are translated. In the wider English-speaking discussions on Lacanian psychoanalysis, Miller is mostly discussed and criticised in relation to a few political or public interventions without sustained study of his teaching on psychoanalysis. For these reasons it is useful to read Miller not without the work of those who have studied and worked with, or been taught by, Miller himself.

In this chapter, I ask what it means to say that jouissance is non-negativisable. To contribute to attempts to answer this question, I focus on three seminal lectures for the Lacanian orientation of psychoanalysis by Jacques-Alain Miller, delivered in Brazil in April 1998 and published under the title *L'os d'une cure* (2018).[7] As Véronique Voruz proposes in her work closely tracing Miller's late trajectory, this is where Miller first develops the perspective for a non-negativisable jouissance

(Voruz, 2022).[8] However, during these three lectures Miller neither uses the term non-negativisable nor speaks of the positivity of jouissance, and only once directly refers to [a] jouissance that cannot be annulled. Yet, it is within these three lessons that he offers a new perspective for Lacanian psychoanalysis: the connection between the signifier and jouissance is to be re-thought theoretically (Miller, 2018, p. 48).[9] My reading is oriented by the work of Alexandre Stevens and Véronique Voruz from the Freudian field in constructing this trajectory.

Through this chapter, I trace what is changing for psychoanalysis of the Lacanian orientation when the perspective of non-negativisable jouissance is introduced. The theoretical movement underlying these clinical shifts in contemporary psychoanalysis is one that moves away from the Freudian paradigm of libidinal investment and disinvestment in signifying articulations, and towards the Lacanian paradigm of the production of jouissance by the signifier's impact on a living body. This can also be articulated as a logical movement away from a prioritisation of language's effects of *mortification*, towards a foregrounding of the *production* of jouissance by the signifier in the living body – a shift, in other words, from a view of language as subtracting something, and having a negative effect (–), to one that views it as adding something, giving it a positive effect (+). Lacan comes to articulate this changing landscape during his twentieth seminar, *Encore* (1972–1973), but its development in his teaching had been underway since much earlier. The question that engages Miller in *L'os d'une cure* (2018) is, how did Lacan think about the attraction of the libido by the signifying articulation? As Freud already realised, language does not only serve to express meaning. Signifying articulation also attracts libido; it is libidinally invested. It is noteworthy that this perspective poses a major problem for psychoanalysis: what is in fact possible for psychoanalysis once the signifier is conceptualised in its inability to annihilate jouissance fully for a speaking being, and instead comes to be conceived as producing it?

Incalculable Libido: From Contingency to the Cut

In *L'os d'une cure* (2018) psychoanalysis is re-conceptualised as an operation of reduction against the proliferation of speech in the register of meaning. Miller begins his first lecture by introducing the novel concept of *reduction-operation* [*óperation-réduction*] into Lacanian psychoanalytic theory (p. 33). Alongside this, he makes a particular distinction between a reduction to the symbolic (formalisation) and a reduction to the real (jouissance). This distinction is introduced through three different mechanisms Miller identifies as potentially present in the speech of an analysand: repetition, convergence and avoidance. The first two mechanisms, repetition and convergence, allow a reduction to elementary symbolic formulas.[10] The third, avoidance, makes possible a reduction to the real (p. 41). Avoidance is opposed to the mechanisms of repetition and convergence, but at the same time, both of these other operations make avoidance possible (p. 34). This is to say, the symbolic reduction is not without a relation to the reduction in the register of the real.

Regardless that these three lectures are extremely demanding in terms of the theoretical shift Miller develops throughout them, he nevertheless articulates the advances he is making in close contact to the actuality of psychoanalytic practice. From dense theoretical movement Miller underlines a practical orientation for the analytic encounters:

> The analyst should not let himself be fascinated by repetition and convergence, repeated and constant presence, but should also focus on the repetition of absence, of avoidance, of circumvention, which constitutes precisely for the subject a stumbling block.
>
> (Miller, 2018, p. 41)

It is worth noting that the paradigm of the reduction-operation is constructed by Miller on the basis of a logical opposition. Symbolic reduction refers to a reduction on two levels: a reduction to the necessary primordial statement of the subject (what does not cease to be written), and another reduction, to those formulas that, though correlative to the necessary formulations, are impossible to articulate (what does not cease not to be written). In making these two levels codependent on one another, Miller makes impossibility appear as the binary opposition of necessity. This logic of opposition implies a duality, which also introduces the possibility of *discontinuity* into this formalisation. One element can be in opposition to another on the condition that it is distinct from it: S1 // S2. For this reason, the paradigm of the reduction-operation can be seen as distinct from the logical *continuity* introduced by the Borromean framework orienting Lacan's very last teaching.

As Miller articulates it in 1998, whether a signifying formula for a particular subject is necessary or, on the contrary, impossible to articulate, it nevertheless operates in the same logical dimension, that of *deduction* (p. 42). Reducing the analysand's discourse – which is encountered mostly as random, confused and abundant – to elementary symbolic formulas allows a confrontation in the analytic experience with something that escapes the operation of deduction (p. 42). To something that cannot be calculated, and which introduces itself, therefore, in the logical dimension of contingency. This is the dimension of jouissance. That is to say, countering the process of symbolic reduction is something that is both possible and incidental, rather than continuous or altogether impossible.

The reduction to jouissance, in other words to the libidinal value of a particular signifying articulation, is not a matter that is applicable to the (symbolic) process of deduction. As Miller points out, when we ask why such-and-such a signifier or expression has taken on a fundamental value for a subject, we do not arrive at the necessary and the impossible at all:

> Everything in an analysis that concerns jouissance, the emergence of subject's mode of jouissance, is a matter of contingency, [. . .] in the human being, what is of the order of jouissance is open to encounter and is not programmed.
>
> (Miller, 2018, p. 43)

It is absolutely necessary, Miller argues, to grasp the opposition between these two registers: that of the necessary and the impossible, on the one hand, where the *symbolic formula* is *isolated*, and that of contingency, on the other, where the *experience of jouissance* is *situated* (p. 44). This also clarifies Freud's distinction between a qualitative factor (i.e. the order of the signifier) and a quantitative factor (i.e. libido) at stake in the speech of an analysand. I will address this distinction in the next part of the chapter. Within the framework of Miller's logic, however, the qualitative factor of speech operates in the logical dimension of necessity and impossibility, whereas, quantitatively speaking, the libidinal value a subject grants to a certain signifying articulation is always a matter of contingency (what ceases not to be written). Something comes to be inscribed that could either have been inscribed in another way, or not have been inscribed at all. It is also on this level that the immeasurability of the experience of jouissance disrupts the prevailing subjective (in the actuality of the analytic experience) as well as theoretical (in the actuality of constructing how to think about what takes place in the psychoanalytic experience) formulations. One cannot deduce how much libido is invested in any given signifying articulation.

The first inscription of the horizon of non-negativisable jouissance is articulated within this non-calculable aspect of the libido. And even if jouissance is not yet introduced in its complete positivity, and not yet distinguished from the Freudian concept of libido, I find myself asking if the perspective of non-negativisable jouissance introduces in fact a relation between positivity and logical continuity. It is a question that targets how to map the positivity of jouissance, which concerns the conjunction of a living body and the signifier, in the topology of tori Lacan was utilising for psychoanalysis at the very end of his teaching. A logical dimension for which, strictly speaking, there is no discontinuity without the external operation of a cut.

Radical Disjunction: S // a

During the second lecture of *L'os d'une cure*, Miller properly introduces the question of the incalculable contingency of jouissance, with reference to Freud's *Some Neurotic Mechanisms in Jealousy, Paranoia and Homosexuality* (1922). In this text, Freud distinguishes the unconscious signifying formation from the libido it is capable of attracting. This attraction of libido is what Freud called 'investment' [*Besetzung*], which is translated as 'cathexis' in the English *Standard Edition*. During this second lecture, Miller underlines how the quantitative factor [*das quantitative moment*] refers to "the amount of cathexis that these structures are able to attract to themselves" (Freud, 1922, as cited in Miller, 2018, p. 44).[11]

The first essential point that emerges from this distinction is that there is, in the psychoanalytic experience, a *break in causality* between signifying articulation, on the one hand, and libidinal investment, on the other (p. 45). This break was already recognised by Freud. A signifying articulation is a formal construction, which can never of itself indicate what value of jouissance the subject grants to it (p. 45). Here we see how libido, in this instance still aligned with jouissance, is distinct from the signifier. But it is precisely this relation between libido and the signifier that starts to shift in the theory Miller is laying out during these lectures.

The division between a qualitative and quantitative factor in analysis was put forward by Freud in *Some Neurotic Mechanisms in Jealousy, Paranoia and Homosexuality*. Freud, in working through paranoid delusions with structural similarity to persecutory ideas in general, comes to realise here that classical persecutory ideas may be present "without finding belief or acceptance" by the patient himself (Freud, 2001, p. 228). Freud describes how, when persecutory ideas flashed up occasionally during an analysis with a particular patient, this patient always regarded them as "unimportant and invariably scoffed at them" (p. 228). The persecutory ideas, he surmises, were not necessarily libidinally invested from the start. Freud points out that, as a result of this potentially unaccepted, uninvested status of these paranoid ideas, "it may be that the delusions which we regard as new formations when the disease breaks out have already long been in existence" (p. 228). This realisation leads Freud, making use of an Aristotelian logical distinction, to put forward a *qualitative* and a *quantitative* factor along his theory of the libido. Freud attributes more significance to the latter, quantitative factor, because it for Freud refers to "the *degree of attention* or, more correctly, the *amount of cathexis* that these structures are able to attract to themselves" (p. 228).[12]

In a closing intervention to the Colloquium of the Clinical Section in 1984,[13] Miller points out how Freud's starting point with regards to the question of psychosis was precisely to take into account the libidinal dimension in psychosis (Miller, 1984). Lacan's contribution to this question, Miller (1984) continues in saying, was the notion of the psychoanalytic handling of jouissance, in the form of object *a*. But, as Freud works out in *Some Neurotic Mechanisms*, not all signifying articulations – be they of delusion or not – carry libido by the mere fact of structure. As Freud becomes aware here, libido instead associates itself with the semantic effect of the signifier (Miller, 2018, p. 52). For Freud, libidinal investment occurs at the level of meaning. What Lacan, as Miller points out, called 'enjoyed meaning' [*sens joui*] is precisely the Freudian libido associated with the semantic effect of the signifier – that is to say, the signified. This, however, does not introduce a complementarity between signifying articulation and jouissance. On the contrary, as already pointed out, there is a radical disjunction between these two planes in Freud's work.

In light of this disjunction, the signifier cannot be conceived as producing libido, as this would close the gap Freud appreciated to exist between signifying articulation and libidinal investment. Instead, the signifier only attracts libido through the signified effect. For this reason, Miller comes to ask how Lacan thought about the libidinal investment of signifying articulation. The signifier can exist in two possible ways with respect to libido: (1) signifier *plus* libido, through libidinal *investment* of the signifier, and (2) signifier *minus* libido, through separation of the signifier and the libido, or what Freud called *disinvestment* (p. 48). Libido, then, does not merely obstruct the signifier, but instead invests in it. For this reason, the connection between the signifier and jouissance (i.e., the question of libidinal investment) introduces a major problem for the operation of reduction in psychoanalysis. How can a subject disinvest from jouissance? This question is not solved at the level of mere formalisation, or reduction to the symbolic. Miller illustrates this through an example of the obsessional structure, in which the subject is restrained by certain signifying formulas. The question here is, Miller points out, not so much how to isolate these formulas, but how the subject may come to cede the jouissance they bring to him. The time required for this cession cannot be calculated (p. 48).

> The time it [disinvestment] takes is not calculable. We see this in accounts of the pass. Certain subjects have elucidated their repetition, identified their destinal signifier, but their analysis is not complete until they have yielded the jouissance that for them remains attached to this repetition and to this signifier.
>
> (p. 48)

The most important consequence of this view of libidinal disinvestment is that it requires us to appreciate the Freudian libido as a constant quantity; one not necessarily compliant to transformations on the level of the signifier (p. 73). Analytical work cannot then be conceived as a mere movement against jouissance; as a progression of libidinal disinvestment measured, as Miller puts it, by the effects of mortification (p. 73). Approached in this way, traversing the fantasy would be tantamount to disinvesting it. But this, we can now appreciate, would not solve much, precisely because the quantity of libido in Freud's sense would not change. The positivity of jouissance is not the same as the pathogenic plasticity of the Freudian libido, and, as proposed earlier, jouissance in its positivity is ultimately to be distinguished from the Freudian libido. Even so, in its potential independence from signifying formulations, the idea of non-negativisable jouissance has a strong root in the Freudian concept of the libido.[14]

Direct Relationship: From Antinomy to the Symptom

It is from what he calls the *antinomic effects*[15] of the signifier – on the one hand, the *effect of mortification* (barred S), and on the other, the *jouissance effect* (petit *a*, which presupposes life) – that Miller invites a change of perspective: "It consists in positing that the signifier does not have a mortifying effect on the body, which is what the theory of fantasy supposes" (p. 57). What now becomes essential is that the signifier is a *cause* of jouissance. The signifier does not merely attract libido, as Freud discovered, but produces it under what Miller calls the 'species' of surplus enjoyment [*les espèces du plus-de-jouir*] (p. 57). This means, as he explains, that the signifier fundamentally has an effect of jouissance on the body (p. 57). This effect of jouissance on the body is what Lacan called the symptom. This clarification has implications, as Miller cautiously proposes, on the idea of how an analysis ends. Considered from the perspective of antinomic effects of the signifier – mortification and jouissance – it is possible to realise the necessity for the formula of fantasy, barred S in relation to *a*, which combines these two effects. It is in the fantasy, as Miller reiterates, that Lacan envisages the libido to be conjoined with the mortifying effect of the signifier. Fantasy, in this sense, is the resolution of this particular antinomy. In other words, the fantasy is the libidinal resolution of the contradictory effects that language imposes on the speaking being.

Fantasy, as Miller continues, supposes a body *mortified* by the signifier, while the symptom refers to the body *vivified* by the signifier. It is in this sense that the symptom goes beyond the fantasy. If we are concerned with the symptom today, Miller states, it is because Lacan has shown us that the *signifier refers to the body under the modality of the symptom* (p. 57). Here we already have, in a way, the articulation of the symptom as a body event, which is given in full within *Lacanian Biology* (2000).[16] Furthermore, this leads Miller to realise that the theoretical location of the symptom in Lacan's work is exactly where Freud had inscribed the drive. The drive, as Miller points out, is a concept for thinking about the relationship of the signifying articulation on the body (p. 58). He explains that the drive in Freud's work is the interface between psychic and somatic, while the symptom in Lacan's work is the connection between the signifier and the body (p. 58). The essential difference is that for Freud the drive is a myth, whereas in Lacan the symptom is real (p. 58).

The symptom for Lacan is now described as appearing in a way in the same logical place as the fantasy. The only exception is that, as Miller says, the latter presupposes *a radical distinction* between the order of the signifier and that of jouissance, and appears as the mediation between these two orders (pp. 57 and 66–67). The symptom, on the contrary, inscribes what Miller calls a much more *direct relationship* [*un rapport beaucoup plus direct*] between the signifier and jouissance (pp. 66–67). The symptom supposes that one cannot define the signifier without jouissance, nor jouissance without the signifier (p. 67). This is already an articulation of the conjunction between signifier and jouissance that Miller uses, during his last course *L'Un tout seul* (2011), to define the sinthome.

Finally, Miller arrives at a new definition of the Lacanian signifier: the signifier as such refers to the body, and this reference is made in the modality of the symptom (p. 67). That is to say, in the symptom, there is no radical distinction between the signifier and jouissance. This perspective also involves clarifying the very term 'subject', insofar as the subject of the signifier, distinct from the subject of the jouissance, is a mortified element (p. 69). This is why, when Lacan brings the living body into psychoanalysis, he substitutes the term 'subject' with *parlêtre* (p. 69). Parlêtre, simply stated, is the opposite of the lack of being. It is the subject *plus* the body, that is to say, the subject plus the enjoying substance (p. 69). These developments lead Miller to re-articulate the stakes for the end of analysis as follows: the pass is not a simple matter of libidinal disinvestment (p. 73). To say that analysis leads to identifying with the symptom, as Lacan proposed in the first lesson of *Seminar XXIV*, means, in this perspective, "I am as I enjoy" (p. 73). Analytical work is no longer conceived as a mere progression of libidinal disinvestment, insofar as the progress of an analysis is not measured by the extent of an annihilation of jouissance.

The question is therefore, as Miller puts it, where does the libido go if it withdraws from the fantasy? Libido in Freud's sense is a constant quantity. During the lectures of *L'os d'une cure* (2018), Miller introduces this as the real question of the pass: "Assuming that the libido is badly invested, that it can disinvest from this bad place, where will it invest itself?" (p. 73). His answer is that no disinvestment can prevent the symptom from remaining a mode of enjoyment. Here we see the movement from a framework of *negativity* (disinvestment) to one of *positivity* (the symptom as a mode of enjoyment where libido remains a *constant* quantity). This is precisely what Lacan introduced as early as 1964 during his *Seminar XI* on the *Four Fundamental Concepts of Psychoanalysis*. Towards the end of the final lesson, on 24th of June 1964, Lacan asks, "What, then, does he who has passed through the experience of this opaque relation to the origin, to the drive, become? How can the subject who has traversed the radical fantasy experience the drive?" (Lacan, 2004, p. 273). And Lacan continues by saying that is precisely this beyond of any analysis that has never been approached (p. 273). In this sense, the 'beyond the pass' [*outrepasse*][17] of the traversal of fantasy is already inscribed by Lacan before formalising the procedure of the pass in 1967.

The importance of these three Brazilian lectures published under the title of *L'os d'une cure* (2018) is further clarified by Alexandre Stevens in his argument for the XIXth Congress of the *New Lacanian School* (NLS), titled *Bodily effects of language* (2020). In the argument, Stevens situates the movement from the idea of the signifier's antinomic effects – both deadening and enlivening – to the idea that the signifier itself produces jouissance, in the context of what he calls the 'diachrony' of Lacan's teaching. In the very beginning of the argument, Stevens points out how the effects of language on the body are articulated according to a variation that goes from signifying mortification, in the classical period of his teaching, to the effect of jouissance arising from the impact of the signifier on the body, in his later teaching (Stevens, 2020). What Miller – by making reference to a logical opposition for which there is no immediate resolution in *L'os d'une cure* – first describes as antinomic effects of the signifier, is inscribed by Stevens as part of a gradual movement in Lacan's teaching, in a way that is carefully elaborated within the argument. With reference to Miller, Stevens shows how this movement leads from the conception of the signifier as a cause of jouissance, to a new definition of the body.

As Miller argues in *Lacanian Biology*, Lacan's return to the effect of satisfaction in relation to language and the body leads Lacan to pass from the concept of language, to that of lalangue (Miller, 2000, p. 23). That is to say, as Stevens reads Miller, the signifier as such works not for signification but for satisfaction (Miller, 2000, as cited in Stevens, 2020). This goes, as Stevens points out, in the direction of posing what Miller calls "an equivalence between signification and satisfaction" (Miller, 2000, as cited in Stevens, 2020). The antinomy of the two distinct effects of the signifier, coming together in one and the same conception of the body, starts to dissolve.

Conclusion

During the lessons published later as *Lacanian Biology* (2000), which follow the concerns of the three Brazilian lectures, Miller proposes that there are *two movements* present in the links between the body and the signifier (Miller, 2000, p. 44). The antinomic effects of the signifier are no longer contrasted to one another, but distinguished as two separate logical movements through which the signifier comes to associate with the body. First, as Stevens clarifies, there is a *significantisation* of the body present from the first period of Lacan's teaching (Stevens, 2020). The principle example is the signifier of the phallus, which raises an organ to the dimension of the signifier. But in the last period of Lacan's teaching, there is also a *corporisation* of the signifier to be considered (Stevens, 2020). This, on the contrary, is the signifier grasped as *affecting* the body of the speaking being. Furthermore, it is the signifier becoming body, "dividing up [*morcelé*] the body's jouissance and making surplus jouissance spurt from it" (Miller, 2000, as cited in Stevens, 2020). This, according to Stevens, allows us to grasp that the signifier affects the body other than through a set of meanings.

The *corporisation* is, Stevens quotes Miller, "*the bodily effect of the signifier*". It is neither the signifier's semantic effect (that is to say, the signified), nor its effect as a supposed subject (in other words, all the signifier's effects of truth) (Miller, 2000, as cited in Stevens, 2020). On the contrary, corporisation refers to the signifier's effects of jouissance. This double movement of *significantisation of the body* and *corporation of the signifier* is described by Lacan in *Radiophonie* (Stevens, 2020). A being has his body only because of language, otherwise it wouldn't even be there, but it is the *incorporation* of the signifier that gives him this body caught up in the effects of jouissance (Stevens, 2020). It is to be noted that we have moved from a perspective viewing the antinomic effects of the signifier, and opposing its mortifying and libidinal effects, to a view of the relation of the signifier and the body as a double movement, whereby the body is *signifierised* and the signifier is *incorporated*. But what also appears to take place is the emergence of two distinct and discordant conceptions of the body. There is a body, distinct from language, but amenable to the signifier, and to its meaning effects – that is to say, a theoretical conception of the body that comes from seeing the symbolic and imaginary as quite closely tied together – and there is another idea of the body whose relation to language constitutes a conjunction, a conception of the body that places emphasis on the dimension of the real.

In light of this new view on the relationship between the signifier and jouissance, and this new conception of the body, this chapter proposes that *non-negativisable* implies a positivity that would not stand in a logical relation to negativity, as its alternative. In other words, this positivity is not a surplus produced by a prohibition, negation or displacement of libidinal satisfaction – all of which are terms that imply a structural negativity at the heart of subjective experience that would be amenable to the symbolic. On the contrary, the idea of this non-negativisable positivity points to those bodily effects of language that, on one hand, are singular to each speaking being and escape straightforward symbolic reduction, and that, on the other, close the theoretical gap between signifying articulations and libidinal investment, upon which the classic psychoanalytic operation located itself. If the conjunction between negativity and positivity is necessarily dissolved in order to speak of the positivity of jouissance, this dissolution is made possible by an erasure of the gap between signifying articulation and libidinal investment.

These 'clinical consistencies',[18] or concepts that conjugate theoretical precision with the specificity of clinical observation, differ widely between psychoanalysts from different schools and orientations. Through this chapter, I have tried to demonstrate how different psychoanalytic orientations, even within Lacanian psychoanalysis, have very specific theoretical 'consistencies' that orient clinical work. For this reason, it is becoming increasingly difficult to speak of 'psychoanalysis' as such. And yet, it is necessary that psychoanalysis is distinguished from psychotherapy, and from mere therapeutic work. In this sense, the positivity of jouissance – that is to say, positivity that cannot be conjugated with negativity – further distinguishes the irreducible specificity of psychoanalysis from the normative logic, operating in the register *for all*, of psychotherapy.[19] In contrast to that normativity this conception of jouissance pushes psychoanalysis further towards a non-standard clinical practice, insofar as non-negativisable jouissance constitutes a paradigm that centers on the singular norm of a particular speaking body. In other words, this idea of the positivity of jouissance leads psychoanalysis of the Lacanian orientation further towards the utmost singular consistency, that which 'holds' a particular speaking body vis-a-vis its real, and which exists for each speaking being. In this paradigm, what used to be considered merely pathological, and thus amenable to a variety of elimination operations under the aegis of healing, becomes the principal source of a know-how when putting in operation the function of the psychoanalyst.

Notes

1 As Lacan articulates in the second lesson to his *Seminar XX* (1972–1973), "(i)ndeed, the signifier is first of all that which has a meaning effect [*effet de signifié*], and it is important not to elide the fact that between signifier and meaning effect there is something barred that must be crossed over" (Lacan, 1999, p. 18).

2 A little later in the same second lesson to *Seminar XX*, Lacan points out that the relationship between signifier and signified was incorrectly qualified as arbitrary by Saussure, and continues in saying that "what passes for arbitrary is the fact that meaning effects seem not to bear any relation to what causes them" (Lacan, 1999, p. 19). For Lacan (1999), if they seem to bear no relation to what causes them, that is because "we expect what causes them to bear a certain relation to the real" (p. 19).

3 This certainly poses its own difficulties for anyone taking up the question of psychoanalysis in an academic publication and context, and the least that should be done, when the question of psychoanalysis is taken seriously enough, is to not remain unaware of such logical difficulty.

4 During the third lesson of *Seminar XX*, Lacan further clarifies the function of the signifier in saying, "Distinguishing the dimension of the signifier only takes on importance when it is posited that what you hear, in the auditory sense of the term, bears no relation whatsoever to what it signifies" (p. 29). We therefore come to distinguish signification

from what is heard, and further from what can be read, the dimension that the letter introduces into psychoanalysis.

5 This distinction implies, as Véronique Voruz has outlined, towards a real *fixity* of jouissance that is to be distinguished from the pathogenic *plasticity* of the Freudian libido (Voruz, 2022).

6 This trajectory finds its quilting point towards the end of Miller's final *Course* at the University of Paris 8, *L'Un tout seul* (2011). It is with the teaching from this *Course* that Alexandre Stevens delivers his conference *The real of the body as an effect of language* (2020), given as a video conference for the *Lacanian Compass* USA, and which is a remarkable reference in order to follow Miller's trajectory from 1998 onwards. I am in gratitude to colleagues Azeen Khan, An Bulkens and Samya Seth for reminding me of this conference.

7 These three lessons were delivered as part of the VIII Brazilian meeting of the Freudian Field in Salvador de Bahia, 18–21 April 1998. The published text was drawn up by Christiane Alberti and Phillippe Hellebois, unread by the author, but published with his permission.
   Miller's *L'os d'une cure* (2018) has been published by the *Libretto Series* (LP) of the World Association of Psychoanalysis (WAP) in English translation by Alasdair Duncan, retitled by Jacques-Alain Miller as *Analysis Laid Bare* (2023).

8 The paper published online as part of the preparatory work towards the twentieth Congress of the *New Lacanian School* (NLS) *Fixation and Repetition* (2022) is a revised version of a paper Voruz presented on 12th of February 2022 at the *Kring voor Psychoanalyse*, titled "Root of the Symptom" (Voruz, 2022).

9 It is noteworthy that these three conferences (which take place only a couple of months before) lead to the central themes of the 1998–1999 course *Le reel dans la experience analytique*, during which Miller redefines the symptom as a body event during six lessons extracted from his 1998–99 course and published under the title of *Lacanian Biology* (2000). It is also from this 1998–1999 course that the lessons published under the title *Six Paradigms of Jouissance* (1999) have been extracted. The three conferences of *L'os d'une cure* (2018) open this perspective which finds a quilting point during Miller's final course, *L'Un tout seul* (2011) which remains unpublished.

10 At the very end of the first lecture, Miller points out that in analysis the astonishing effects of the inscription of spoken words in the history of the subject can be seen. "The analysand sometimes knows this major statement as soon as he enters the analysis, and gradually discovers how much truer it was than he could have known, and to what extent he has carried its mark and weight. He thus discovers that the mishaps of his life are reducible to the effect of the mark of this statement" (Miller, 2018, p. 32). Another possibility is that this statement upon which the discourse of the analysand converges, is not given by the analysand but is up to the analyst to produce it in the form of an interpretation. This interpretation is then inscribed in the same place as the primordial statement (Miller, 2018, p. 32).

11 The quote is from *Some Neurotic Mechanisms in Jealousy, Paranoia and Homosexuality* (1922), published in English in the XVIIIth Standard Edition of the Complete Psychological Works of Sigmund Freud (Freud, 2001, p. 228).

12 Italics mine.

13 This intervention was introduced as part of the work in the *Delusions* seminar by the organising committee of the *London Workshop of the Freudian Field* (LWFF), Susana Huler, Gabriela van Der Hoven, Peggy Papada and Philip Dravers woking under the direction of Jacques-Alain Miller. The text of the intervention was translated to English by Philip Dravers (for the use of the workshop) and discussed by Susana Huler during the second instalment of the workshop.

14 As Véronique Voruz notes (2022) "(w)hat I think is interesting with regards to the Freudian libidinal fixation is that we know that for Freud libido is characterised by its

utmost plasticity, by its capacity in constantly displacing itself and invest a multiplicity of objects. A libidinal fixation is therefore pathogenic in and of itself because it prevents the free movement of the libido and builds dams in the body where the libido remains entrapped" (Voruz, 2022).

15 "(L)e deux effets antinomique du signifiant: l'effet mort, l'effet de mortification signifi-ante $ et, à l'opposé, l'effet jouissance *a* qui suppose la vie" (Miller, 2018, p. 56).

16 These three lectures lead to the central themes of the 1998–1999 Course *Le reel dans la experience analytique*, during which Miller redefines the symptom as a *body event* during six lessons extracted from his 1998–99 Course and published under the title of *Lacanian Biology* (2000).

17 This French term refers (1) literally to the beyond of the pass, and (2) conceptually to what could be called the pass of the sinthome. This second theory of the pass refers to the end of an analysis taken beyond the traversal of the fantasy. But of course it is a problem, as Miller points out in several occasions, to have a rigid theoretical definition of what the pass is, insofar as it risks production of testimonies of the end of analysis in those precise terms. And at the same time, it is an epistemological, ethical and political necessity for psychoanalysis to have an idea of the end of an analysis.

18 A term Miller introduces during his final Course *L'Un tout seul* (2011), and which I find particularly useful for thinking about the relation between theory and clinical practice in psychoanalysis. For Miller, this term is quite specific and I am making more broad use of it here, with a slightly different emphasis.

19 My academic research concerns this distinction between psychoanalysis and psycho-therapy in the context of contemporary practices of psychoanalysis, and I acknowledge that I am making a very general use of the term here for the purpose of providing some concluding remarks to this chapter.

References

Freud, S. (2001). Some Neurotic Mechanisms in Jealousy, Paranoia and Homosexuality (1922). *The Standard Edition of the Complete Psychological Works of Sigmund Freud, Volume XVIII* (1920–1922). The Hogarth Press.

Lacan, J. (1999). Encore, the Seminar of Jacques Lacan, Book XX. On *Feminine Sexuality, the Limits of Love and Knowledge, 1972–1973*. W.W. Norton and Company, Inc.

Lacan, J. (2004). *The Four Fundamental Concepts of Psycho-Analysis (1973)*. Karnac.

Miller, J.-A. (1984). Montré à Prémontré. *Analytica*, 37, pp. 27–31.

Miller, J.-A. (2000). Biologie lacanienne et évènement de corps (1998–1999). *La Cause freudienne: Revue de psychanalyse*, 44, pp. 5–45.

Miller, J.-A. (2011). *L'un-tout-seul. 2010–2011* (1st ed.). La Martiniere. https://www.decitre. fr/livres/l-un-tout-seul-9782732467276.html

Miller, J.-A. (2018). *L'os d'une cure*. Navarin.

Stevens, A. (2020). Bodily Effects of Language. https://uqbarwapol.com/bodily-effects-of-language-xix-th-congress-of-psychoanalysis-nls/.

Stevens, A. (2021). The real of the body as an effect of language. *Lacanian Compass*, 5(6). https://lacaniancompass.com/wp-content/uploads/2022/02/AlexandreStevens.pdf.

Voruz, V. (2022). Root of the Symptom. www.amp-nls.org/nls-messager/tuche-the-root-of-the-symptom/#m_-1409673662910620861__ftn8.

Chapter 10

Badbeing

What's So Bad about Resistance in the Clinic?

Ian Parker

Introduction

This chapter pits itself against popular therapeutic discourse about 'well-being,' arguing that psychoanalysis resists such ideological verities attuned to the task of adaptation. Against well-being, we value 'badbeing' in our clinical work, and we will see that notions of symbolic castration – the conceptual bedrock of psychoanalytic subjectivity – and hystericisation, acting out, passage to the act and our understanding of resistance as being on the side of the analyst, each lead us from positively inflected well-being to productively negative badbeing. There is, nevertheless, a danger that therapeutic discourse, including its psychoanalytic variants, will still succeed in recuperating such negativity, and so the final section of the chapter addresses this political problem.

Well-being in Society

Psychoanalysts are neither psychotherapists nor psychiatrists, and psychoanalysis is not a 'health profession', which is one reason why we are not concerned with boosting self-esteem or promoting 'well-being' in our clinical practice (Parker, 2011). The other reason, of course, is that the 'well-being' project is a corollary of an attempt to make us all healthy and happy, and that attempt operates within taken-for-granted moral and moralising parameters that govern how we should live. Well-being is at the core of 'positive' psychotherapy.

We are told, for example, on a United States Air Force website that there are 'four dimensions' of positive well-being – spiritual, emotional, physical and social 'wellness' – as part of a 'campaign initiative' that is 'designed to establish a proactive, healthy, and war-fit' team (Edwards Air Force Base, 2022). A little more apparently innocuous is the injunction on a United Kingdom local county website that we attend to 'five ways to well-being' in which you 'connect' through building relationships, 'be active' to improve your physical health, 'keep learning' in order to boost self-confidence, 'give' even a smile to others to increase your self-esteem and 'take notice' for which awareness can be assessed with a National Health Service questionnaire (Derbyshire County Council, 2022).

DOI: 10.4324/9781003375920-13

These superegoic injunctions at least make explicit what a positive pro-gramme for mental health consists of, and the slippery slope into conformity that psychoanalysis needs to beware of. Psychoanalysis that turns itself into a form of psychotherapy, and which thereby attaches itself to other healthy life-style initiatives, could thereby endorse some of the suggestions made by those who tell us to be more positive. But psychoanalysis as such is grounded in a quite different ethics, one in which we wish no particular good on analysands (Parker, 2019).

Psychoanalysis, on the contrary, refuses and questions such societal impera-tives, and instead of adapting people to society, enables them to navigate moral-ideological, institutional and familial requirements in a way that takes a distance from them, it is intrinsically negative. A necessary consequence is that we focus on 'badbeing', on what in us rebels, including rebellion against what there is in us that tells us that we must be well and well-behaved. It is in that respect that psychoanalysis connects with radical politics outside the clinic (Parker and Pavón-Cuéllar, 2021). That also means that inside the clinic we treat 'negativity' as, as it were, a positive condition for the psychoanalytic work to happen.

Badbeing in the Clinic

Psychoanalysis, remember, is an impossible profession, and it is this very impos-sibility that lies at the deepest core of its negative approach to subjectivity, and this is the reason why we value negativity rather than attempt to replace it with positiv-ity. This is clearest in clinical practice in the role that resistance plays. Resistance is a positive condition for psychoanalysis, the place where negativity is handled in such a way that the 'direction of the treatment' is not also the education or adapta-tion of the analysand to dominant ideological nostrums about their mental health (Lacan, 2006).

Symbolic Castration

We cannot wish away the different forms of symbolic castration – necessary sub-jection to language that enables us to attempt to speak to others in a human com-munity – that turn us into the kind of subjects fit for psychoanalysis. That symbolic castration, enacted through the 'no' of an authority figure, stereotypically the father in the nuclear family, functions as a 'third', a point from which the subject is able to break from the often-suffocating dyadic relation with the primary caregiver (Mul-ler, 1996).

That 'third' position is itself a 'no' that can, if idealised, function only as a 'yes', only as if only something positive. Then, in transference, the analyst who is posi-tioned in that way has the task of enabling the negative as well as positive aspects of the third to appear; the 'no' must be available to function also as a 'no' for the subject in analysis to themselves experience and enact.

Hystericisation

One of the signature strategies of the Lacanian psychoanalyst is to make this aspect of the 'no' of the third position function, even to encourage it. This, in place of the reassuring ameliorative attempts of the humanist therapists seeking to 'understand' what their client is saying and to bring about the illusion that analysand and analyst are engaged in an egalitarian task designed to enable them both to be positive about what they are doing and about who they are.

This strategy is a 'hystericisation' of the analysand, something very different from the labeling of a resistant client as 'hysterical' (Fink, 1997). This hystericisation is to bring the analysand closer to speaking as a subject, questioning, rebelling, and tracing a trajectory from complaint at what has been done to them to reflection on what their place in that complaint is. In other words, this is to refuse the 'positive' agenda of psychotherapy and speak with the negative, acknowledging what is negative about themselves as speaking subjects.

Acting Out

That negativity is channeled into speech, of course, but there are moments when the analyst makes missteps, errors that are particular to each analysand, and so not predictable and always avoidable. Those missteps are noticed by the hystericised analysand – that is precisely what they are sensitised to in the transference – and though responses may take exaggerated form, and the temptation of the analyst is to make sense of what is happening through the motif of a 'negative therapeutic reaction', they are not to be so pathologised.

The analysand may then respond by action rather than speaking – being late, walking out, missing sessions and so on – and this 'acting out' is then something 'negative' that can actually be productive in the analysis if it can then be put into words. Acting out is an opportunity to work with what is negative about the subject, productive negativity.

Passage to the Act

A more complex and, for psychoanalysts, controversial enactment of resistance to the analysis and to speaking to an analyst, is 'passage to the act', something that is all the more tempting to place on the side of a destructive negativity that is then often pathologised. The 'clinical structures' of neurosis, psychosis and perversion are usually the mainstay of Lacanian psychoanalytic training, and the categories are rehearsed in preliminary sessions and in supervision, even if the analyst warns themselves not to make definitive fixed diagnosis and not to resort to a quasi-psychiatric framing of distress.

If we are not be evangelists, insisting that every subject in the world be amenable to psychoanalysis, we need to keep open the possibility that even 'passage to the act' – an extreme and apparently self-destructive form of 'acting out' – may be a message to us, the message being that our psychoanalysis is an offer that is being refused, and that what we may well experience as a hostile 'negative' attitude is not; it is something negative that may be more helpful and productive to the subject we cannot ourselves reach.

Resistance Is on the Side of the Analyst

Lacanian psychoanalysis does at least have at its disposal a reflective conceptual apparatus that should encourage the analyst to avoid pathologising responses to bad behavior in the clinic. Instead of blaming the analyst for their lack of adaptation to analytic procedures – the kind of blame that is expressed in pop-psychoanalytic talk about 'resistances' that are obstructing the work and that should be interpreted so that they are no longer functional in a supposedly 'negative' way – we learn that resistance is on the side of the analyst.

This is an aspect of our work that more productively reconfigures the talk of 'counter-transference' in other psychoanalytic traditions of work. While 'counter-transference' pretends to theorise the analyst's responses – an imaginary line mirror image of the analysand's transference – it usually has the effect of interpreting, and encouraging the analyst to reinterpret their own responses as something positive. Counter-transference is often a conceptual and experiential machine for turning what is negative on the side of the analyst into something positive and using that positive knowledge to then tackle and reengineer what remains negative on the side of the analysand. Lacan's insistence that resistance is on the side of the analyst, on the contrary, is an opportunity for working with negativity as such.

Recuperation into Dominant Discourse

A degree of resistance is tolerated in much psychoanalytic practice on condition that it be channeled and reframed in a positive way. In this way, what is most radical about negativity is absorbed and neutralised, and we – patients, clinicians and adepts and enthusiasts for psychoanalytic discourse – are provided with manifold strategies for recuperating what might, at first glance, function as critique so that it is turned into yet another endorsement of usual clinical technique.

We may be told, for instance, that the analysand walking out of session, or refusing to return to analysis, is a message that must be understood within the frame of the transference, as a message about some error that the analyst has committed. There is then a potentially fruitful opportunity for the analyst to reflect on their own resistance, that which has been admitted as being on the side of the analyst.

Such failures can be reconfigured as an indictment of the analyst, an indication that the pull of analysis on the analysand was not sufficiently strong, perhaps as an index of the lack of 'desire of the analyst'. This is the usual reflexive and generous therapeutic reframing of what has happened, one that comes into play after reluctant suggestion that the analysand is themselves unable to tolerate the session. Speculation about 'clinical structure' that does not immediately blame the analysand – as psychotic or perverse – may focus on the way they are intent on holding something in reserve, obsessional, or rebelling, hysteric. Notice the twisting, once again, of negative into positive, of refusal into a valuable lesson.

We have no idea what is going on inside the head of the analysand, what their underlying motives are, what numinous stuff accompanies the trail of the signifiers that compose a session and turn it, in the analyst's reading and sense-making of it, into a narrative. That narrative, told by the analyst, is then instantiated in the 'case presentation' in which all that may have been negative, either guessed at or completely unknown to the analyst, is then rendered into a smooth positive form. Even when the lessons learnt may jar with received knowledge, as all the best case presentations should do, it is often with the effect of validating or supplementing what positive knowledge we already think we have (Parker, 2018).

There is, of course, a possible point of rupture in the treatment, when there is a putative 'end of analysis' but, once again, among the many allusive and elliptical formulations of this 'end' that Lacan gives, this reconfigures what may seem to be negative as a positive. This, of course, is where what might possibly be conceived of as the 'end of analysis' is where the analysand themselves takes the fateful step of becoming an analyst (Lacan, 1967–1968).

The hermeneutic circle of psychoanalytic discourse then folds around itself to provide final confirmation in the 'passe' for instance, that what was said in and about the analysis was meaningful or, better said, that the reduction to non-meaning can be appreciated as something positive (Lacan, 1964/1973). What 'absolute difference' there may be in the meaningless signifiers that are produced, potentially negative phenomena, are then wrapped up into a self-congratulatory appreciation of the work of the analyst. What 'absolute difference' there may be between analyst and analysand is then also sutured as the analysand enters the circle of those permitted to contribute something positive to the discourse that bore them.

Conclusions

In this way what is 'badbeing' about us, what is most productively negative, threatens to be transformed into 'well-being', and the tragic sensibility of psychoanalysis is lost, rendered into a therapeutic story of redemption, and to 'fail better' turned into another variety of personal success. If are really to attend to 'lack' we have to find ways of living with what is impossible about psychoanalysis itself, recognising – as Wilhelm Reich and many other radical analysts since have declared (Žižek, 1989) – that analysis is impossible in a society in which it is necessary and possible only in conditions where it will be unnecessary.

This badbeing inside the clinic does connect with political resistance outside the clinic, and our refusal of the project of adaptation, to which most mainstream psychotherapy and psychiatry is committed, is then also profoundly political. The 'Red Clinic' project, for example, neither injects radical politics into the clinic nor does it turn politics into a clinical phenomenon, 'analysing' politics. However, the concern with negativity is a linking concept, enabling us to conceptualise how the refusal of adaptation inside the clinic and the refusal of capitalism outside it are each, in very different domains, expressions of a political sensitivity that we consider to be 'communist' (Pospihalj, 2022).

Those critics ranging from Ernest Gellner (1985) to Paul Preciado (2021) who are irredeemably 'negative' about psychoanalysis and who call for an 'end to analysis', are then most in tune with the ethos we practice. Their critiques chime with the experience of analysands who have been able to put their saintly analysts into the bin, break from their transferential attachment to them, and, having made use of analysis, are able to move on, kicking, in a classically Wittgensteinian move, the ladder they have climbed away and kicking against psychoanalysis itself.

References

Derbyshire County Council. (2022) 'Five Ways to Wellbeing', www.derbyshire.gov.uk/social-health/health-and-wellbeing/mental-health-and-wellbeing/five-ways-to-wellbeing/five-ways-to-wellbeing.aspx

Edwards Air Force Base. (2022) '4 Dimensions of Wellness', www.edwards.af.mil/About/4DW/

Fink, B. (1997) *A Clinical Introduction to Lacanian Psychoanalysis: Theory and Technique.* Cambridge, MA: Harvard University Press.

Gellner, E. (1985) *The Psychoanalytic Movement, or the Coming of Unreason.* London: Paladin.

Lacan, J. (1964/1973) *The Four Fundamental Concepts of Psycho-Analysis: The Seminar of Jacques Lacan, Book XI* (translated by A. Sheridan). Harmondsworth: Penguin.

Lacan, J. (1967–1968) *The Seminar of Jacques Lacan, Book XV, the Psychoanalytic Act* (unpublished translation by C. Gallagher from unedited French manuscripts).

Lacan, J. (2006) *Écrits: The First Complete Edition in English* (translated with notes by B. Fink in collaboration with H. Fink and R. Grigg). New York: Norton.

Muller, J. P. (1996) *Beyond the Psychoanalytic Dyad: Developmental Semiotics in Freud, Peirce and Lacan.* London and New York: Routledge.

Parker, I. (2011) *Lacanian Psychoanalysis: Revolutions in Subjectivity.* London and New York: Routledge.

Parker, I. (2018) 'Psychoanalytic Clinical Case Presentations, the Case Against', *Lacunae: APPI International Journal for Lacanian Psychoanalysis*, 17, pp. 6–36.

Parker, I. (2019) 'Psy ethics' in Y. Stavrakakis (ed.) *Routledge Handbook of Psychoanalytic Political Theory*, pp. 369–379. London and New York: Routledge.

Parker, I. and Pavón-Cuéllar, D. (2021) *Psychoanalysis and Revolution: Critical Psychology for Liberation Movements.* London: 1968 Press.

Pospihalj, D. (2022) 'For a Communist Clinic', *Sublation Magazine*, www.sublationmag.com/post/for-a-communist-clinic

Preciado, P. (2021) *Can the Monster Speak?: Report to an Academy of Psychoanalysts: A Report to an Academy of Psychoanalysts.* London: Fitzcarraldo Editions.

Žižek, S. (1989) *The Sublime Object of Ideology.* London: Verso.

Chapter 11

Singularity and the Real that Cannot Be Written

On Lacan's Use of Frege in His Later Work

Stijn Vanheule

A Plea for the Symptom

In the field of psychiatry, diagnosis is dominated by the medical semiological model, which is rooted in Hippocrateon medicine (Eco, 1976). Symptoms are seen as signs that refer to an underlying illness entity or disorder. This implies that all attention is directed towards the condition that causes the complaint. In this model, symptoms only play a secondary role, and have no inherent truth-value: they are mere signals of searched-for conditions. As a catalogue of potential disorders, the *Diagnostic and Statistical Manual of Mental Disorders*, in particular, bears witness of such an approach.

Lacanian psychoanalysts often indicate that a mere symptom-oriented approach is not characteristic of their practice (Verhaeghe, 2004), implying that the aim of their treatment does not consist in removing or mastering symptoms. On the other hand, it is remarkable that psychoanalysts take the symptom very seriously. In *Seminar XVIII* Lacan (1971) does so by stressing several times that, in line with Marx, Freud placed the symptom centre stage, and valued it as an autonomous object of inquiry. Freud no longer thinks of the symptom as a semiological sign, but as a rebus that must be read, independent of its associated illness or condition. In this line of reasoning the symptom obeys internal laws that have nothing to do with underlying illness entities, but with a presumed underlying subject: through the symptom repressed representations and desires are expressed, affecting the subject who suffers. In line with Lacan, the internal law the symptom follows can be thought of as the (clinical) structure a subject is marked by (Vanheule, 2011; Verhaeghe, 2004; Fink, 1995).

Clinical structures, of which Lacan characterized neurosis, psychosis and to a lesser extent perversion, are modes of functioning. In Lacan's early work these modes of functioning concern a logic in the relation between subject and Other (Lacan, 1959), and in his later work it refers to the way in which a so-called speaking-being[1] is positioned in discourse (Lacan, 1972–1973). In any case, clinical structures should not be thought of as underlying entities to which symptoms refer, but as modalities that only obtain a status because they are continually actualized via symptoms. By means of the symptom, the subject/speaking-being appears, and it is this mode of appearance that Lacan characterizes with his concept of structure.

DOI: 10.4324/9781003375920-14

The idea that psychoanalysis has a specific theory of the symptom is not novel, but remains most relevant for clinical thinking on psychic suffering. In a number of texts Jacques-Alain Miller (1998, 2011) suggests that with the aid of Frege's concepts of *Sinn* and *Bedeutung* two constitutive dimensions of the symptom can be discerned. Miller (1998) connects these to Lectures 17 and 23 from Freud's (1915–1917) *Introduction to Psychoanalysis*. In these lectures attention shifts away from the sense or message the symptom contains, to the *jouissance* it includes. In this line of reasoning the *Sinn*, or sense, refers to the repressed signified that the symptom qua signifier brings to the fore, while the *Bedeutung*, or referent, concerns an element of corporeal jouissance. The *Bedeutung* of a symptom is the libidinous enjoyment that is included in human suffering. It makes up the point around which the fundamental fantasy and pathological fixations are organized: "*Sinn* is the effect of sense, what is determined by the signified, and *Bedeutung* concerns the relation to the real" (Miller, 1998). Whereas *Sinn* can be interpreted, such is not the case for the *Bedeutung*. Miller (2011) indicates that *Bedeutung* and fixation should be *read* instead of interpreted. The underlying idea is that jouissance is not expressed in the semantics of speech, but in the way in which the Real is dealt with.

Indeed, in his work from the early nineteen seventies Lacan frequently refers to the works of Gottlob Frege and to his concepts *Sinn* and *Bedeutung*. With the aid of these constructs Lacan points to two components in the symptom, as well as to two dimensions in the discourse of the analyst. In this chapter I explore what Lacan aims at making clear as he discusses the concepts *Sinn* and *Bedeutung* in the nineteen seventies. Central to this discussion are Lacan's seminars XVIII, XIX and XX. My paper starts with a short discussion of Frege's concepts *Sinn* and *Bedeutung*, which will make clear that he also discerns a related third dimension: the *Vorstellung* or idea. Next I move to important lines of thought in Lacan's work from the nineteen seventies, and to his specific use of Frege's concepts *Sinn* and *Bedeutung*. Towards the end of the chapter I examine how Frege's dimension of the *Vorstellung*, which was not discussed by Lacan, could be thought of in Lacanian psychoanalysis.

Sinn, Bedeutung and Vorstellung: From Frege to Lacan

The distinction between *Sinn* and *Bedeutung* is central to two texts from Frege (1892a, 1892b), in which he discusses the nature of linguistic signs. Crucially, he discerns three components in linguistic signs: the referent or *Bedeutung*, the sense or *Sinn* and the idea/representation or *Vorstellung*. What he doesn't discuss in these texts is the material nature of the linguistic sign. His focus is on what the sign indicates.

From the perspective of Lacan's earlier work, his choice to focus on precisely this part of Frege's work is somewhat surprising. After all, Lacan used to emphasize the materiality of speech by directing all attention to the signifier. Just like de Saussure, who defined the signifier as the acoustic image of a word (de Saussure, 2006), Lacan uses the concept to refer to the material nature of the elements that make up language. He argues that at the level of the unconscious, the signifier is predominant, which, for example, can be seen in slips of the tongue. These are produced when the metonymic line of speech is interrupted and a signifier that the speaker didn't intend to say is uttered unexpectedly. In Frege's work, by contrast, the materiality of the linguistic sign is not a real issue. This might bear witness of the different concerns both authors have: Lacan starts from speech in the context free association during psychoanalytic treatment, and pays special attention to equivocality. Frege, in his turn, is concerned with questions concerning logics and scientificity, and is more concerned with univocality.

As Lacan incorporates the work of Frege into his own thinking, he does not explicitly address the question as to how his own concept of the signifier relates to the Fregean sign. However, in my view, his paper *The Signification of the Phallus – Die Bedeutung des Phallus* makes clear that for Lacan (1958) the Fregean sign is a synonym of the signifier. In this text Lacan defines the phallus as a signifier with particular characteristics ("The phallus as a signifier provides the ratio [*raison*] of desire" Lacan, 1985: 581), to which he refers with the concept *Bedeutung*. In this text Lacan does not explicitly refer to Frege, although he later indicates that he acquired the concept *Bedeutung* from Frege's work (Lacan, 1971). Whereas signifiers usually generate meaning by virtue of their reference to other signifiers, the phallus is unique in that it refers to the existence of signification as such: "it is the signifier that is destined to designate meaning effects as a whole" (Lacan, 1958: 579). Within this view, Lacan makes a clear distinction between the signified and signification, to which he refers with the term *Bedeutung*. Both are presented as two opposing categories: one possibility is that a signifier refers to other signifiers and generates signifieds via punctuation; the other possibility is that a signifier refers to the existence of signification effect as such. In terms of the latter, only one specimen exists, and that is the phallus. The phallus has no signified, i.e. no meaning, but it does have a referent, which is the signification effect of language.

In Frege's work, the *Bedeutung* concerns the object in the real world that the sign designates. It is the thing as knowable via direct sense impression (Frege, 1892b). Frege attributes a truth-value to this object: a statement is 'true' when it faithfully depicts the referent, and 'false' when this is not the case. For example, the message 'this is not a pipe' from Magritte's famous painting is 'true' when we take the material smoker's requisite as a referent, but 'false' if we accept that the depiction of a pipe is a good enough referent. Or, as Lacan says: "this is the sense that Frege gives to *Bedeutung*; it is denotation" (Lacan, 1971–1972: 55).

The sense or *Sinn*, in its turn, concerns "the mode of presentation" of a sign (Frege, 1892a: 153). It is the meaning commonly attributed to a sign: "The sense of a proper name is grasped by everybody who is sufficiently familiar with the language or totality of designations to which it belongs" (Frege 1892a: 153).

The classic example Frege (1892a) uses to differentiate between *Sinn* and *Bedeutung* is the ancient distinction between the 'morning star' and the 'evening star.' The morning star is the name given to the planet Venus when it appears east before sunrise, and the evening star is the name given to Venus when it appears west after sunset. In both cases the reference is the same, i.e. the planet Venus qua celestial body, while the sense in people's discourse differs depending on whether it is called morning star or evening star. Starting from the discipline of logics, Frege believes that the goal of science consists of disambiguating language by putting the *Bedeutung* to the fore, and by formulating as exactly as possible to which object a linguistic sign refers, which bears witness of a neopositivist attitude to signs and science (Eco, 1976). Or, as Lacan indicates with reference to logical positivism: "it consists putting a signified to the test of something that decides by yes or no" (1971: 13).

Frege's notion of the *Vorstellung* is the least well-known component he distinguishes in a sign. It concerns the representation or idea that takes shape in the mind of an individual. He describes it as: "an internal image, arising from memories of sense impressions which I have had and acts, both internal and external, which I have performed. Such an idea is often imbued with feeling; the clarity of its separate parts varies and oscillates" (Frege, 1892a: 154). Whereas *Sinn* concerns the shared concept or common sense that a sign evokes, the *Vorstellung* concerns an individual's associative memory network, with subjective impressions and affective connotations. Frege thus concludes:

> The idea is subjective: one man's idea is not that of another. . . . This constitutes an essential distinction between the idea and the sign's sense, which may be the common property of many and therefore is not a part or a mode of the individual mind.
>
> (Frege, 1892a: 154)

Indeed, while one can presume that the *Sinn* of a sign is identical for all members of a community, the *Vorstellung* is personal and context-dependent. The value and meaning of a representation are determined by the other representations a person has, which, in their turn are influenced by the individual's affective state and the precise moment in time at which representation is evoked. Frege believes that the *Vorstellung* is of minor importance for the logician and the scientist, which brings him to exclude this dimension from further reflection.

On the Sexual Non-Rapport, the Semblant and Sexual Jouissance

With the aim of discussing how Lacan uses Frege's concepts I will first discuss a number of crucial ideas from Lacan's work in the nineteen seventies.

As we already indicated with the aid of Miller (1998), Lacan connects the concept *Bedeutung* to the Real: the referent is something that cannot adequately be named, and in relation to which language is structurally failing:

> It is of the nature of language, I am not saying of speech, I am saying of language itself, that as regards approaching anything whatsoever that is signified in it, the referent is never the right one, and this is what makes a language.
>
> (Lacan, 1971: 45)

While Frege suggests that sensory perception can grasp the object that makes up the referent of language, Lacan, with reference to his psychoanalytic practice, believes that such is not the case. In his view, language use implies that all relationships with the referent are indirect.[2] In this context he also suggests that his concept of the Real is related to Aristotle's *ousia*, of which he says "[w]hat is proper to ousia . . . is that it cannot in any way be attributed, it is not sayable" (Lacan, 1971: 27). In other words: whereas Frege uses the *Bedeutung* with the aim of disambiguating the *Sinn*, Lacan believes that the dimension of *Bedeutung* simply cannot be disambiguated. The intangible nature of the referent cannot be mastered, but can only be compensated for by making use of discourse. Indeed, discourse doesn't reach the Real, but only gives shape to a sense of reality: to a world of appearances and semblances in which the discourse user can believe. In such a discursively structured world the Real is covered up, but not grasped. The Real continues to be manifested at the level of impossibilities in logical deductions, and in the inconsistencies of our experience of reality (Lacan, 1971: 27–30).

More particularly, Lacan links the concept *Bedeutung* to sexuality such as it takes shape at the level of the unconscious.[3] Sexuality cannot simply be understood in terms of the biology of the sexes – "the genotype of the body carries something that determines sex/gender [*le sexe*], but that's not enough" (Lacan, 1971–1972: 43) – but gravitates around what Lacan calls 'the sexual relationship' and 'sexual jouissance.' Characteristic of the sexual relation and sexual jouissance is that they are not regulated by instinctual biological forces, but make up a gap that always needs to be bridged. For him, the sexual opens up a field of 'non-rapport.' This does not mean to say that Lacan denies the relational issues that play between partners, but emphasizes that the factors that connect a man and a woman cannot be described unambiguously: "When I say *there is no sexual relationship*, I put forward very precisely this truth, that sex/gender [*le sexe*] defines no rapport at all in speaking beings" (Lacan, 1971: 13).

In this line of reasoning the concept 'rapport' has a specific meaning. Lacan defines the relationship between two elements in terms of a 'rapport' if the laws that govern their bond are fixed. If this is the case, the relationship "can be written" (Lacan, 1971: 65). For example, within this view, gravitation is a relationship that can be written: starting from knowledge on the physical properties of an object, like its mass and its density, formulas make it possible to calculate how long it will take to touch the ground when the object falls down from a given height.

Applied to sexuality it could be argued that the way male and female animals interact is fairly uniform, and depends only marginally on how two specific specimens behave. Yet as soon as our focus is on humans, the nature of relationships is not a priori given. In this context Lacan (1971–1972: 18) notes "the inability to formulate a precise rule at this point." A sexual relation is not installed on the basis of the correct triggers being projected, but is always contingent, and shaped through the encounter between two speaking-beings: "So it is in a discourse that natural men and women, as one might say, have to valorize themselves as such" (Lacan, 1971: 146). Thus, in humans the sexual relationship cannot be written: it cannot be formalized in terms of fixed rules that apply to each particular relationship: "The Other is absent from the moment that what is at stake is the sexual relationship" (Lacan, 1971–1972: 104). That's why Lacan qualifies the sexual relationship as a non-rapport. In this context he also mentions a "deficiency of the sexual rapport" (Lacan, 1971: 167), which indicates that there is no signifier that might name what a sexual relation consists of. The only things humans are left with are speech and discourse, which for Lacan (Lacan, 1971: 83, 148) should be thought of as an effect of the non-rapport. Indeed, all speech on the sexual non-rapport is a mere "half-saying" (Lacan, 1971–1972: 12), meaning speech that is ever beside the point. The fundamental impossibility that is inherent to the sexual relationship cannot be solved by means of the signifier: "sexual encounters always fails" (Lacan, 1971–1972: 27), which produces a state of desperation (Lacan, 1971–1972: 115). The only option individuals are left with is inventing ways of dealing with the non-rapport: "That they sort out themselves as best as they can" (Lacan, 1971–1972: 18).

In Lacan's view the sexual relationship is Real. It is "that which does not stop not being written" (Lacan, 1972–1973: 57), which implies that in order to establish a bond between individuals, speech must always be mobilized. Indeed, given the non-rapport at the basis of all relationships, the speaking-being cannot but make use of discourse, which opens up a field of semblance:

> For the boy, what is at stake in adult age, is being-a-man [*faire-homme*]. This is what constitutes the relation to the other party . . . one of the essential correlates of this being-a-man, is to indicate to the girl that one is so. In a word, we find ourselves put right away in the dimension of the semblant.
>
> (Lacan, 1971: 32)

A male person is not automatically 'man' in relation to a woman. Only by manifesting oneself as a man or a woman in discourse can a bond between partners take shape. In other words: *the* sexual relationship is Real and cannot be written; what remains open is the possibility of engaging oneself in *a* sexual relation. This is only possible through the use of discourse, and by identifying oneself as man or woman.

As already suggested, Lacan indicates that the use of discourse implies the dimension of the *semblant*. Crucial for our understanding of this concept is that throughout his teaching Lacan interpreted it in various ways (Grigg, 2007). In the nineteen fifties he uses the concept *semblant* to refer to the world of appearances that is installed by means of the Imaginary. At that moment semblance is an imaginary phenomenon that needs to be distinguished from the Symbolic. As Lacan developed his discourse theory this all changes profoundly. Henceforth, the *semblant* refers to a position through which an agent enters discourse. At this point "there is no discourse that is not of the semblant" (Lacan, 1971: 146). In seminar XIX he more specifically defines the four positions in discourse as shown in Figure 11.1 (Lacan, 1971–1972: 67).

Upon making a comparison with the position he discerned in Seminar XVII (Lacan, 1969–1970) it might strike one that he calls the position of the agent, top

Semblant	Jouissance
Truth	Surplus Jouissance

Figure 11.1 The four positions in Lacan's discourse formulas.

left in the discourse formula, the place of the *semblant*. It is the place from which all further acts are determined, and the point at which one of the elements of discourse is taken seriously (S_1, S_2, $ or *a*). In this line of reasoning an element of discourse starts to function as a *semblant* when an agent identifies with it, and starts functioning in the name of this discourse element. In each of the four discourses that Lacan discerns semblance takes shape in a particular way. In the discourse of the master semblance takes shape by positing an idea/signifier as a fact (S_1); in the discourse of the university this proceeds by coming out with knowledge (S_2); in the discourse of the hysteric by putting the division of the subject on the foreground ($); and in the discourse of the analyst, in its turn, by bringing an objectal sign of life to the fore (*a*).

In terms of the sexual non-rapport Lacan indicates that a sexual relation takes shape starting from one of these elements in discourse. For example, his idea of 'being-a-man,' mentioned earlier, indicates that one identifies with masculinity qua S_1 in the discourse of the master (Lacan, 1971–1972: 108). 'Being-a-man' means that one adopts a prevailing idea of masculinity and acts from the assumption that one coincides with this idea. The effect of such use of semblance is that an interaction with another person, who will henceforth be qualified as man or woman, can begin, and that a sexual relation can take shape. Above all, such a sexual relation is a product of discourse, and a compensation for the actual non-rapport. Moreover, in line with his Hegelian schema of subjective recognition (Lacan, 1955–1956) he believes that each use of the *semblant* is not simply a matter of using characteristic self-references 'I am a man,' but a result of how one thinks of the other. The following quote makes this clear: "[s]exual identification does not consist in believing oneself to be a man or a woman, but in taking account of the fact that there are women, for the boy, and that there are men, for the girl" (Lacan, 1971: 34).

In terms of Lacan's discourse formula the concept of *semblant* also indicates that the element one starts from in making use of discourse is only the apparent motor of the process. Indeed, the *semblant* is determined by yet another element, which is the *truth*. Just like the *semblant*, *truth* is a position in discourse. It is the lower left position in the formula (Figure 11.1), and in each of the four discourses another element occupies this position. For example, in the discourse of the master subjective division ($) can be found behind the decisiveness of a statement (S_1), and in the discourse of the analyst the knowledge that makes up the unconscious (S_2) is what guides the seemingly objectal presence of the analyst (*a*).

In his discussion of sexual jouissance, Lacan starts from a similar logic: similar to the sexual relationship, jouissance cannot be thought of in purely biological terms, nor can the dynamics that govern jouissance be written in law-like terms.

In this context he mentions "the impossibility of subordinating the enjoyment described as sexual to that which, *sub rosa*, would specify the man and the woman taken as the carriers each one of a precise batch of genotypes" (Lacan, 1971: 148), and he also indicates that "sexual jouissance is found not to be able to be written, and it is from this that results the structural multiplicity" (Lacan, 1971: 107). Just like the sexual relationship, sexual jouissance is biologically dysregulated, which drives the human being into the arms of language and discourse. The net result is that sexuality takes shape in variable ways.

In this line of reasoning, 'pure' jouissance is an impossibility that can only be imagined mythically. Yet, as soon as representations of it are made, jouissance is linked to images and signifiers, thus losing its direct nature. An iconic example Lacan frequently refers to for illustrating the idea of pure jouissance is the primal father from Freud's paper *Totem and Taboo*. The primal father is a male figure in a horde of primitive individuals who, without any limitation, would have enjoyed all women. To the extent that he is a pre-discursive being that is not subjected to any cultural law, this primal father has a pure jouissance, and is not a "slave of the phallic function" (Lacan, 1971–1972: 108). However, by thinking, speaking and writing, sexual jouissance is conditioned by discourse and is no longer limitless in nature. As this happens jouissance obtains a phallic character: "[t]he phallus is very properly sexual jouissance in so far as it is co-ordinated to a semblant, in so far as it is solidary with a semblant" (Lacan, 1971: 34). Indeed, by evoking from what, and in relation to whom one enjoys, sexual jouissance obtains an image and a name, and starts being a semblance. This implies that, on the one hand, the experience of jouissance can be actualized at the level of one's representations. On the other hand, the use of discourse implies that direct access to jouissance is lost. As soon as jouissance obtains a place in discourse via the *semblant*, it is castrated and subjected to limits.

Other examples Lacan refers to as he discusses pure jouissance include the texts of Marquis de Sade. For example, in his novel *120 Days of Sodom*, forty women and boys are held in captivity and subjected to the pleasures of four libertarians. These libertarians merely use the bodies of their captives in terms of their own satisfaction and don't feel restricted to any taboo. Lacan suggests that such use of the body bears witness of an unlimited jouissance:

> [t]o enjoy [*Jouir*], is to enjoy a body. To enjoy, is to kiss it, is to embrace it, is to cut it in pieces. In law, to have the jouissance of something is exactly this, it is to be able to treat something as a body, namely to demolish it.
>
> (Lacan, 1971–1972: 32)

In this context, pure jouissance is equated with enjoying and taking advantage of a body, which in the end results in the destruction of bodily integrity. By making use of discourse jouissance is subject to the *semblant* and to the laws of discourse. Hence Lacan's idea that "language functions, from its origin, as a stand in for sexual jouissance. Along this way it organizes the intrusion of jouissance in corporeal repetition" (Lacan, 1971–1972: 44). Language tempers the unbridled nature of jouissance and submits it to cultural habits and taboos. It is for denoting this point of submission to the *semblant* that Lacan uses the term phallus in his later work.

The Phallus and the *Bedeutung*

The phallus, which he represents with the symbol Φ, refers to the intersection between jouissance and the *semblant*. It indicates that both an experience of lack and compensation are created when language and discourse enter the field of jouissance. An experience of lack is created because the *semblant* cuts something from the purity of jouissance, which is why sexual jouissance can be qualified as castrated. An experience of compensation, in its turn, is created when a speaking-being starts to believe that by means of language something can indeed be told about sexual jouissance, and about the way in which it plays between partners. In Lacan's view, all human speech is grafted on this intersection between jouissance and the *semblant*:

> Language . . . , in the end, only connotes the impossibility of symbolizing the sexual rapport among the beings that inhabit it, this language, by reason of the fact that it is from this habitat that they are able to speak.
>
> (Lacan, 1971: 148)

The phallus represents this impossibility.

In Seminar XVIII Lacan on the other hand notes that the title of his earlier paper *La signification du phallus – Die Bedeutung des Phallus* (Lacan, 1958) is in fact a pleonasm. He then suggests that the phallus itself can be thought of as the *Bedeutung* all speech attempts to get hold of: "[i]n language there is no other *Bedeutung* than the phallus" (Lacan, 1971: 148).

As both lines of reasoning are combined it can be noted that Lacan in fact uses the term phallus in two ways.

On the one hand he indicates that in the system of language, the phallus is the *Bedeutung* all other signifiers refer to. While Frege thought of the linguistic sign in terms of a link with the external world, Lacan holds on to the idea of intralinguistic reference: signifiers refer to signifiers. This is an idea he starts from in the nineteen fifties and holds on to in the nineteen seventies. The nuance he adds to this basic idea is that one signifier, the phallus, is exceptional in that all other signifiers refer to it. The phallus is "the sign for the 'passion of the signifier'" (Lacan, 1970: 399). In terms of Lacan's mathemes this idea can be depicted as follows: $\Phi \leftarrow S_2$.

On the other hand, Lacan indicates that the phallus itself is a most remarkable signifier in that it does not refer to anything substantial, but only points to the *non-rapport*. This means that from a Fregean point of view, the phallus has no referent, and cannot 'write' the Real the human subject has to deal with. It only names the impossibility: "[t]he Real of sexual jouissance, in so far as it is detached as such, it is the phallus" (Lacan, 1971: 34). Indeed, the phallus points to the Real but doesn't help overcoming it. Note that in making a link between the phallus and the Real of sexuality Lacan made a substantial change compared to his works from the nineteen fifties, where the phallus merely referred to the existence of meaning effects (Lacan, 1958). In Seminar XVII Lacan refers to the impossibility of writing jouissance with a triangle or a double slash, which he places at the lower level of his discourse formula, between 'truth' and 'product.' In line with this notation, we can depict the Real the phallus points to as follows: $\blacktriangle \leftarrow \Phi$ or $// \leftarrow \Phi$. Summarized, this brings us to the scheme shown in Figure 11.2.

In this line of reasoning, the phallus can be thought of as an elementary mode of defense against the non-rapport. For example, in his paper *L'Étourdit* Lacan (1972: 458) writes that the phallic register compensates the non-rapport. He then describes the phallus as "the function that makes up for the sexual rapport," which, as already indicated, doesn't exist. Hence the idea that the function of the phallus consists of "dealing with the absence of the sexual rapport" (Lacan, 1972: 458). It seems that in this line of reasoning the phallus refers to an act of faith: i.e. the belief that it makes sense to use discourse in dealing with the Real and jouissance. Indeed, henceforth the phallus can be defined as making use of the semblant in dealing with jouissance and with the non-rapport. With his mathemes Lacan expresses this use of the phallus as follows: Φx. In this formula, Φx is the variable that refers to jouissance (Lacan, 1971: 170). The combination x makes clear that *jouissance* is approached through the angle of phallic signification.

What does this line of reasoning about the phallus and the use of semblance imply for Lacan's discussion of the sexual relation? The core idea seems to be that which plays between man and woman is phallic in nature, which implies a castrated relation to the sexual object: "For men, the girl is the phallus, and this is what castrates them. For women, the boy is the same thing, the phallus, and this is what castrates them also" (Lacan, 1971: 34). In this line of reasoning, man and woman have a different and non-complementary relation to the phallus. In Seminar XX Lacan (1972–1973) expresses their respective positions with his formulas of sexuation. These formulas indicate that the masculine position consists of the attempt to approach *jouissance* entirely from the phallic register (Grigg, 2005). In this context

The *Bedeutung* of language	$\Phi \leftarrow S_2$
The *Bedeutung* of the phallus	$\Phi \blacktriangle \leftarrow \Phi$ or $// \leftarrow$

Figure 11.2 The *bedeutung* of language and the *bedeutung* of the phallus – version 1.

masculinity does not refer to someone's biological equipment, but to a position in discourse. Lacan expresses this position with the following formula: $\forall x \Phi x$. The formula indicates that all ($\forall$) that plays at the level of *jouissance* (x), is approached via phallic signification (Φx). Characteristic for the female position, in its turn, is that approaching *jouissance* via discourse is only partial. Not all *jouissance* is approached from a phallic angle: $\overline{\forall X} \bullet \Phi X$. A part of it, which Lacan qualifies as feminine jouissance, is not mastered via the *semblant*.

A further effect of assuming the phallic function is that *jouissance* itself obtains a discursive position. In Seminar XIX Lacan more specifically qualifies the upper right position in the discourse formula as the place of *jouissance* (see Figure 11.1). In making this point he indicates that by making use of the *semblant*, pre-discursive jouissance is partly made discursive. The part that fails to be integrated in discourse, in its turn, is indicated by the absence of an arrow between the positions 'truth' and 'surplus jouissance,' or by the triangle or double slash that he sometimes puts there.

Interestingly, in Seminar XVIII Lacan also picks up the discussion of the relation between the concepts phallus and Name-of-the-Father. From the start he qualifies them as closely related (Lacan, 1971: 34), and as he goes on, he concludes that the function of the phallus consists of *naming* what remained Real. In his discussion he addresses an example from Russell, who claimed that 'the author of Waverly novels' is not just a synonym for 'Sir Walter Scott,' just like 'the morning star' is not just a synonym for 'Venus': "*The author of Waverley novels* carries a sense, a *Sinn*, while *Sir Walter Scott* designates a *Bedeutung*" (Lacan, 1971: 171). 'Sir Walter Scott' is a proper name, and not just a signifier. Proper names designate a speaking-being, and introduce the speaking-being qua subject in discourse. The actual signification, which indicates who the subject actually is, takes place only in a second step, via the chain of signifiers that is mobilized with reference to the proper name. The following quote from Lacan demonstrates this line of reasoning, and makes clear that qualifying someone as 'father' only has an organizing effect if that person actually identifies with this nomination and produces signifiers that place it in a broader speech context: "What is named Father, the Name-of-the-Father, if it is a name that is efficacious, it is precisely because someone stands up to answer" (Lacan, 1971: 172). In a similar vein, the proper name 'Sir Walter Scott' only signifies something if signifiers are produced like 'the author of Waverley novels,' which make clear who 'Sir Walter Scott' precisely is:

> If the *author of Waverley novels*, is a *Sinn*, it is precisely because the *author of Waverley novels* replaces something else, which is a special *Bedeutung*, the one that Frege thinks he should pinpoint with the name of *Sir Walter Scott*.
>
> (Lacan, 1971: 172)

In this line of reasoning, the phallus can be thought of as the nomination a speaking-being uses for the Real of the sexual non-rapport. In Lacan's line of reasoning, psychoanalytic treatment aims at detecting such nomination; at discerning the name or names someone has given to the non-rapport. The S_1 the analytic discourse (Figure 11.3) produces, refers to the concrete name(s) someone has been giving to this Real. It pinpoints the non-rapport, but doesn't clarify it.

Characteristic of the analytic discourse is that via the position of object he/she occupies (symbolized by a in Figure 11.3) the analyst stimulates free association. Free association allows signifiers to circulate, such that an experience of surprise is created for the ego, and the question of who the subject ($) is comes to the fore. On the one hand this mode of speech digs up the unconscious knowledge that makes up someone's truth (S_2). Indeed, associative speech that explores the signifiers included in symptoms and in productions of the unconscious brings a body of knowledge to the fore that was repressed until then; a knowledge of which analysts presume determines symptoms. On the other hand the analytic discourse also creates something specific, and that is the S_1. Through free association, the analysand encounters 'esoteric' (sic. Deleuze, 1969) signifiers that function as crossroads or end points of diverse associative lines. Such signifiers are senseless, and cannot be translated in terms of unconscious knowledge (indicated by the double slash between S_1 and S_2). They are without rhyme or reason, but name the Real of the sexual non-rapport. Thus, the concept of *Bedeutung* in Lacan's work can be expanded as shown in Figure 11.4.

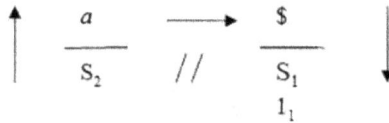

$$\uparrow \quad \frac{a}{S_2} \quad \longrightarrow \quad \frac{\$}{S_1} \quad \downarrow$$
$$1_1$$

Figure 11.3 The discourse of the analyst.

The *Bedeutung* of language and of unconscious knowledge	$\Phi \leftarrow S_2$ or $S_1 \leftarrow S_2$
The *Bedeutung* of the phallus and of the master signifier	$\blacktriangle \leftarrow \Phi$ or $\blacktriangle \leftarrow S_1$ or $// \leftarrow \Phi$ or $// \leftarrow S_1$

Figure 11.4 The bedeutung of language and the bedeutung of the phallus – version 2.

Sinn and *Vorstellung* in Lacan's Work

Now that we have discussed how the concept of *Bedeutung* can be thought of we will address how *Sinn* and *Vorstellung* are henceforth used by Lacan. Starting from Seminar XII Lacan (1964–1965) situates *Sinn* at the level of unconscious knowledge. *Sinn* is not an unambiguous message that could be derived from the signifiers of a symptom, but a set of signifiers and signifieds that repeatedly emerge in someone's speech. Sense is never unequivocal but equivocal, and dispersed over the collection of signifiers that come to the fore in free association. Free association deconstructs symptoms and productions of the unconscious, such that what remains is a collection of signifiers and signifieds that represent aspects of desire.

Whereas symptoms can be thought of as *manifestations* of sense, *Sinn* is only articulated and obtains a place when it is articulated via free association. Sense is articulated when, through the deployment of the discourse of the analyst, repressed or fended of signifiers come together and open up a field of signifieds that concern the person who is speaking. In terms of the discourse of the analyst, *Sinn* is the knowledge (S_2) that makes up the truth of this discourse.

The *Vorstellung*, which Frege discusses as the third dimension of the sign, doesn't obtain an explicit place in Lacan's work. However, in my interpretation this dimension can be meaningfully integrated into Lacan's reflection on *Bedeutung* and *Sinn*. Considered from the discourse of the analyst, the labor of free association, which brings the divided subject ($) to the fore, can be thought of as the dimension of the *Vorstellung*. While Frege, as a logician, excluded the *Vorstellung* qua person-specific and situation-specific aspects of the linguistic sign from his further reflections, Lacan, in line with Freud, actually puts it to the fore. Free association invites the analysand to leave aside common sense, and to explore signifiers that emerge through symptoms and productions of the unconscious. Along this way the person- and situation-specific use of the signifier comes to the fore, and the subject is connoted in specific terms.

Conclusion

While Lacan starts from Frege when he incorporates the concepts *Sinn* and *Bedeutung* into his own work, it is striking that he defines and uses these terms in completely different ways. For Frege, *Bedeutung* refers to the extra-linguistic object the linguistic sign refers to. For Lacan, by contrast, *Bedeutung* refers to the dimension of the Real, as primarily expressed at the level of sexuality and the sexual relation. Characteristic of the Real is that it 'cannot be written,' meaning that no laws underlying the Real can be articulated. Yet Lacan indicates that human beings give names to the Real and to the non-rapport they are confronted with. This attempt of the speaking-being to name the Real can be qualified as phallic. In terms of the discourse of the analyst, the singular signifiers (S_1) free association ends up with are the names a speaking-being gives to the Real. Indeed, the sexual non-rapport is the *Bedeutung* S_1 names, and in its turn S_1 is the *Bedeutung* to which all other signifiers used in free association (S_2)

refer. *Sinn*, in its turn, refers to *common sense* in Frege's work: it is the meaning that is commonly attributed to a linguistic sign. In Lacan's work *Sinn* refers to the signifiers that make up the unconscious, and to the equivocality of the signifieds that are associated with these signifiers. In the formula of the analytic discourse, sense can be located at the level of the unconscious knowledge (S_2) that makes up the truth of someone's speech. The third component Frege discerns in the linguistic sign is the *Vorstellung*, which refers to the personal ideas and feelings a speaker connects to a sign. Lacan doesn't discuss this component explicitly, but in terms of the logic of the discourse of the analyst I suggest that the *Vorstellung* can be situated at the level of free association all analytic work starts with.

Notes

1 The concept of 'speaking being' [*être parlant*] or 'speaking-being' [*parlêtre*], which Lacan uses quite frequently in the nineteen seventies, should clearly be distinguished from the concept of subject. In Lacan's work, the subject is a mere project of determination by signifiers. It is the aspect of self-experience that arises via connotations of signifiers. The concept of speaking-being, in its turn, refers to the tension between speech and *jouissance* qua corporeal fact: "the speaking-being to put it plainly, is this disturbed relationship to one's own body which is called jouissance" (Lacan, 1971–1972: 43).
2 "[T]he reference to all what has to do with language is always indirect" (Lacan, 1971: 58).
3 "The Real, properly speaking, is incarnated by what? By sexual jouissance, as what? As impossible" (Lacan, 1971: 33).

References

de Saussure, F. (2006). *Writings in General Linguistics*. Oxford: Oxford University Press.
Deleuze, G. (1969). *The Logic of Sense*. New York: Columbia University Press, 2001.
Eco, U. (1976). *A Theory of Semiotics*. London: Macmillan.
Fink, B. (1995). *The Lacanian Subject*. Princeton: Princeton University Press.
Frege, G. (1892a). On *Sinn* and *Bedeutung*. In M. Beaney (Ed.): *The Frege Reader*, pp. 151–171. Oxford: Blackwell, 1997.
Frege, G. (1892b). Comments on *Sinn* and *Bedeutung*. In M. Beaney (Ed.): *The Frege Reader*, pp. 172–180. Oxford: Blackwell, 1997.
Freud, S. (1915–1916). Introductory lectures on psycho-analysis. In J. Strachey (Ed. & Trans.): *The Standard Edition of the Complete Psychological Works of Sigmund Freud* (Vol. 15). London: Hogarth Press.
Grigg, R. (2005). Lacan and Badiou: Logic of the pas-tout. *Filozofski Vestnik*, 2, 53–65.
Grigg, R. (2007). Semblant, phallus and object in Lacan's teaching. *Umbra*, 1, 131–8.
Lacan, J. (1955–1956). *Le Séminaire de Jacques Lacan, Livre III, Les psychoses*, texte établi par J.-A. Miller. Paris: du Seuil, 1981.
Lacan, J. (1958). The signification of the phallus – Die Bedeutung des Phallus. In J. Lacan (Ed.): *Écrits: The First Complete Edition in English*, pp. 575–84. Trans. B. Fink. New York & London: W.W. Norton, 2006.
Lacan, J. (1959). On a question prior to any possible treatment of psychosis. In J. Lacan (Ed.): *Écrits: The First Complete Edition in English*, pp. 445–88. Trans. B. Fink. New York & London: W.W. Norton, 2006.

Lacan, J. (1964–1965). *Le Séminaire de Jacques Lacan, Livre XII, Problèmes cruciaux pour la psychanalyse*. Unpublished seminar.

Lacan, J. (1969–1970). *Le Séminaire de Jacques Lacan, Livre XVII, L'envers de la psychanalyse*, texte établi par J.-A. Miller. Paris: du Seuil, 1991.

Lacan, J. (1970). Préface à une thèse. In J. Lacan (Ed.): *Autres Écrits*, pp. 393–402. Paris: du Seuil, 2001.

Lacan, J. (1971). *Le Séminaire de Jacques Lacan, Livre XVIII, D'un discours qui ne serait pas du semblant*, texte établi par J.-A. Miller. Paris: du Seuil, 2006.

Lacan, J. (1971–1972). *Le Séminaire de Jacques Lacan, Livre XIX, Ou pire . . .*, texte établi par J.-A. Miller. Paris: du Seuil, 2011.

Lacan, J. (1972). L'Étourdit. In J. Lacan (Ed.): *Autres Écrits*, pp. 449–495. Paris: du Seuil, 2001.

Lacan, J. (1972–1973). *Le Séminaire de Jacques Lacan, Livre XX, Encore*, texte établi par J.-A. Miller. Paris: du Seuil, 1975.

Miller, J.-A. (1998). The Seminar of Barcelona on *Die Wege der Symptombildung*. *Psychoanalytical Notebooks, 1*. Retrieved from: www.londonsociety-nls.org.uk/JAM_barcelona.htm

Miller, J.-A. (2011). Reading a symptom. *Hurly-Burly – The International Lacanian Journal of Psychoanalysis*, 6, 143–152.

Vanheule, S. (2011). *The Subject of Psychosis – A Lacanian Perspective*. London & New York: Palgrave Macmillan.

Verhaeghe, P. (2004). *On Being Normal and Other Disorders*. New York: Other Press.

Section 4

Spare Parts

Chapter 12

To Create, Perform, Produce Psychology from Scratch

Negativity in the Work of
Wolfgang Giegerich

Nicholas Balaisis

Introduction

In a recent book on psychology that draws on Jung, Wolfgang Giegerich, and the novelist Joseph Conrad, Greg Mogenson (2019) argues that while modern psychology is significantly versed in the positive and empirical, it does not have much to offer in terms of the *negative*. He states that academic and clinical psychology "knows a tremendous amount" about "memory, perception . . . sexuality, and attachment behavior" but doesn't much address what Conrad describes as "that glimpse of truth which we forgot to ask for" (p. 9). Much of psychotherapy works in the realm of the *positive* – treatment goals, acute symptoms, scaling assessments – but more rarely attends to the *negative* in the patient. This is reinforced by many patients themselves, who are increasingly armed with psycho ed. and are well-versed in their knowledge of psychological terms like attachment styles and come with specific treatment plans, goals and even notions of what qualifies as successful therapy. As Mogenson suggests, however, the therapeutic process often elicits that which we didn't ask for, or as Jung frequently asserts: the other picture that looms up in the background behind the analysand. It is this *negativity* that often matters most in psychotherapeutic practice.

In making this claim, Mogenson draws on the notion of the negative in psychotherapy advanced at length by Wolfgang Giegerich. For Giegerich, the negative identifies the non-empirical heart of psychology – psychology's true object of focus, and a focus which stands at odds with much contemporary psychotherapy, Jungian analysis and clinical psychology. In stressing the negative in psychotherapy (and recovering the negative in Jung's work itself), Giegerich pushes against contemporary goal-oriented psychotherapy. This focus has implications for many aspects of psychotherapeutic practice such as its temporal orientation (its tense) as well as the stance and role of the therapist. Working in the space or tense of the negative, he argues, is to be backward-looking and performative; it is an ephemeral labor produced and reproduced by both analyst and patient, effecting not results or goals, but temporary "glimpses" of psychological truth.

DOI: 10.4324/9781003375920-16

The Negative in Fairy Tales: Integrating Hegel

Giegerich's use of negativity draws greatly from Hegel and the *Phenomenology of Spirit*. In Volume 3 of his Collected Writing in English, *Soul-Violence*, Giegerich uses a fairy tale to exemplify the work of negation or negativity in psychology. He recounts the tale of the *Robber Bridegroom*, a folk tale about a miller's daughter who is promised to a rich suitor. In the tale, the daughter sets off to visit the suitor in a forest and comes upon the den of an ancient woman, who warns the daughter that she is in a murderer's den and so conceals the daughter behind a barrel. The daughter then witnesses the robbers violently dismembering another girl who they have led into the house thinking it to be the promised bride. The girl remains behind the barrel and ultimately escapes and marries the suitor, producing the ring finger of the chopped-up girl as proof of her ordeal. For Giegerich, this fairy tale and, in particular, the girl's stance toward the event, exemplifies the role of negativity in psychology, and most significantly, the successful engagement *with* the negative on the part of the girl in the tale. What stands out most for Giegerich is that the girl in the fairy tale is able to witness and withstand the horror of the dismemberment without fleeing.

> She is obviously up to the horror that takes place before her eyes. She is able to bear the "unbearable" sight. She does not experience the horror as absolute trauma. She demonstrates quite literally what it means "to look the negative in the face and to tarry with it."
>
> (Giegerich, 2020b, p. 148)

For Giegerich, the negative figures importantly in psychotherapy as something that must be lingered within or tarried with. In invoking tarrying with the negative, of course, he draws upon Hegel's famous sentence in the *Phenomenology*, a passage that Giegerich returns to frequently in his work. In this same passage, Hegel (1977) describes the life of Spirit as that which does not "shrink from death and keep itself untouched by devastation, but rather the life that endures it and maintains itself in it" (p. 19). This "maintaining" itself in the face of the negative is what Giegerich (2020b) identifies in the fairy tale, as a dialectical "integration" in psychological work, often experienced or expressed through violence: "the witnessing of the dismemberment of another always implies one's own annihilation namely through the narcissistic insult, indeed the killing of one's own ideal inherent in this *sight*" (p. 149). Tarrying with the negative in psychology involves a dialectical devastation that has been "withstood, been received by consciousness" and which consciousness "has grown in the experience" (p. 149). Giegerich's work stresses the violence or cut implied in Hegel's description of "devastation," and places it at the center of psychological work. To think or experience something psychologically for Giegerich is precisely to be "touched" by devastation in the way that the girl does in the fairy tale.

Tarrying with the Negative in the Perfect Tense

This cut of devastation for Giegerich assumes a particular tense in the psychological scene, a tense that puts his argument about psychology in opposition to contemporary models of psychology. Giegerich frequently speaks against the developmental – or future-oriented – model of therapy so prevalent in modern modes of clinical practice. The developmental model is rooted in positivism and empiricism, which for him are not the work of psychotherapy.

> What I conceive, by contrast, is a "psychotherapy of the perfect tense." No ideal. No wishing and hoping. No Sollen and striving. Because there is nothing to strive for, no goal set for us. Any developmental goal envisioned by psychology can be seen through as an ego program, our own agenda. What is needed instead of all this is merely our "catching up with" what has already become real.
>
> (2020a, p. 416)

The negative inhabits the space of "the catching up." Psychotherapy in the perfect tense means to catch up and tarry with that which *already happened* but which the ego has not yet realized, or from which it often flees. Psychotherapy thus always looks backward, a tense that puts it at odds with many applications of contemporary therapy and many clients' wishes and plans for betterment, improvement or even more "meaningful" or purposive forms of existence. Giegerich sees the desire for "meaning" or purpose as a neurotic formation precisely because it is *positively* conceived. Meaning in the contemporary psychological scene is largely *positivized* as some external Other based on a lack.

This is true of clinical practice that promises evidence-based metrics or SMART goals that seem to provide empirical proof of psychic improvement. We achieve meaning as a result or effect of satisfying a series of psychological goals. Here we can think of common prescriptions or treatment for depression as existing empirically *in front* of the client – if only they walk or exercise more they will find greater meaning and purpose out there in the world. Positive psychology is one that presents the cure on the horizon in front of the client rather than as something more immanent and, in Giegerich's terms, already embedded in the client's logical negativity. In speaking directly on the question of "meaning" as a clinical goal, Giegerich argues that it is always only *immanent* rather than *transcendent* (or logically negative). "Is it really so terrible to live without a higher meaning? Is it really the void that yawns before us when we are without it? After all, Homer, Dante, Shakespeare, Goethe . . . etc. etc. Are they not enough? More than enough? (2020a, pp. 230–231). In other words, we do not *make* meaning through psychotherapy as a kind of positive empirical enterprise.

Psychotherapy in the *perfect tense* mirrors in some ways the Freudian arc of analysis as gaining recognition of one's false or outgrown childhood illusions and aspirations (recognition of one's castration). Giegerich often cites a parallel quote from Roland Barthes where he states that being modern "is to know what is no longer possible" (2020c, p. 179). We might say the same thing in the work of psychotherapy, an insight that echoes the Freudian view that therapy leaves us sadder, but wiser. For Giegerich, this knowledge is also the work of psychological thinking, but with the additional cut of violent recognition. For Giegerich, *knowing* what is no longer possible represents a negation, or a killing which initiates a new mode of knowing (and a letting go of ego-illusions). Greg Mogenson (2005) describes it this way: "Psychological reflection above all knows itself, even if the reflective moment of that knowing changes it, [kills it] requiring yet other reflective acts *ad infinitum*" (p. 12).

The distinction that Giegerich draws between the developmental modes of psychotherapy and "psychology with soul" is akin to the distinction that Hegel draws between his dialectical method and the insights drawn through science, positivism or Schelling. Dialectical insight for Hegel (1977) cannot be achieved "like a shot from a pistol" as immediately graspable (p. 16). Rather, "true thoughts and scientific insight are only to be won through the labor of the Notion" (p. 43). In other parts of the dialectic Hegel speaks about truth being "ripened to its properly matured form so as to be capable of being the property of all self-consciousness Reason" (p. 43). For Hegel, philosophy enters after the fact, looking backward, following the Owl of Minerva. For Giegerich, similarly, psychology happens as a catching up after the fact and a truth borne through a labor with the negative, a *coming home* to that which *already is* (or has become true).

Recovering the Negative in Jung

In making the case for a psychotherapy in the perfect tense Giegerich recovers an orientation towards the negative that he sees and underlines in Jung. Giegerich frequently returns to a passage in Jung where he describes psychology as something which happens in the background of the clinical scene: "behind the impressions of daily life – behind the scenes – another picture looms up, covered by a thin veil of facts" (1997, p. 8). Giegerich conceives the "other picture" that looms up as what he calls the *psychological difference*, mapping the space between the empirical/factual presentations of the patient (their statements, their symptoms) and what Jungians often refer to as the *objective psyche*. Drawing on a line from Joseph Conrad, Greg Mogenson refers to this looming picture (always negative) as "that glimpse of truth for which you had forgotten to ask" (p. 9). Psychology always has an ear for this other picture that looms up, between the lines, or even against the grain of what the patient *positively* identifies as the therapeutic goal or presenting problem. The art of therapy often consists of drawing attention to this other picture or forgotten question that can frequently break the alliance and create the appearance that the therapist isn't listening to the client's real (*positive*) concerns.

Attending to that which occurs in the background distinguishes this kind of psychology from what Giegerich describes as the technician approach in much of clinical psychology. He speaks of hatching or circumambulating as verbs to describe therapeutic work, actions that seek not to isolate the symptom and its direct resolution but rather to encourage the patient to *think psychologically*. Here again he draws upon particular passages in Jung where he sees attention to the negative. He often reiterates a central claim by Jung that the therapist meets the patient not as a technician or even physician but empty-handed like an attendant, nurse or servant: "*Therapon* means first of all servant, caretaker, attendant, nurse. Only that! Nothing heroic or magnificent" (Giegerich, *Dreams*, p. 38). The dangers of the current psychological modality (or psychological epistle), for Giegerich, is to reify the symptom – to limit the symptom as a *positivity* or a *thing* – a thing that can be categorized and to which one can apply the treatment systematically. As he argues, "soul" or Geist "does not have a permanent (thing-like) existence" (*Geist*, p. 33). It is not empirically given.

Psychology and psychological thinking must therefore also be ephemeral and performative. Giegerich hangs on a particular line from where he notes that psychological interpretation involves a retelling of the symptom in the analytical space – to "say it again, as well as you can". This *retelling* is where the negative *glimpse* of psychology resides. Psychology is thus linguistic, performative, ephemeral and of course always approximate. In speaking about dreams as psychological phenomena, for instance, he challenges the often-used symbology that Jungian analysts use as guides to interpreting client dreams. Against this, he argues that dreams are not in themselves psychologically important (as positive matter); they become psychologically meaningful only in what Jung described as their interpretive retelling. He compares this to works of art like poetry or painting, noting that they are not empirically given things. Works of art come into being or into existence through their being thought by the viewer: it "needs to be re-created afresh by the viewer. And it exists only in this act of re-creation and only as long as it lasts and maintained, kept alive" (*Geist*, p. 33).

Psychology's Lack of Archimedean Point

In stressing the ephemeral and performative/linguistic notion of psychology, Giegerich refines another subtle but crucial aspect of Jung's psychology: psychology's lack of an Archimedean point. Giegerich (following Jung) troubles psychology's self-embrace as a positivistic science, adopting the Archimedean point of observation and knowledge similar to other sciences like biology. Distinguishing psychology from the other sciences, Giegerich (2020a) argues that it is not a discipline constituted "through a structural difference between subject and object" (p. 570). In science, he continues, the object of study is irrevocably outside of itself. In depth psychology there is no Archimedean point outside of itself: "This means that psychology is logically so constituted that it operates within a fundamental identity. It is structurally not different from itself. Symbolically expressed: it is uroboric. It bites its own tail" (p. 570). Greg Mogenson (2017). describes this notion in Giegerich using the figure of total immersion in the sea without a boat:

> In contrast to other sciences which theorize from a position that is supposedly outside the phenomena that they are concerned with (for which they may be

called "dry land" or "ship's deck" sciences), psychology is immersed in itself as in an infinite sea inasmuch as everything it says about its subject matter, the psyche, is but a further phenomenal expression of the psyche, strokes of the swimming it must learn in order to build itself at sea.

(Psychology as Discipline, p. 200)

Psychology, as Sheldon Cashdan argues (1988) must start from scratch in every instant and build itself up from the bath of the patient's content (p. 152). This is co-constructed by the patient as well, and psychology *happens only* in the fleeting instances where this co-construction occurs. It is not made visible through diagnostic or assessment – it is not positively *there* in the patient for the therapist to identify or discover. Psychology only happens when the patient is touched by that which is logically negative. It is performative and linguistic. As Giegerich (2021) argues "it is only in my and the patient's or any person's actual achieving here and now a *psychological understanding* of something" (p. 62). It is a happening, a momentary event and not something empirically given.

Thought as Mediation of the Empirically Given

Thought occupies a central place in Giegerich's notion of psychology's "happening," and is what he interprets Jung to mean in his notes to analysts on how to interpret patient symptoms such as dreams: "[w]hat the dream, which is not manufactured by us, says is *just so*. Say it again, as well as you can" (p. 591). Giegerich highlights the last part of Jung's passage to stress Jung's notion of "thinking *again*" that is the work of psychology: a production that always occurs after the fact of the symptom. "Thinking is the art to allow the matter that we are dealing with to speak for itself" (Giegerich, 2020a, p. 16). One way we might think about this is in terms of clinical psychology accounts of disorders or pathologies and their seemingly factual existence. For instance, in the PHQ9 assessment for depression, we explore whether or not a client *has* certain symptoms like sleep issues, lack of motivation or appetite. A greater quantity of these indicates the likelihood that the patient *has* depression or *is* depressed. Giegerich's point is that this is not yet psychology. Psychology, citing Hegel (2020a), "only begins its flight at dusk, when the day is over. Thinking thinks what has already happened and now is" (p. 17). It is the *thinking again* of the symptoms that allows the psychological phenomena to "be released into their truth" (p. 17). This again involves the patient and the therapist in a different relation than in modern clinical psychology. The symptom is not identified and discovered in the patient but is produced and mediated *after the fact*. Assessment may be useful in mapping some of the terrain, but it is not yet psychology in Giegerich's sense.

Patients know this intuitively as well since there is rarely an experience of decisive satisfaction as a result of assessment or diagnosis – knowing what it is they *have*. We may even offer that there is little satisfaction to be gained from causality theory such as may be found in attachment history or family of origin work.

Knowing that one may be predisposed to relational anxiety does not necessarily produce satisfaction. Satisfaction, if it is to arrive, comes not from identifying and quantifying the symptoms but, in another Hegelian allusion – in letting that empirical knowledge *come home to itself.* Here Giegerich's notion of psychology closely resembles Hegel's notion of speculation, which he distinguishes from reflection. Reflection, for Hegel, is categorical and scientific, producing "in thought, a world that is dead" (Verene, 2007, p. 2). We could argue that much of clinical psychology operates in this mode, where "psycho education" operates as a kind of scientific schema where all psychological "objects are fully categorized and rendered lifeless, labeled, like parts of a skeleton, or pigeon-holed, like boxes in a grocer's stall" (Verene, 2007, p. 2). This for Giegerich keeps the symptoms at bay, as empirical objects outside the subject. *Coming home to oneself* mirrors more closely what Hegel means in speculative thinking where we know something as a subject through thought's reflection *into itself.* It is this dialectical or "circular" speculative knowing that Giegerich casts as psychology or psychological work. In Hegel, speculative truth exists uroborically, it "is the process of its own becoming, the circle that presupposes its end as its goal, having its end also as its beginning" (Verene, 2007, p. 18). Giegerich names this process in psychology as *absolute negative interiorization,* which like Hegel's dialectic, moves in the direction of sublation and the restored position.

Looking at this phenomenon clinically, this dialectic can be seen as a series of negations in the patient that work in the direction of sublation – "a negation which maintains the key dimension of the negated phenomenon and elevates it into a higher level" (Žižek, 2020, p. 61). In this process, what matters is that the *externality* – the thingness – of the symptom is dissolved and negated (as something that has inflicted and befallen me like an illness). The symptom is allowed to come home to itself, integrated into the life world of the patient and de-literalized and dispersed into larger narratives of the self. The patient begins to see depression, in one example, as an expression of a life trajectory, an affective expression of a combination of regrets, sadness, feelings of shame, guilt and built-up resentments. This work involves the tracing, mapping and *thinking* of these thoughts in the presence of the affects associated with depression – and building it afresh in each session. Tarrying with the negative, psychologically, for Giegerich, is thus to build psychology *from scratch* in each session. It is not a process that is fixed or finite, but because it is logically negative, remains an ongoing production performed anew in each session. It is a labor that begins with the empirical situation – the presenting problem – but labors always in that which looms up behind the analytical scene.

References

Cashdan, S. (1988). *Object relations therapy: Using the relationship.* Norton Press.
Giegerich, W. (2020a). *The soul always thinks.* Routledge.
Giegerich, W. (2020b). *Soul-violence.* Routledge.
Giegerich, W. (2020c). *Neurosis: Logic of a metaphysical illness.* Routledge.

Giegerich, W. (2021). *Working with dreams*. Routledge.

Hegel, G. W. F. (1977). *Phenomenology of spirit*. (A. V. Miller, Trans.). Oxford University Press.

Jung, C. (1997). *Notes of a seminar given in 1930–1934*. (C. Douglas, Ed.). Princeton University Press.

Mogenson, G. (2005). *A most accursed religion: When trauma becomes a god*. Spring Publications Inc.

Mogenson, G. (2017). *Afterword: 'Bringing them the plague 2.0.'* In *Psychology as discipline of interiority*. (J. Sandoval & J. Knapp, Eds.). Routledge, pp. 198–203.

Mogenson, G. (2019). *That glimpse of truth for which you had forgotten to ask*. Dusk Owl Press.

Verene, D. P. (2007). *Hegel's absolute: An introduction to the reading of Hegel's phenomenology of spirit*. SUNY Press.

Žižek, S. (2020). *Hegel in a wired brain*. Bloomsbury.

Chapter 13

(Un)Mourning the End of History

Mark Featherstone

How are we to understand the chaos of the present? Since the turn of the 21st century we have witnessed a series of traumatic global events, from 9/11 through the financial crash and the global pandemic up to the war in Ukraine, which have destroyed the global system that provided a degree of social, political, and economic certainty from the late 1980s to the end of the 20th century. The moment that ushered in this period of relative stability, certainty, and confidence was, of course, the fall of the Berlin Wall, the end of the Cold War, and the emergence of the American led-global hegemony that Frances Fukuyama (1992) wrote about in terms of the end of history.

According to Fukuyama, the Hegelian story of dialectical change through opposition and struggle was over. The collapse of the so-called socialist or communist system in Eastern Europe, coupled with what seemed like inevitable social and political change in China, signaled the rise of the American empire. In the wake of the end of the Soviet Union, which had been the main challenger to American global power since the end of World War II, it seemed as if there was no alternative to the liberal, democratic, capitalism system. There would be no more large-scale ideological transformation. American ideas were the only ideas in town. We remember that this turn to uni-polar global power led to a period of enormous optimism through the 1990s. It was imagined that the growth of capitalism could eliminate poverty, hunger, and misery around the world. There would be no more *haves* and *have nots*.

At the same time the internet came into popular use in rich Western societies supporting the wider sense of social, political, economic, and cultural optimism. Under conditions of entirely free communication, it was thought that the individual would escape from the suffocating systems of identification that had developed over the course of human history. We could now be who we wanted to be, not who society expected and demanded we should be in order to maintain social order. Alongside the rise of what it was imagined might end up becoming a kind of Habermasian ideal public sphere capable of challenging the deep structures of social, political, and economic power, the ability to become somebody else on the internet seemed to represent escape from Freudian repression and the Oedipalised self. Perhaps we had moved beyond the problem of the ego tormented by on the one hand, the

DOI: 10.4324/9781003375920-17

authoritarian super-ego, and on the other hand, the primitive id, that represented the true self, but that could never see the light of day.

If Freudian history was over, Deleuze and Guattari's (1983) Anti-Oedipal, Schizoid self seemed about to take centre stage in the new global cyber-utopian system. As Baudrillard (1988) wrote in the late 1980s, the American system of pure positivity was 'utopia realised'. What the moderns had dreamed about since Thomas More, and the Marxists had labored to try to create in socialist and communist states that quickly lapsed into nightmarish dystopias, had been achieved by Americans. In the 1990s we were all Americans and we were living in utopia. In my view the story of the 21st century is the story of the unraveling, or the unbinding, of this global system, the end of the end of history, and the posing of key questions about how we might move beyond utopia. In this short chapter, I want to suggest this is precisely what we might be able to achieve through a negative psychoanalysis, or a form of psychoanalysis that emphasises the value of negation and negativity, and has the potential to enable escape from the unmourning of the end of history.

With the benefit of hindsight it is clear that the end of the Cold War, George Bush senior's famous vision of the New World Order, and Fukuyama's (1992) declaration of the end of history and the abolition of negativity also represented the failure of the American global utopia that was essentially stillborn. We remember that the unravelling or unbinding of this system began in spectacular fashion in the fires of 9/11, continued through the invisible collapse of the financial markets in 2008 and the deadly contagion of the Covid-19 pandemic, and has now brought us to the point where we occupy a new Cold War characterised by the confrontation between Russia and the West in Ukraine. At the same time, the cyber-utopia of the 1990s, which we thought would endure as a space of freedom, democracy, and the expression of the self, has become a kind of dystopia of behaviour control marked by algorithmic authoritarianism, toxic hate speech, information overload, confusion, and disorientation.

Given that projection into the future requires processes of rational understanding and calculation, the ways in which the new cybernetic dystopia seems to have destroyed knowledge and collective competency in a maelstrom of non-knowledge and dis-information has created a sense that we, humanity, have no pathways into a predictable future. Beyond the Hegelian dialectic, beyond the relationship between thesis and antithesis or positive and negative polarities, which has sustained human reason since the Ancient Greeks, the future appears to have vanished. Moreover, this sense of living in a dark, dystopian, futureless state is reinforced by the problem of the Anthropocene, and recognition that the American global utopia also represented the total humanisation of the planet. Although we might imagine that this means that civilisation has finally won out over the brutality of nature, and this would have been how Hobbes would have understood this situation, the reality of the situation is very different. Running into the planetary limits of growth, we know that the Anthropocene basically names a situation characterised by the radical incompatibility of the human system premised on infinite modernisation and expansion and the natural system that is marked by organic limits and ecological balance. Under these conditions, we cannot escape the feeling that negativity is back on the scene in the form of tendencies towards regression, destruction, collapse, annihilation, and ultimately extinction. As Byung-Chul Han (2015) notes, the world of positivity has passed and we are now living in a state of burn-out, exhaustion, and entropy. It is precisely this situation that has led Stiegler (2018) to declare the end of the human adventure, which began when primitive proto-humans first made use of stone-age tools, machines, and technologies to overcome their constitutive lack relative to other animals. For Stiegler, this Promethean story is over and what we need now is the invention of a theory and practice of the neganthropocene or negation of the anthropocentric system and the figure of the human constantly looking to grow into the future.

Although Stiegler is never clear about exactly what this neganthropocentric revolution would like look, I would suggest that it would have to involve a future founded upon principles taken from prehistory, certainly prior to the moment when everything solid began to melt into air and perhaps even back before we somehow came to believe that we exist above and beyond the environment that sustains our existence. Before Descartes imagined the separation of the doubting subject and alien object, before Hobbes wrote of a state of nature that is nasty, brutish, and short, and before Locke suggested that humanity owes a debt to God to put nature to profitable good use, I think Stiegler's neganthropocene would require an acceptance of and coming with to terms with co-dependence, vulnerability, finitude, and reliance upon others and nature, which is precisely what the Promethean story seeks to deny and negate. As Freud reminds us in *Civilization and Its Discontents* (2002), humans have come to imagine they are Promethean Gods.

Rational thought, machines, and technology have enabled us to rise above the natural world and perform astonishing feats, but we cannot escape our reliance upon environmental systems. We cannot live without the biosphere and for this reason we are defined by limitation, lack, and negativity. Considering the psychology of the Promethean God, Freud explains that despite his enormous technological achievements, he remains emotionally stunted and marked by a kind of primitive fear founded upon his deep sense of vulnerability and weakness. It is, of course, precisely this fear that drives his efforts to escape from himself, and his limitation and finitude, into something more fitting of divinity. What is this, but an immortality project! It is, however, impossible to become a God, which means that the Promethean's desperate desire to overcome his humanity simply exacerbates his obsessive concern with his animal vulnerability with the result that he is haunted by spooks, specters, and monsters that rise up in the darkness and threaten to expose him for what we he is – lacking. According to the American psychoanalyst, Laurence Rickels (1988), this inability to accept loss, lack, and finitude reflects a state of aberrant or unmourning that we must overcome if we are to ever come to terms with the reality of human existence. This is, in large part, exactly what Stiegler wants to achieve. Referring to Plato's story of the creation of humanity from his *Protagoras* (2009), Stiegler's (1998) view is that our constitutive lack means that we have never been Promethean Gods. We have always been Epimethean fools, desperately trying to make up for what we think is missing in humanity, without realising that this missing element, what Lacan calls the real, is precisely what makes us what we are – human.

In a sense, of course, psychoanalysis has always been about coming to terms with lack. The whole point of analysis is not to cure the analysand, but rather to enable them to understand their symptoms, to understand how their behaviours are an effect of a desperate attempt to overcome some traumatic episode that cannot be overcome because it has already happened. In this respect, there is no escape, there is no utopian world where we are no longer troubled, but only a state of realism and acceptance, where we make sense of and come to terms with our symptoms, our negativity, and understand that these are definitives of our humanity. This is why what Andre Green (1999) calls 'the work of the negative' is never finished. Moreover, this key insight, the idea that we never overcome once and for all, that we never emerge into a space of pure positivity which is not somehow marked by the negative, is not simply one that refers to the individual analysand working to make sense of their own symptoms, but rather also a wider meta-psychological understanding that Freud and his followers introduced, and which, I believe, may help humanity to come to terms with its current predicament unmourning the end of history. In sketching out this psychoanalysis of the contemporary catastrophic moment, we should start with consideration of Hegel, who first imagined the idea of the end of history, and, in Jon Mills' (2002) view, was a key figure in the pre-history of psychoanalysis on the basis of his philosophy of humanisation, death, desire, and recognition set out in *The Phenomenology of Spirit* (2019).

Long before Freud developed the psychoanalytic idea of the unconscious, Hegel imagined humanity's emergence from a primitive state through the transition of consciousness into self-consciousness based upon the confrontation of what would become the master and the slave. In this story of the birth of humanity, Hegel envisions the struggle between two proto-humans in the state of nature. During the battle, one party shows willingness to fight to the end, while the other chooses the path of self-preservation. In this regard, the latter demonstrates their attachment to nature, which they are unable to overcome, while the former shows the desire to win at all costs, and thus transcends the natural tendency to prioritise self-preservation. Given their willingness to die, rather than accept subordination, the master is born. At the same time that this extremism ensures the defeat of the slave who is unwilling to go all the way, it also creates a fissure in the master's relationship to nature. On the basis of his willingness to give up on life itself, the master rises above nature, experiences estrangement from himself, and emerges into self-consciousness. By contrast, the slave is born in their inability to face down the possibility of death. The result of this lack of will is that they remain shackled to nature and become the master's laborer. They must work upon the world. However, this is not pointless, meaningless, toil. Hegel imagines that the slaves find themselves reflected in their work, which eventually results in their own humanisation and movement towards self-consciousness. At this point, they leap from the status of object to subject and confront the master as an equal who demands recognition on the basis of their subjectivity. The result of this situation is that the master-slave dialectic is finally abolished in a state of inter-psychic/inter-subjective communication characteristic of a classless society.

Beyond their original engagement with negativity, which we should understand in terms of first, the dialectical struggle between the two parties, and then second the slave's work upon the objective world, in the final moment master and slave become self and other and subsume their common negativity within a state of mutual recognition. In other words, they become other-wise. Following Hegel, however, Freud's intervention demonstrated that the leap from consciousness to self-consciousness is forever compromised by the emergence of the unconscious that would prevent the self from ever becoming fully transparent to itself. In this state intra-psychic communication is forever limited and lacking and inter-subjective interactions similarly crash upon the rocks of the unconscious nature of the self. If we are never fully aware of ourselves, how can we ever hope to communicate with the other in a manner which effectively conveys our state of being. In this context, the role of psychoanalysis becomes about making sense of symptoms emerging from, in Hegelian terms, the shift from consciousness to self-consciousness, which simultaneously generates the unconscious that remains a primitive left-over of a state before we were fully human.

Despite our Prometheanism, titanic efforts to construct civilisation, and high-tech modernity, the point of psychoanalysis is, therefore, to emphasise the need to recognise our inability to ever overcome our primitive past. While Hegel writes about the emergence of the human from the state of nature, Freud's primal scene involves childhood and the Oedipal struggle over mother and father. In Hegel's philosophy, unhappy consciousness emerges from estrangement and an inability to fully escape from nature. We know that Freud sees this as constitutive of the Oedipal self. We are always miserable, and civilisation is always discontented, because we have been separated from mother and must live our lives marked by lack. For Freud, there is no point pretending otherwise, because the negative, the reminder of our loss, is always with us. Indeed, the problem with the pretense that we can somehow overcome this loss and become whole is that it generates an obsessive compulsion to escape from the self that eventually transforms into a death drive that confuses the fantasy of the lack of lack and a state of serene satisfaction with self-destruction and non-existence. Freud (2002) did not believe in the idea of satisfaction. Happiness is a myth. The same is true of Lacan. In Lacanian theory (2007), negativity emerges in the mirror stage when we become estranged from ourselves and persist in the form of the real that haunts first the imaginary and then the symbolic self that can never find a way to extinguish the lack that troubles its existence. As we have seen, Stiegler (1998, 2018) takes this Lacanian self organised around a psychic economy of lack and excess, and projects it through the history of humanity, including modernity, and high-tech globalisation, until the Anthropocene or totally humanised world, which overwhelms the planetary, biospheric system that supports organic life. Against the backdrop of this Promethean history, concerned with escaping from bottomless lack through endless excess, Stiegler imagines the return of the negative in a big way.

From Stiegler's point of view, stupidity, madness, and death are everywhere and the only way to contain them is to face up to our own constitutive negativity, the Epimethean lack that represents the unconscious other side of the Promethean story. We must move beyond denial. We must move beyond the strategy of negation, which Freud (2001) explains in order to show how we seek to deny negativity ('it's definitely not that!'), because this is precisely what has led us to the catastrophic moment we occupy today. In other words, the denial of negativity, and the refusal to take care of it, has resulted in a situation where the negative is overflowing everywhere. In Lacanian psychoanalysis the Oedipalised subject seeks to manage the negativity introduced into psychic life through the process of individualisation by pursuing the object that might make them feel whole again. This strategy is sustainable because desire never runs out. Even though the object never measures up to the loss sustained in the mirror stage and then later the Oedipal moment, the very pursuit of the thing or person who seems to represent what is missing is enough to ensure that the subject is able to cope with their lack in a state of motion.

However, problems occur when it becomes clear that this, that, or the other object will never hit the mark. At this point, the deferral of lack in motion no longer functions effectively and the subject's relationship to the world moves from one conditioned by desire to one concerned with drive, which describes the situation where the identity of the object becomes irrelevant and its ability to sustain the subject in motion is negligible. Under these conditions the subject finds itself caught in a vicious cycle of lack and excess and comes to resemble a binary switching machine endlessly oscillating between oppositional states of being and nothingness to the extent that it falls into a kind of twilight zone somewhere between life and death (Lacan, 1991). In this borderline state, which describes the experience of the addict, there is no space for change or transformation. The subject is trapped in a nightmarish cycle where efforts to escape only ever seem to reinforce the fatal situation they occupy. Upping the stakes, and seeking out bigger and better highs, becomes pointless because it is clear there is no escape. As William Burroughs explained across a range of books, but perhaps most famously *Junky* (2012), the Junky lives out a life of gray monotony and boredom, because they know that their high is only ever a temporary respite from the misery of lack which they simply cannot endure.

We remember that this psychological complex was first explored by Freud in his *Beyond the Pleasure Principle* (2003), which details how his grandson Ernst sought to escape from the trauma brought about by the departure of his mother Sophie by playing a game of *fort/da* and imposing symbolic mastery over a traumatic situation he could not control in reality. Adorno and Horkheimer (1997) expanded this theory of the compulsion to repeat into a theory of consumer capitalism and addiction to buying stuff in order to try to overcome the lack brought about by the misery of life under capitalism. Building upon this tradition, Stiegler's (2011, 2012, 2014) point is that the spirit of consumer capitalism, the belief that this, that, or the other object will take away our pain, has now run out of road. We have reached a state of peak stuff. Marx's (1990) magical commodity, the object of desire able to fascinate, is no more. It is now so much junk polluting the environment. In other words,

Stiegler explains that we have entered the space of death drive capitalism, in the sense that we have lost belief in the idea that we can consume our way into a better future, and realise that our consumerism represents a kind of fatal strategy. We are caught in the space of the junky, consuming ourselves to death, even though we know that this will never take away the pain of our constitutive lack. But we carry on, because we must. We have nothing else.

From a Freudian point of view, we know that this ends one of two ways. We either remain within the coordinates of drive and end up destroying ourselves in a kind of apocalyptic cataclysm, which would, of course, represent one way to eliminate the lack of humanity once and for all, or we turn back towards the miserable structures of civilisation that were set up to incubate and contain negativity and live with the finitude and limitation that make us human. This is the choice we face today. Once upon a time the Hegelian master seemed to overcome his mortality. He became human. However, Lacan knew that death is the absolute master (Borch-Jacobsen, 1991). There is no way to escape our finitude. Living through the end of the end of history, and the collapse of the global system of total positivity, this is what we must realise. We must overcome the strategy of negation ('even though it appears that this is what's happening, it's not really that'), which enables us to deny the truth that is blindingly obvious, and learn to live with our constitutive negativity, rather than endlessly seeking to escape.

My final words: we are living in a period of unraveling, unbinding, and disorganisation that Freud, Lacan, and Stiegler connect to Thanatos. We know that negativity is everywhere in the world. This is the case because we have never been able to accept that it is deep within us. Even now, we imagine Prometheus will save us, that we will be able to escape the planet for some other world, but I think this is simply another example of Epimethean foolishness. There is no future in this kind of science fiction, which is, I believe, simply a contemporary representation of what Rickels (1988) calls unmourning or the inability to live with lack. Instead, we should embrace our finitude, limitation, and lack and start to mourn our loss. We must come to terms with our humanity if we are to survive, which is precisely why we need psychoanalysis, a psychoanalysis of the negative, or a negative psychoanalysis, today more than ever before.

References

Adorno, T. W. and Horkheimer, M. (1997) *Dialectic of Enlightenment*. London: Verso.

Baudrillard, J. (1988) *America*. London: Verso.

Borch-Jacobsen, M. (1991) *Lacan: The Absolute Master*. Stanford, CA: Stanford University Press.

Burroughs, W. S. (2012) *Junky*. London: Penguin.

Deleuze, G. and Guattari, F. (1983) *Anti-Oedipus: Capitalism and Schizophrenia: Volume I*. Minneapolis: University of Minnesota Press.

Freud, S. (2001) 'Negation' in *The Standard Edition of the Complete Psychological Works of Sigmund Freud: Volume XIX: 1923–1925: The Ego and the Id and Other Works*. London: Penguin. 235–243.

Freud, S. (2002) *Civilization and Its Discontents*. London: Penguin.

Freud, S. (2003) *Beyond the Pleasure Principle*. London: Penguin.

Fukuyama, F. (1992) *The End of History and the Last Man*. New York: Free Press.

Green, A. (1999) *The Work of the Negative*. London: Free Association Books.

Han, B.-C. (2015) *The Burnout Society*. Stanford, CA: Stanford University Press.

Hegel, G. W. F. (2019) *The Phenomenology of Spirit*. Cambridge: Cambridge University Press.

Lacan, J. (1991) *The Seminar of Jacques Lacan: Book II: The Ego in Freud's Theory and in the Technique of Psychoanalysis, 1954–1955*. New York: W.W. Norton and Co.

Lacan, J. (2007) 'The Mirror Stage as Formative of the I Function as Revealed in Psychoanalytic Experience' in *Ecrits*. New York: W. W. Norton and Co. 75–82.

Marx, K. (1990) *Capital: Critique of Political Economy: Volume I*. London: Penguin.

Mills, J. (2002) *The Unconscious Abyss: Hegel's Anticipation of Psychoanalysis*. Albany: SUNY Press.

Plato. (2009) *Protagoras*. Oxford: Oxford University Press.

Rickels, L. (1988) *Aberrations of Mourning: Writing on German Crypts*. Detroit: Wayne State University Press.

Stiegler, B. (1998) *Technics and Time: Volume I: The Fault of Epimetheus*. Stanford, CA: Stanford University Press.

Stiegler, B. (2011) *The Decadence of Industrial Democracies: Disbelief and Discredit: Volume I*. Cambridge: Polity.

Stiegler, B. (2012) *Uncontrollable Societies of Disaffected Individuals: Disbelief and Discredit: Volume II*. Cambridge: Polity.

Stiegler, B. (2014) *The Lost Spirit of Capitalism: Disbelief and Discredit: Volume III*. Cambridge: Polity.

Stiegler, B. (2018) *The Neganthropocene*. London: Open Humanities Press.

Chapter 14

Trauma, Negativity, and Death Drive in Spielrein, Heidegger, and Buddhist Thought

Wanyoung Kim

Introduction

"Positive psychology" is a term that first appeared in Abraham Maslow's book *Motivation and Personality*, and emerged within the movement of humanistic psychology in 1950's Europe and the United States. Positive psychology explicitly focuses on the good aspects and emotions of life such as courage and happiness, and in building patient strengths rather than weaknesses. While it is beneficial to consider positive emotions as something humans strive for generally, an exclusive focus on these emotions neglects important issues such as death, negativity, and trauma and leaves them to the wayside. Positive psychology alone leads to an avoidance of negativity, death, and trauma that are important for the patient to confront and resolve in order to establish stability and a healthy mode of functioning in everyday life. Unresolved, these issues will continue to arise in therapy and are necessary for the patient to confront with the help of the therapist. It is known that unresolved trauma at any point in life can cause mental, emotional, and behavioral symptoms and issues that need to be resolved. This chapter will compare the needed role of negative psychoanalysis as articulated in the work of Sabina Spielrein and Martin Heidegger, and within Buddhist beliefs, and discuss and critique their clinical merits and usefulness.

Death and Negativity in Spielrein

An associate of Carl Jung and Sigmund Freud, Sabine Spielrein was a pioneer of psychoanalysis who wrote on the death drive ten years before Freud first covered the death instinct in his work *Beyond the Pleasure Principle* in 1920. It is notable that Spielrein influenced, and was closely influenced by the work of both Jung and Freud after spending time as their patient in turn. However, her work on the death drive differs from the two. Rather than conceiving of aggression or death and libido as opposing forces, as in the work of Freud, or relegating death instinct to a problematic dimension of inner mental life such as "introversion," in Jung's work, Sabine views destruction as an inherent force or process within the human drives or libido that needs to be confronted (Freud, 1982). Indeed, she champions the view

DOI: 10.4324/9781003375920-18

that life must die before one fully comes to life. Death and life are inextricably intertwined. Within her essay, Spielrein identifies a dual destructive and reproductive impulse within the sexual instinct. She not only notes the negative feelings of disgust and anxiety associated with the sexual drive (*Fortplanzungstrieb*) and how some animals die after reproducing; she also notes that times of war, destruction, and morbidity are often associated with neuroses and disruptions to people's sexual lives. Neurotics often have destructive fantasies associated with representations of war. Spielrein states that: "The destruction component predominates in neurosis and expresses itself in all the symptoms of resistance against life and natural fate" (Spielrein, 1912/1995, p. 14).

Within the individual, Spielrein differentiates between the ego-psyche (the Self) and a deeper psyche, known as the "species-psyche" (*Artpsyche*). There are two opposite psychical tendencies – a "tendency towards dissolution and assimilation" and a "tendency towards differentiation" – which represent the preservation of the species (*Arterhaltungstrieb*) and the self-preservation drive (*Selbsterhaltungstrieb*), respectively. She writes,

> The type-preservation drive is a reproduction-drive and also expresses itself psychically in the dissolution and assimilation tendencies (transforming of the I into a we) with the following new differentiation out of "primal matter" [*Urstoffe*]. "Where love rules, the I, the sinister despot, dies." With love the dissolution of the I in the beloved is at the same time the strongest self-affirmation, a new I-life in the person of the beloved.
>
> (Spielrein, 1912/1995, p. 15)

In other words, Spielrein sees destruction of the egoic or narcissistic tendencies of the "I" as a necessary driving vehicle within the process of human self-creation and recreation and love, rather than a hidden force that is dialectical to the human drives. Thus, Spielrein's death instinct offers a radically more promising, life-affirming, and resilient view of the human psyche than Freud's view. In Spielrein's thought, the death instinct between the ego and sexual drives would not annihilate life, as Freud wrote in his work on death drive and the pleasure principle in 1920. Rather, this death instinct would destroy the Self and turn it into the Collective Self. The proposition that destruction and creation are intertwined means that there is no drive that is inherently or purely negative.

Death and Negativity in Heidegger

The philosopher Martin Heidegger first addresses *Gelassenheit* in "Conversation on a Country Path about Thinking," written between 1944 and 1945. The "Conversation" is structured as a dialogue between a scientist, a scholar, and a teacher. The scientist reasons in a deductive mode of thinking. The scholar is an academic who is trained as a philosopher and thinks according to a metaphysical perspective. The teacher is the person through whom Heidegger presents his idea of a "thinker." The three speakers dialogue about the nature of thinking, and try to see if it is possible to achieve a form of thinking that does not involve the will. The structure of their dialogue is not linear, but rather circular, and it is in the interaction of their ideas that the mode of being and thinking called *Gelassenheit* presents itself.

The thought of the thinker in the dialogue is what Heidegger calls "meditative thinking" [*das besinnliche Denken*], which can be distinguished from calculative reasoning [*das rechnende Denken*]. *Gelassenheit* is revealed to be an unfolding, a path that leads to an opening described as the following: "Where else but in that-which-regions, in relation to which releasement is what it is" (1966, p. 70). Within *Gelassenheit* is a "resolve" [Entschlossenheit] (ibid., p. 81), which can be compared to Heidegger's resolve in *Being and Time* as a "letting oneself be called forth" (1996, p. 283) to one's ownmost possibility of being. Arguably, death, trauma, and negativity are ownmost possibilities of being. An authentic being *with Gelassenheit* opens themselves up authentically to death, trauma, and negativity rather than being closed off to them in an insular positivity. In *Being and Time*, Heidegger further speaks of authentic being as an orientation toward the possibility of its death, as being-towards-death (*Sein-zum-Tode*). However, Being-towards-death is a way of being rather than simply an orientation. The task of an authentic thinker in the "Conversation" is to meditate upon the truth of being, which includes the real possibility of death, negativity, and trauma.

The various translations of *Gelassenheit* are "equanimity," "serenity," "inner poise," "stillness," or "waiting," but it can more literally be translated as "leaving," "letting be," or "releasement," *gelassen* in German. *Gelassenheit* is an acceptance of one's Being-toward-Death where a being has accepted and integrated the possibility of their mortality and is calm in the face of its impending approach.

Death, Trauma, and Negativity in Buddhism

Now I will compare Heideggerian equanimity with Buddhism. Within Buddhist thought there are four sublime attitudes: love or loving-kindness, compassion, sympathetic joy, and equanimity, which are practiced towards all living beings. German Buddhist monk Nyanaponika Thera writes,

Equanimity is a perfect, unshakable balance of mind, rooted in insight. [. . .] Looking into life we notice how it continually moves between contrasts: rise and fall, success and failure, loss and gain, honor and blame. We feel how our heart responds to all this happiness and sorrow, delight and despair, disappointment and satisfaction, hope and fear. These waves of emotion carry us up and fling us down; and no sooner do we find rest, than we are in the power of a new wave again. How can we expect to get a footing on the crest of the waves? How shall we erect the building of our lives in the midst of this ever restless ocean of existence, if not on the Island of Equanimity.

(1999, p. 9)

While a less Enlightened being would be easily shaken and affected by long-lasting damage from trauma due to negative events and emotions, a person who is equanimous is able to meet negative events with a sense of inner peace, strength, and resoluteness.

As in Heidegger, equanimity in Buddhist thought is achieved and cultivated through meditative thinking as a higher, Enlightened state. More specifically, equanimity is the Enlightened self's ability to remain mentally and emotionally composed and stable despite exposure to worldly phenomena, *dharma*, a great deal of which is negative and produces mental anguish or suffering. In Buddhism, death, like birth, is viewed as a necessary state within the process of reincarnation, and it is necessary for an individual to have to come to terms with the reality of suffering and death to become Enlightened or to escape the cycle of rebirth and samsara.

It is important to note that Buddhist equanimity can be utilized as a clinical technique to help neurotic and depressed patients with emotional regulation. In a statistical study of 644 patients with neurosis and perceived stress, the utilization of equanimity as a clinical technique was shown to moderate depressive symptoms. As Wongpakaran, et al. write:

> Clinically, equanimity may be perceived as a balanced emotional reaction toward stimuli, along with a tolerant and nonjudgmental attitude towards one's fellow humans. As equanimity is found to be integrated in mindfulness meditation method, it should hypothetically help control disruptive emotions among people with psychiatric problems. One study showed that equanimity results in fewer difficulties with emotional regulation, and this may explain the positive effect of mindfulness-based meditation on the emotional regulatory effect of mindfulness, as well as on neuroticism and alexithymia.
>
> (2021, p. 2)

It is apparent that as it relates to the death drive or to death itself, acceptance of trauma and of negative feelings associated with death such as anxiety or depression is a necessary step toward their resolution, and toward an end goal of making peace with negativity. Although it is Buddhist mindfulness that is specifically integrated into this clinical technique of equanimity, we might note its similarity to Heideggerian *Gelassenheit* as a form of meditative reflection upon the truth of being, means that the latter can also be integrated into a clinical practice of equanimity to help patients resolve negative emotions, depression, and anxiety. As noted before, *Gelassenheit* is characterized by a healthy resolve or resoluteness in the face of death, negative life events, or trauma, and this way of being can be successfully cultivated in psychiatric patients similarly to Buddhist equanimity.

As for Spielrein's psychological view of the death instinct, we can note that her view can also be clinically integrated into an approach that helps depressed and neurotic patients resolve traumas and negative emotions associated with sexuality, love, war, and creativity. It is by accepting the place of destruction of ego, a former unhealthy self tied up in inhibitions and depression or anxiety, that there can be made room for a new, higher self to be actualized – one that is integrated into social being; a self with a far greater capacity to overcome its fears, love others fully, and exercise creative potential in its accomplishments.

References

Freud, S. (1982). Jenseits des Lustprinzips. In S. Freud, Ed., Sigmund Freud Studienausgabe (Vol. III, pp. 213–272). Frankfurt, Deutschland: Fischer.

Heidegger, M. (1966). Conversation on a Country Path about Thinking. In M. Heidegger, Ed., Discourse on Thinking. Trans. John M. Anderson and E. Hans Freund. New York: Harper and Row.

Heidegger, M. (1996). Being and Time. Trans. Joan Stambaugh. Albany, NY: State University of New York Press.

Spielrein, S. (1912/1995). Destruction as a Cause of Becoming. Translated by Stuart K. Witt. Psychoanalysis and Contemporary Thought, 18:85–118. Retrieved from www.alsf-chile.org/Indepsi/Articulos-Clinicos/Destruction-as-cause-of-becoming.pdf

Thera, N. (1999). The Four Sublime States. Penang: Inward Path Publishing.

Wongpakaran, N., Wongpakaran, T., Wedding, D., Mirnics, Z., & Kövi, Z. (2021). Role of Equanimity on the Mediation Model of Neuroticism, Perceived Stress and Depressive Symptoms. Healthcare (Basel), 9(10):1300. https://doi.org/10.3390/healthcare9101300

Chapter 15

Why Positive Thought Must Be Negated in the Analytic Session

Negative Dialectics as Therapeutic Technique

Joel Michael Crombez

Psychosocial Diagnosis and Scenic Landscape

Freud (1920/2012) noted that patients often resist the therapeutic process even when they are suffering and enter analysis of their own free will. Confronting the psyche and subjecting it to scrutiny involves challenging the internalized fiction of the self – the image we imagine others perceive of us (Cooley, 1902) – that we construct throughout the life course and attempt to project and protect in performative social situations (Mead, 1934/1972; Goffman, 1959). This internalized self-image is not, however, fully of the conscious domain. At the core of this construct is, as Lacan (1966/2006) framed it, "a function of misrecognition" (p. 560), insofar as this image that resides within the imaginary is an idealized ego. On the one hand this is developed out of the echoes of primary narcissism and on the other hand as a protectionary mechanism to insulate the self from the realities of everyday life, such as when we fail to live up to our own fictionalized image. As such, it is largely unconscious. Working through this register in the analytic session reveals uncomfortable truths to the patient, including how the one we are most often dishonest with is our own self.

Modern society, however, insulates the individual from working to uncover and engage with truths that would rattle and disturb the fictions we construct of ourselves. It does so, not to protect us, but to protect its own functioning because these self-constructions are built upon the distortions of a society structured around the totalizing logic of capital. Such a logic is totalizing insofar as it organizes and trains our thoughts through a dominant ideology that is oriented toward its own ends rather than those of individual subjects or the human species as such (Crombez, 2021). Critical self-reflection runs counter to capital's aims because it reveals the alienating function of capital (Marx, 1961/2007) and calls into question the so-called "individualism" of modern societies; which is about atomizing people and dismantling the power of the social, not about the construction of authentic individual selves. Capital, therefore, requires a population that is disconnected and/or distracted from the pursuit of authentic individualism because such a pursuit is incompatible with an economic system that relies upon the exploitation of labor and the focus on productive ends *qua* capitalist profit under the banner

DOI: 10.4324/9781003375920-19

of individual survival. Pushing an ideology of positive thinking protects capital from these truths entering the conscious register which would be a necessary pre-condition for a true democratic reorganization of society's structuring principles. The culture industry accomplishes this task for capital by presenting positive think-ing as the de facto legitimate vehicle to individual success and by supporting a brand of negativity aimed at either nihilistic pessimism or at demonizing the very forms of social organization which would enable the pursuit of authentic individu-ality. Modern society, therefore, obscures the desire that is produced by its inherent lack of human fulfillment by misdirecting the desire for meaningful and fulfilling individuality toward the provisions of a culture industry that gives us ready-made identities to mask our hollow interior lives as it demonizes thoughts that call posi-tive thinking under the current societal conditions into question because this would run counter to its aims.

Mainstream psychiatric practices support this endeavor by overwhelmingly fol-lowing the biomedical model of treatment – despite limited and in many cases no evidence that the roots of many mental health afflictions are biological in nature (Horwitz, 2020) – because these treatment methods fit hand-in-hand with the logic of capital. Likewise, mainstream psychoanalytic practices have jettisoned the most critical components of the practice in favor of an analytic method that better con-ditions analysands to function within the status quo. These two models of men-tal health treatment primarily do this by placing the root cause of mental distress within the individual patient by insisting, whether there is supporting scientific evidence and rational argument, or not, that the problem is because of the patient's internal functioning. Capital supports the biomedical model through pharmaceuti-cal and insurance lobbying to control what third-party payment for psychiatric care covers, maintaining a system that does not need to be primarily based on what is best for the patient's mental well-being but rather one that is weighted toward what is most beneficial to these companies' bottom line. Government intervention for patient rights is therefore rare, as this model prioritizes the rapid reintegration of the patient into the labor system and keeps them from questioning the legitimacy of a social system that does not prioritize their well-being. Per Durkheim's discov-ery, a society *sui generis* (1895/1982) does not need to focus on individual needs for its own survival and can tolerate a significant amount of anomie (1897/1997) especially once the human component has largely become superfluous to the func-tioning of capital (Postone, 1996). So not only is this about maintaining the com-petitive edge of business over labor, but without a strong social safety net people are dependent upon wage labor for survival. Missing work or long bouts of unem-ployment due to mental distress places survival itself into jeopardy, and if one finds themselves in this desperate situation the fault is laid squarely upon their own shortcomings. Mass marketing of anti-depression and anti-anxiety medica-tions instills in the patients' minds that these are the desired solutions for their ills because they can be seamlessly integrated into the patient's life without any need for critical and painful self-reflection, cause little or no disruption in their day-to-day activities, and set them back on the path of positive thinking. By promoting an agenda in which this mode of positive thought is rewarded and legitimated by the system, capital has melded with the psychiatric field to form one of its biggest ideological propagandists.

From the perspective of modern society, what do individuals have to be positive about beyond the limited accomplishments of their own personal sphere of action? From a planetary perspective, rather than representing a healthy mode of thinking, positive thought appears downright neurotic and narcissistic at best and psychotic at worst. From 1970 to 2018, in the time it took the human population to double in size from 3.7 to nearly 8 billion – a mark we passed in 2022 – the biodiversity of nonhuman plant and animal populations declined by an average of 69% globally (WWF, 2022). Meanwhile, the year over year rise in global temperature continues to climb, often at a rate that exceeds scientific modeling. As highlighted in the *6th Assessment Report* by the Intergovernmental Panel on Climate Change (2022), without immediate planetary changes we have a high likelihood of blowing past 2°C increase in average global temperature by 2050: a threshold long held by the scientific community as the point when there will be irreversible and catastrophic consequences for life itself. Accelerating strain on an already taxed ecosystem, the fate of the natural world upon which we depend looks grim.

Shift our view to the artificial world of modern society and our landscape is even bleaker. With Russia's invasion of Ukraine in 2022, Westerners began to wake up to the reality that peace in their countries is not guaranteed and war is not only a fearful reality for those nation-states who fall under the dreaded gaze of the United States' foreign policy. Suddenly, the threat of nuclear weapons – which never went away but only faded from the collective conscious upon the collapse of the Soviet Union – is now reignited as the fate of Ukraine is only an epiphenomenon to most Western onlookers of the real war which was only ever "Cold" in name. Bringing back the ill-fated echoes of George W. Bush's "Mission Accomplished" speech, the COVID pandemic is here to stay despite world governments patting themselves on the back for implementing half measures that saw drastic death tolls and the world's richest multiply their wealth while the world's poorest teeter on the brink of economic devastation yet again. Advertisements for psychiatric medications may sell us on the virtues of positive thinking as they promise new sexual partners, puppies, and an endless smile on our face, but given the facts of our planetary forecast, how is positive thought anything more than ideological delusion for a world spiraling out of control?

Negative Dialect as Therapeutic Technique

Most patients have already exhausted other avenues of psychiatric care without experiencing the desired results when they enter analysis as a "therapy of last resort" (Fink, 2014, p. 220). Analysts first encounter them at a point where their distress is often compounded by the impotence of previous treatments which they have interpreted as personal failure. The whole point of their seeking help is because something (or everything) in life has lost its luster, this is in point of fact a desirable starting point for negative psychoanalysis[1] because they are typically already sensitized to the darker side of modern society and the human condition therein by sensing the lack that it has produced within themselves. Life itself under these conditions cannot help but produce a situation in which both the patient and their thoughts are stagnant. Introducing dialectical thinking in the analytic session is a way of breaking through that stagnation by placing thought and the material conditions from which it arises in tension so as to produce movement between the two. However, dialectical thinking is typically a foreign pattern for patients as modern society does not nurture this kind of thinking in either its positive (as in Hegel, 1807/1977) or its negative variants (as in Adorno 1966/2007, 2003/2008) so developing this kind of thinking is a necessary first step.

Recognizing that the Hegelian model is rooted in positive thought – beginning and ending from a position of idealism – we do not need to go through this form in the therapeutic session and can go straight to negative dialectics. "To think is to identify" (Adorno, 1966/2007, p. 5), but the identification of the patient with their idealized ego is, like all concepts, rooted in contradiction. Thinking that life is supposed to be a certain way, with the fulfillment of certain socially produced expectations, is the contradiction upon which the idealized ego is constructed and maintained by the system of capital as the unobtainable carrot that hides the more insidious stick of social control. Especially under present conditions the imagined thing and its material form are irreconcilable. The analysand must reveal this kernel of truth for themselves; it cannot be thrust upon them by the analyst. They do so by first coming to think, not in terms of identity, but in terms of *non-identity*: that is, in terms of what is non-identical between their "self" as a subject and their "self" as an object constructed by the material conditions in which we live. Only by exposing the inherent contradiction between the two will their thought invert from a positive affirmation to one which progresses via negation. What remains after the contradictions are revealed between the concept of the self as object and the material self as subject is the core of thought upon which the patient can begin a serious analysis of the ways that, on the one hand, society fails to create the conditions for their flourishment and, on the other hand, the ways that they as a subject both think and take actions that are not in line with the thoughts they so assiduously defend as their own prior to analysis.

Whereas dialectical thinking in the ultimate instance of the Hegelian model resolves itself by constructing a more perfect philosophical ideal, negative dialectics recognizes that positive thinking betrays the material conditions that form our thoughts and in which we are compelled to live our lives. "A life that had any point would not need to inquire about it," wrote Adorno (2007, p. 377). It is precisely this point that has eluded the patient who is blinded by positive thinking insofar as they are socialized to believe that the point of their life must be inherent to the system itself. However, because the system categorically denies the needs of the individual by demonizing the foundations upon which authentic individuality could be built, the point of life must not be positively affirmed from within the given conditions. This does not imply that there is no point to life, that life is not worth living, or that nihilistic doom should unburden us from the shackles of morality in the pursuit of happiness. Rather, it implies that facing the negative of modern life requires training in negative thinking so as to agitate our minds from the ossification that capital conditions within those who demand something better than the current circumstances provide. Idealistic (i.e. positive) thought is bound to drive the patient back to the brink of mental anguish for any such transformations cannot be accomplished at the level of false individuality cherished by the logic of capital. Only history shows what changes are possible within material reality and negative dialectics provides a tool for patients to embark upon a lifetime of working through the false ideals of a modern world racing toward our collective extinction. It is only upon this condition that when and where we may be able to take action which would advance the conditions for authentic individuality and mental well-being would we ever even know to act in the first place.

Note

1 It must be noted in the strongest of terms, that this does not apply to patients who are experiencing a high degree of suicidal ideation. Whether or not those patients may be candidates for using the negative dialectics as a therapeutic technique, and what that would entail, must be addressed elsewhere due to space constraints.

References

Adorno, T.W. (2007). *Negative Dialectics* (E.B. Ashton, Trans). Continuum.

Adorno, T.W. (2008). *Lectures on Negative Dialectics: Fragments of a Lecture Course 1965/1966* (R. Tiedemann, Ed; R. Livingstone, Trans). Polity.

Cooley, C.H. (1902). *Human Nature and the Social Order*. Charles Scribner's Sons.

Crombez, J. (2021). *Anxiety, Modern Society, and the Critical Method: Toward a Theory and Practice of Critical Socioanalysis*. Brill.

Durkheim, E. (1982). *The Rules of Sociological Method* (S. Lukes, Ed; W.D. Hall, Trans). The Free Press.

Fink, B. (2014). *Against Understanding, Volume 1: Commentary and Critique in a Lacanian Key*. Routledge.

Freud, S. (2012). *A General Introduction to Psychoanalysis*. Renaissance Classics.

Goffman, E. (1959). *The Presentation of Self in Everyday Life*. Doubleday.

Hegel, G.F.W. (1977). *Phenomenology of Spirit* (A.V. Miller, Trans). Oxford University Press.

Horwitz, A. (2020). *Between Sanity and Madness: Mental Illness from Ancient Greece to the Neuroscientific Era*. Oxford University Press.

IPCC. (2022). *Climate Change 2022: Impacts, Adaptation and Vulnerability* (H.-O. Pörtner, D.C. Roberts, M. Tignor, E.S. Poloczanska, K. Mintenbeck, A. Alegria, M. Craig, S. Langsdorf, S. Löschke, V. Möller, A. Okem & B. Rama, Eds). Cambridge University Press.

Lacan, J. (2006). *Ecrits: The First Complete Edition in English*. W.W. Norton & Company.

Marx, K. (2007). *Economic and Philosophic Manuscripts of 1844* (M. Milligan Ed and Trans). Dover Publications, Inc.

Mead, G.H. (1972). *Mind, Self, and Society: From the Standpoint of a Social Behaviorist* (C. W. Morris, Ed). The University of Chicago Press.

Postone, M. (1996). *Time, Labor, and Social Domination: A Reinterpretation of Marx's Critical Theory*. Cambridge University Press.

WWF. (2022). *Living Planet Report 2022 – Building a Nature-Positive Society* (R.E.A. Almond, M. Grooten, D. Juffe Bignoli & T. Petersen, Eds). WWF.

Chapter 16

The *Hau* Must Be Returned

The Exile of the Dead and Its Effects on the Western Imaginary

Juliette Tocino-Smith

Today, the specter of death looms over our phantasies of biomedical modernity: first, we tried to conceal it, then to repress it; now we find ourselves in a complete state of denial. The dead are no longer solely buried in their graves, abandoned in segregated spaces at the margins of our cities: they have also now been *cremated* in our minds, in our imaginaries. Self-inflicted 'biomanagement' has become the normative paradigm of our times, and so we suffer, for the *return of the repressed* lurks. Mourning has become ob-scene[1] and awkward (Baudrillard, 1993:128) and even if we try to display the torturing realities of our minds, there is no collective to sustain us. By disrupting the law of symbolic exchange, we have Othered death, and on the flipside, we have drowned our bodies in the great illusion of Immortality.

In this chapter I argue that capitalism, alongside with biomedicine, have contributed in eliminating death from the social, visual and symbolic landscape of the Western imaginary by means of negation, cremation of the dead and the deployment of multiple strategies aiming at the extension of human life at all costs. Following Baudrillard, I suggest that capital also came to infiltrate the *unconscious* of the population, by having changed its organizing principle into an economic one of accumulation of life surplus and excess, this also providing an interpretation for the disbelief in mortality that has grown at the very heart of the West. As we will see such developments have had severe repercussions on the psychological well-being of bereaved individuals, who no longer enjoy the collective forms of meaningful rituals or convivial relations with the dead that were prevalent in the Middle Ages. I terminate the chapter by concluding that the problem of endless and pathologized-medicalized mourning can only be resolved through a collective resocialization death, and a restoration of the symbolic exchange principle that would liberate the unconscious from the fears that have been accumulated it inside of it by restoring to the living a sense of ontological security ensured by the incorporation of a healthy dose of death into everyday life.

The tone adopted here is almost by necessity, provocative, if not experimental; it stems from an intention to express hostility towards 'rational-scientific' orthodoxy and to espouse a fresh stance towards the problematization of the relationship between death and 'modernity'. Such an approach is in sum more of a critique of

DOI: 10.4324/9781003375920-20

current cultural attitudes towards death rather than an analysis of how people have succeeded to come to terms with bereavement by their own means.

The Exile of the Dead

In the Middle Ages, death was viewed as something banal, expectable and familiar (Bryant, 2003). *Memento mori* suffused art, architecture and clocks with skulls and bones to remind people of the evanescent character of their existences, and the recurring appearance of the plague, smallpox and influenza between the 16th and 17th centuries ensured that death remained visible in and central to everyday life. In the 15th century in Poland, throwing crumbs of food under the table for the deceased was one of many practices of offering (Korpiola and Lahtinen, 2015:43) in which the living partook in order to stay on good terms with their dead. In exchange these were expected to be guardians of the family hearth and warrantors of a good harvest (Korpiola and Lahtinen, 2015). Neglecting, or 'forgetting' the dead could have severe repercussions, and thus was to be avoided at all costs: for this this effect, the Slavic calendar of annual rites was imbued with symbolic ritual contacts with the dead to ensure between both 'realms' continuity, regularity and, most importantly, *bonne entente*.

Commencing in the 17th century, modernization generated an 'engineering mentality' (Lock, 2004:16), one manifestation of which was a concerted effort to establish increased control over the natural world through the application of scientific methodologies, for instance as is found in exaggerated hospital practices of treatment and diagnosis (McCue, 1995). The flourishing biomedical culture gradually removed the 'spectacle of death' from the streets and public plazas into hospitals, while cemeteries were banished from the center of the peripheries (these having been previously the epicenter for local festivities: in 1231, the Church Council of Rouen in France had to take action to forbid dancing in cemeteries (Ariès, 1975:32)). Hospitals became institutions committed to healing, and dying patients obstructers to the enforcement of the norm. In a similar vein to the threat of madness to reason (Foucault, 1988), the threat of the 'unpredictable nature of biological death' (Bloch and Parry, 1982:15) became one in need of being managed and controlled (Baudrillard, 1993). Illustratively, cremation, which had been in the Middle Ages prohibited by law – or rather the type of treatment that would have been reserved to heretics, sodomites and witches – became a mainstream practice in Italy and Great Britain by the end the 19th century. Far from the dark times of the Black Death in which up to six hundred bodies could be thrown into the same grave, this sanitizing practice was tellingly 'the most radical means of getting rid of the body, of forgetting and nullifying it' (Ariès, 1975:91), and perhaps also allegorically, an effective way to ensure that the deceased would not resurrect and return to disturb the living from the new *enlightened* order these were manufacturing for themselves.

Death, once tamed and part of the city landscape, mutated into something populations came to experience as *isolating, frightening, privatized, medicalised and meaningless* (Howarth and Jupp, 2016:xviii). Thus, while stubborn pursuits for developing technologies of prolonging life where carried out attempting to terminally exterminate death (Baudrillard, 1993:162), the obnoxious *mors omnia vincit*[2] suffusing former times was swept out from the consciousness of the collective.

Neglecting the *Hau*

This transition, this repression of death, Baudrillard argued (1993), also unfurled on a psychological level. Previously the anti-economic[3] organizing principle of Western society, 'symbolic exchange', which involved an integration of the dead in the social order, was completely destroyed by the crystallizing forms of capitalism emerging in Europe by the end of the Middle Ages. This profit-oriented economy infected the social order by distorting *within the unconscious* what had previously been a symbolic process characterized by ritual and exchange, into an economic process of redemption, labour, debt and individualization (Baudrillard, 1993:134). To clarify the crucial point made here, I will now bring our attention towards the first organizing principle, that of symbolic exchange.

According to Mauss, exchange is a 'total social fact' (1954) usually involving a relationship between two parties that is fuelled by the practice of gift giving and reciprocity. Each gift contains an element of the spirit (*hau*) of the giver, which haunts the receiver until he has reciprocated the deed by means of a counter gift. Mauss however was only interested in the practical application of exchange, as he did in analyzing economies of gift-giving in so-called 'primitive' societies. However, the theory was taken a step further by Bataille (1985) and Baudrillard (1993), who transposed the significance of the Gift (1954) onto the psychoanalytic concept of symbolic exchange.

Both converged on the idea that the psychological creation of the 'real' is composed by the interplay of symbols operating between an individual's unconscious and conscious (Freud, 1922). The equilibrium of this interplay is ensured by the fact that any form of accumulation or excess is discharged onto the other side, in a similar fashion to the Native American potlatch ceremonies (amongst the Tlingit, Haida, Tsimshian and Kwakiutl, Bataille, 1985). In this context, the gift represents a loss and thus a partial destruction to the receiver, since the desire to destroy is in part transferred onto the recipient (Bataille, 1985:122). If the exchange of expenditure is not reciprocated, problems of disequilibrium can occur, and symbols can accumulate within one side and clog themselves inside of it; this being what would be called repression in psychoanalytic theory.

Death, for instance, is objectively speaking an unavoidable outcome of life, but what the mind and most importantly society decides to make out of it really rests upon subjective criteria. In the Middle Ages, the conscious apparatus was constantly exposed to death in all imaginable forms, there existed a collective structure which allowed individuals to channel their deepest fears and sorrows regarding either their own death or that of a loved one within a ritual or else of symbolic nature. There was an ongoing release, a psychological potlatch which ensured the expenditure of the insecurities of the unconscious into consciousness.

But in the times that followed, curiously Freud came to argue that our 'unconscious behaves as if it were immortal' (Freud in Bauman, 1992:16): desiring immortality for oneself *while still being alive* was completely new. Death then had already been completely banished from consciousness, this reverberating within Baudrillard's theory regarding the shift in the organizational principle of society from an anti-economic to an economic one. Thus, while modernization gradually came to segregate the spatial, biological and symbolic expression of death in everyday life from the visible realm, the collective unconscious became filled up with everything that was not exchanged socially or symbolically (Baudrillard, 1993:134). And so the *hau*, the spirit of the unreturned expenditure came to haunt the living by means of the *return of the repressed* (Freud, Strachey and Gay, 1933), which brought people to fear death itself as the negation of everything that is social and living.

This marked the beginning of a new era, in which mortals had resolved the problem of mortality by becoming immortal themselves and throwing out the dead out of the group's symbolic circulation (Baudrillard, 1993). The idea that *effective* tasks could be performed in order to redefine an unmanageable problem (that of aging and dying) as a series of 'utterly manageable problems' which one can do a lot about (Bauman, 1992:130) began to pervade everyday life. Health magazines, television fitness shows and private health clubs came to promote images of 'bio-management' and promises of eternal longevity. The body, through techniques of surgical enhancement, was made malleable to the laws of modernity and capitalist employment (Blum, 2003). In parallel with the decline of the influence of the Church, the Judeo-Christian legacy of the Immortal soul in the realm of the afterlife came to be distorted into a vain pursuit of the immortality of the body through its commodification and domestication. The hidden contemporary struggle against death therefore became embodied, the body having become the locus for the denial of something that had now become impossible to envision.

Resocializing with the Dead

This glossing of Immortality by popular media and strategies to conceal the wrinkles of death nevertheless left people helpless in front of situations in which mortality revealed its true colors. In the article which asks *Have the British forgotten how to grieve?* (The Telegraph, 2014) an interviewee complains that the moment of death feels 'unrehearsed, because we're used to feeling like we're masters of our own destiny, and suddenly we don't know what to do'. In the Western world, death has never felt so unfamiliar, and the spatial and symbolic void left behind by the dead is left empty, for the rites – or what could also be thought of as collectivized – and thus dis-individualized – *coping mechanisms* – that previously helped the bereaved manifest grief and loss have been removed from circulation of the cycle of symbolic exchange. Thus, on the cruel *skene* of capitalist British society, all that is left to the living is to 'rush back to work' (Stroud, 2014).

Mourning became synonymous to a *morbid state*, that ought to be treated, shortened, erased by the 'doctor of grief' (Ariès, 1975:99–100). No longer is it socially acceptable to publicly display emotions and openly narrate stories of death, as it had been the case with the 'miracle stories' evoked by parents of deceased children in medieval Sweden (Aldrin:91). In such stories the loss of a child was interpreted to be as a result of a divine intervention, and the intensity of the parent's emotional outburst while narrating the story was understood to be proportional to the greatness of the event. Similarly, among the Lancashire working class in Victorian times, the 'drama of death' made apparent through the fervent display of sorrow reflected and reinforced the kin and neighbourhood solidarities of working-class communities (Roberts, 1977).

True, it could be argued that modern funerals constitute mortuary rites in themselves; but I coincide with Baudrillard in saying that 'funerals are acts of exclusion' (Baudrillard, 1993:24), which in contemporary times have for social function that of Othering the dead, for they are indeed performative but do not allow the deceased to be born into another state of 'being' into something else that would be equally meaningful, and thus do not further the symbolic cycle of exchange. Prayers, or what Davies calls the idiom of 'words against death' (1997), are perhaps enounced, but what follows is a profound collective silence, in reality being 'the choking back of sorrow engendered by the prohibition of its public manifestation' (Gorer, 1965:110). Modern funerals leave what Blauner calls 'an unresolved tension in society' (1966:11), for even in the aftermath of the event, the *hau* continues to haunt the imaginaries of the bereaved.

Conclusion

The overarching reflection made in this chapter has been regarding the importance of nurturing a meaningful approach to death in society, and has brought me to make some observations over the 'deregulations' which have unfolded in Western society as a result of the absence of such an approach. As we have seen, in the Middle Ages, the dead and the living then were much more than just two different 'states of being': they coexisted together, and as I have shown, even sometimes shared meals (at least in Poland). A collective conversation and ritualized symbolic exchange made it possible for people to articulate their emotions relating to bereavement or other anxieties related to death within it. This meant that at the heart of the collective psyche, death was brought to the fore of consciousness, and never repressed, as it is the case today in the Western imaginary. As a result of this, the economic drive for accumulation imbued the repressive phenomena with debt, guilt, and fear inside of the unconscious, and saw itself reflected in the anxieties related to death or 'unpreparedness' as to how to cope with death, which today burden the living in capitalist societies. While this disequilibrium of unexchanged debt, this segregation between death excess in the unconscious and life surplus in the conscious remains, and the biomedical industry persists in furthering the shattering of death in all its expressions, the *hau* will continue to exert its most darkest powers on the imaginary of Western population.

Notes

1 In *Symbolic Exchange and Death* (1993), Baudrillard uses the word 'obscene' in the sense of 'offensive to the senses, or to taste and refinement', but also in its Latin etymological sense, 'ob' meaning 'hindrance, blocking or concealment' and 'skene', referring to a theatrical stage. In modern society, mourning is hidden from the modern stage of the theatre of cruelty (Artaud, 1958) of everyday life. It is one of cruelty for it fails to comfort the deepest fears of the unconscious, by upholding an unjust order 'cleansed of death'.
2 Latin. *Death always wins.*
3 The symbolic exchange principle is *antieconomic* in the sense that it does not seek to accumulate, but rather to dispatch the excess of what it possesses, it be whether material or symbolic.

References

Aldrin, V. (2015). Parental grief and prayer in the Middle Ages: Religious coping in Swedish miracle stories. In M. Korpiola & A. Lahtinen (Eds.), *Cultures of Death and Dying in Medieval and Early Modern Europe* (pp. 82–105). Helsinki: Helsinki Collegium for Advanced Studies. Studies Across Disciplines in the Humanities and Social Sciences, 18.

Ariès, P., 1975. *Western attitudes toward death: From the middle ages to the present* (Vol. 3). JHU Press.

Artaud, A., 1958. *The theatre and its double* (Vol. 127). Grove Press.

Bataille, G., 1985. *Visions of excess: Selected writings 1927–1939* (Vol. 14). Manchester University Press.

Baudrillard, J., 1993. *Symbolic exchange and death* (Vol. 25). SAGE.

Bauman, Z., 1992. *Mortality, immortality and other life strategies*. Stanford University Press.

Blauner, R., 1966. Death and social structure. *Psychiatry, 29*(4).

Bloch, M. and Parry, J., 1982. *Death and the regeneration of life*. Cambridge University Press.

Blum, V., 2003. *Flesh wounds: The culture of cosmetic surgery*. University of California Press.

Bryant, C.D., 2003. *Handbook of death and dying* (Vol. 1). SAGE.

Foucault, M., 1988. *Madness and civilization: A history of insanity in the age of reason*. Vintage.

Freud, S., 1922. The unconscious. *The Journal of Nervous and Mental Disease, 56*(3), pp. 291–294.

Freud, S., Strachey, J. and Gay, P., 1933. The dissection of the psychical personality. In *Introductory lectures on psycho-analysis* (pp. 71–100). W. W. Norton & Company.

Gorer, G., 1977. *Death, grief, and mourning*. Arno Press, c1965.

Howarth, G. and Jupp, P.C. eds., 2016. *Contemporary issues in the sociology of death, dying and disposal*. Springer.

Korpiola, M. and Lahtinen, A., 2015. *Cultures death and dying in medieval and early modern Europe: An introduction*. Helsinki Collegium for Advanced Studies.

Lock, M., 2004. Medicalization and the naturalization of social control. In *Encyclopedia of medical anthropology* (pp. 116–125). Springer US.

Mauss, M., 1954. *The gift: Forms and functions of exchange in archaic societies*. Routledge.

McCue, J.D., 1995. The naturalness of dying. *Jama, 273*(13), pp. 1039–1043.

Roberts, E., 1977. Working–class standards of living in barrow and Lancaster, 1890–1914. *The Economic History Review, 30*(2), pp. 306–321.

Stroud, C., 2014. Have the British forgotten how to grieve? *Telegraph.co.uk*. N.p. Web. 7 Jan. 2017.

Tierney, T.F., 1997. Death, medicine and the right to die: An engagement with Heidegger, Bauman and Baudrillard. *Body & Society, 3*(4), pp. 51–77.

Index

American Psychoanalytic Association 4
Aufhebung 65–67, 75, 91
autism 30, 32, 37, 138, 141–144

Badiou, Alain 45, 96n4, 108n4
Barthes, Roland 193–194
biology 4, 7–10, 18, 30, 42, 44, 46–48,
    69–70, 102, 161–163, 166n16
birth trauma *see* trauma
Boothby, Richard 109n9
Brousse, Marie-Helene 124–125, 130
Buddhism 209, 210

certainty 4, 11, 12, 13, 21, 23, 24, 28, 29,
    38–39, 53, 72, 73
Chomsky, Noam 29–31, 49
common knowledge (common sense) 62,
    63, 66, 67, 96, 154, 176, 185–186
constitutive negativity xiv, 111, 116, 124,
    126, 130–131n3, 201, 204–205
Copjec, Joan 108n1
couples therapy 29

Darwin, Charles 8, 66, 79
Dawkins, Richard 9
death xv, 29, 41, 52, 55, 73, 81, 151,
    204–208, 210, 214, 218–223, 223n1,
    223n2; being-toward-death 209
defenses 8, 11–15, 19, 35, 41, 137, 139,
    140, 182
Descartes, René 6–7, 201
dialectics 20, 23, 24, 32, 36, 39, 46, 49,
    52–53, 65, 74, 91–95, 108, 142,
    192, 194, 197, 199–203; master-
    slave 122; negative xv, 215–216;
    see also Aufhebung
discourse 11, 19, 20–24, 28, 63, 118, 152,
    170, 176–180, 184; of the analyst 13,

21, 27, 96, 129, 157, 179, 184–186;
    of the hysteric 21–24, 28, 179; of
    the master (normal) 7, 9, 16, 20–24,
    28, 39, 96; sociological xv, 20; of the
    university 11, 21–24, 28, 179
Dolar, Mladen 109n6
Dora case 13–14, 25–27
drive 78–82, 92, 111–112, 208–209; death
    drive 98–108, 111–112; objet a
    122–123
DSM 16, 17, 40, 53

ego: ego ideal/ideal ego 4, 10, 11, 15, 38;
    ego psychology 5–6, 12, 33; real
    ego 80–81
Ettinger, Bracha L. 112–113, 114, 115
evolution 8, 71, 75
extimacy 31–33

Fink, Bruce 3

generalized foreclosure 34–35

happiness 78, 92–94, 114, 119, 203, 207,
    209, 216; positive thought xv, 195,
    201, 202, 205, 209, 214, 215; *see
    also* toxic positivity
Heidegger, Martin 209, 210
hermit 32
hole 19, 38, 43, 91, 94, 125, 148–152

identification 3, 9–11, 14, 20, 26, 29–30,
    35, 47, 49, 51–52, 73, 131n9;
    projective 64

jouissance xiv, xv, 22–23, 50–51, 152–153,
    180, 186; joui-sens 121; masochism
    93; mortification of 156, 160,

162, 166n15; non-negativisable
154–158; Other 124, 131n5; sexual
176–177, 180, 181, 186n3; surplus
19, 92, 163, 183
Jung, Carl 49, 98, 191–196, 207

Kant, Immanuel 80, 99, 100–103, 108n5,
122
Klein, Naomi 91; and lack 144

lalangue 10, 22, 46–49, 123, 125
Laplanche, Jean 63–64, 142
life coaches 11, 16, 18–19
Locke, John 6, 40, 51, 201
logical time 3, 32, 34, 44, 46

Marcuse, Herbert 108
Marx, Karl 23, 86n23, 92, 95, 98–99, 103,
109n11, 173, 200, 204, 212
masochism 51, 106–107, 109n5, 109n9,
109n11; see also jouissance;
masochism
metonymy 10, 19–20, 22, 34, 37, 41, 46,
48, 49, 80, 94, 122, 150–152, 175
Miller, Jacques-Alain 6, 21–23, 34–35,
119, 124, 129, 149, 155–164,
173–174, 176
mirror stage 9–10, 11, 20, 32, 33, 35–37, 47,
50, 55n2, 64, 73, 170, 197, 204, 205
monk 209
mystical theology 119–120, 123, 128,
130n1; see also theology

New Lacanian School 162, 165n8

object relations 5, 50–51, 55; Klein,
Melanie 64, 78, 83n13
ordinary psychosis 49

parletre 6, 19, 155, 186n1
pleasure principle 67, 92, 107, 108n3, 122,
204, 207
Popper, Karl 63
postmodernism, xv

Red Clinic 171–172
repetition 75–76, 125, 130, 148, 149, 156,
157, 160, 180–181; compulsion
81, 157
resistance 5, 7, 12–16, 29, 31, 33, 34, 37,
41, 44, 48–51, 64, 106, 125, 139,
167, 170; psychotic 36

Revolution 6–11, 19, 40, 43, 98, 101, 106,
109nn7–9, 148, 201
Rorty, Richard 86n23

Schneiderman, Stuart 11, 52
science 6–7, 12, 64, 78, 94, 176, 194–196;
cognitive 70
self-help 4, 28, 33, 92, 118–119, 121
sinthome 35–37, 44, 123, 125, 127–128,
161, 166n17
speaking-being see parletre
Spielrein, Sabine 207, 208
style 39, 44, 147, 168, 191
subject 8, 93; split subject 8, 140; subject
supposed to know 3–5
symbolic order 8, 15, 21, 28–29, 33,
49–51, 85, 122

theology 119, 120, 123, 125, 126, 128,
130n1; see also mystical
theology
topology 8–9, 43–45, 148, 149, 152, 153,
158; torus 44, 94, 148–150, 158
toxic positivity xv, 91–96, 126, 168,
212–216
transference xiv, 3, 5, 6, 12, 13, 20, 24, 27,
28–29, 32, 41, 44, 48–49, 50–52,
54, 128, 152, 170
trauma 3, 14, 18, 19, 92–93, 192, 199, 202,
204, 207, 209–210; birth trauma
18–19
truth 21, 23, 29, 39, 43, 45–46, 49, 54,
63–64, 66, 130, 175–179, 182, 192,
196, 209–210

United States of America 3–8, 11, 16–18,
27–29, 93, 167, 199–205, 207;
see also American Psychoanalytic
Association

void see hole

Western imaginary 222–223
Winnicott, Donald 5, 55, 55n2, 72
world 6, 10, 11, 70, 79, 99, 119, 130, 143,
148, 169, 177, 193, 197, 201,
202, 205, 214; modern world 216;
subject and world 80; as torus 148

Zizek, Slavoj 7, 50, 91–92, 113, 117n1,
117n2, 118, 126
Zupancic, Alenka 45, 100, 111–116, 133

For Product Safety Concerns and Information please contact our EU
representative GPSR@taylorandfrancis.com
Taylor & Francis Verlag GmbH, Kaufingerstraße 24, 80331 München, Germany